✤ **Cross the Threshold to** 1

Once the exclusive secret of the select few, the secrets of magical symbolism are now revealed in *Western Mandalas of Transformation*. Updated and refined through practical experience, the full range of talismans, mandalas, flashing tablets, kameas, sigils, and seals are made understandable and readily available to you. Numerous illustrations demonstrate how to properly create and use these powerful images to positively change your life.

Use sound Qabalistic principles derived from the Tree of Life to fashion powerful, transformative mandalas and seals. Work with a wide range of energies to facilitate healing, personal empowerment, and spiritual development.

From the most basic concepts to the most advanced theories, *Western Mandalas of Transformation* guides you through the process of creating planetary, zodiacal, Qabalistic, and other images for use in meditation, ritual, and magic.

Uncover the mysteries of divine names and the magical power within your own name by learning to convert any name into a magical signature, sigil, or tattwa symbol.

Radically transform your life through exciting new ways of working with numbers, symbols, and the chakras emerging from the cutting edge of modern-day magical practice. Open the magical portal to Daath and the secrets which await the seeker beyond the confines of normal existence.

Western Mandalas of Transformation explains mysteries hidden in the magical squares which have never been published before. Powerful techniques obtained from the experiences of a working hermetic lodge can now be yours. Do you have the will to dare the assay into the silent depths of the unknown?

About the Author

Soror A. L. lives and writes in her niche in the woods with her cat and herb garden. She belongs to a working hermetic lodge on the West Coast and welcomes correspondence on magical squares.

About the Illustrator

After studying Buddhism for five years, Lloyd Nygaard turned to the esoteric traditions of the West and spent seven years in a Fourth Way school practicing the inner disciplines of spiritual evolution. He has studied the writings of Paul Foster Case for the past eleven years with other students from a variety of traditions that have the Golden Dawn as their common source. He works as a design engineer in the aerospace industry, and is currently writing a thesis on transfinite numbers, the mathematics of infinity.

To Write to the Author

If you would like to contact the author or illustrator, or would like more information about this book, please write to them in care of Llewellyn Worldwide. We cannot guarantee every letter will be answered, but all will be forwarded. Please write to:

Soror A. L. or Lloyd Nygaard
c/o Llewellyn Worldwide
P.O. Box 64383-170, St. Paul, MN 55164-0383, U.S.A
Please enclose a self-addressed, stamped envelope for reply or $1.00 to cover costs.
If outside the U.S.A., enclose international postal reply coupon.

Free Catalog from Llewellyn Worldwide

For more than ninety years Llewellyn has brought its readers knowledge in the fields of metaphysics and human potential. Learn about the newest books in spiritual guidance, natural healing, astrology, occult philosophy, and more. Enjoy book reviews, new age articles, a calendar of events, plus current advertised products and services. To get your free copy of the *Llewellyn's New Worlds of Mind and Spirit* magazine, send your name and address to:

Llewellyn's New Worlds of Mind and Spirit
P.O. Box 64383-170, St. Paul, MN 55164-0383, U.S.A.

LLEWELLYN'S GOLDEN DAWN SERIES

WESTERN MANDALAS ✢ OF ✢ TRANSFORMATION

MAGICAL SQUARES ✢ TATTWAS ✢ QABALISTIC TALISMANS

Soror A. L.

Illustrated by Lloyd Nygaard

1995
Llewellyn Publications
St. Paul, MN 55164-0383, U.S.A.

FIRST EDITION
First Printing, 1996

Cover design by Tom Grewe
Editing, design, and layout by Darwin Holmstrom

Library of Congress Cataloging in Publication Data

Soror A. L., 1947-
    Western mandalas of transformation : astrological and qabalistic
talismans and tattwas / Soror A.L. ; illustrated by Lloyd Nygaard. --
1st ed.
        p. cm. — (Llewellyn Golden Dawn series)
    ISBN 1-56718-170-8 (pbk. : akl. paper)
    1. Mandala. 2. Talismans. 3. Magic squares. 4. Tree of life.
 5. Magic. I. Title. II. Series.
 BF1442.M34C66 1995
135'.4—dc20   95-44525
                                                                       CIP

Llewellyn Publications
A Division of Llewellyn Worldwide, Ltd.
P.O. Box 64383, St. Paul, MN 55164-0383

About Llewellyn's Golden Dawn Series

One hundred years ago the original Order of the Golden Dawn initiated a powerful rebirth of interest in the Western Esoteric Tradition that has lasted through this day—this series of books adds new impetus to the Great Work itself among an ever broadening base of sincere students.

> *I further promise and swear that with the Divine Permission, I will from this day forward, apply myself to the Great Work—which is: to purify and exalt my Spiritual Nature so that with the Divine Aid I may at length attain to be more than human, and thus gradually raise and unite myself to my Higher and Divine Genius, and that in this event I will not abuse the great power entrusted to me.*

With this oath, the *Adeptus Minor* of the Inner Order committed him/herself to undertake, consciously and deliberately, that which was ordained as the birthright of all Humanity: *to become more than human!*

This is the ultimate message of Esotericism: that evolution continues, and that the purpose of each life is to grow into the Image set for us by our Creator: to attain and reveal our own Divinity.

These books and tapes will themselves make more easily accessible the Spiritual Technology that is inherent in the Golden Dawn System. It is a system that allows for individual as well as group endeavor; a system based on universal principles that are global in their impact.

And practical. The works in this series are practical in their applications and requirements for application. You need neither to travel to the Mountain Top nor obtain any tool other than your own Consciousness. You need no garment other than your own Imagination. You need no authority other than that of your own True Will.

Set forth, then, into the New Dawn—a New Start on the greatest adventure there is: to become One with the Divine Genius.

This book is dedicated to all my students, and especially to my lodge sisters in Hermetica West, who have been a great source of light and joy in my life: Sarial, La, Tzadkiel, Aimbe, Morning Star, Starel, and Matarah, and to Claire, wherever you are. . . .

Special thanks to: All Golden Dawn friends, both living and dead, and La and Lux for proofreading

✥ TABLE OF CONTENTS ✥

And Mercurius Trismegistus writes, that an Image, rightly made of certain proper things, appropriated to any one certain angel will presently be animated by that angel.

—Cornelius Agrippa

When I sing a song to the sun, it is not because I expect the sun to change its course, but because I expect to put myself into a different cast of mind in relation to the sun.

—Marsilio Fincino

There is no higher form of human freedom than freindship with God.

—St Teresa of Avila

✛ INTRODUCTION ✛

It is widely thought among scientists that beauty and elegance are the most reliable guides to truth; the best theories are the most elegant. Many scientists feel that true inspiration comes from some sort of Platonic realm of archetypal, mathematical, or aesthetic forms which somehow break through our world.

To the scientist, mathematics is the discipline which is most closely tied to nature itself. This may seem strange to the outsider—one to whom math is a bizarre world of numbers and strange symbols—but the idea dates as far back as the ancient Egyptians, who used their understanding of correct proportion of number and ratio to build the pyramids. They could have influenced the ancient Greeks; Plato makes reference in his *Laws* to their sacred canon which served to help preserve their civilization over centuries. Certainly we know that the Greek philosophers perceived numbers and geometry as the ordering principles of the universe. The famous words of Pythagoras echo even today: "Number is the measure of all things." Later Galileo was to say, "The book of nature is written in mathematical language."

In the ancient Near East, numbers were associated with the planets, or even deified. God was thought of as Number One—the Prime Mover—much like the modern Qabalistic concept, where numbers are assigned to attributes of the God-energy on the Tree of Life. Very early in the Old Testament writings the ancient Hebrews displayed a special fascination with certain numbers, and both Gnosticism and medieval Qabalism developed the themes of this mystical relationship with numbers. The Bible is riddled with numerological meaning and Augustine himself studied Biblical numerology for much of his life.

The Pythagoreans imbued certain numbers with mystical properties and had special reverence for numbers such as six, which is the sum of its divisors (6=1+2+3); and the sum of the first four whole numbers, number ten, they called the Divine Tetraktys. The Pythagoreans also discovered a relationship between numbers and harmoniously related tones, which had particular numerical relationships to one another. Some of these principles have been rediscovered, revised, or refined, and are used by numerous healers working on the fringe of what may well be a powerful technology for future mental and physical health. The late Swiss scientist Dr. Hans Jenny and his co-workers have been using sound frequencies in physical regeneration of certain organs of the body. At the turn of this century, the great Christian Qabalist Dr. Paul Foster Case said that in the future, humankind would re-discover the ancient Pythagorean principles of healing through sound and color, and advised meditation on the planetary chakras in the body (which each have a different color) for maintenance of a healthy etheric body.

The wonder-working Pythagoreans also applied their understanding of number to astronomy, devising a system of nine concentric circles or spheres to represent the heavenly bodies. Soon it came to be understood that the relationships existing in these heavenly planets had direct counterparts within the human dimension. This was not just a simple belief in astrology, which was a much more ancient science. It was a more sophisticated understanding of the hermetic principle that through sympathetic correspondences one could temper or augment a planet's effects.

Plato applied numerology to the known elements—earth, air, fire, and water—and thought we did not invent mathematics, we only discovered it. Numbers enjoy an independent existence which transcends the physical senses and belongs to the world of Eternal Forms or Ideas. Many modern mathematicians feel the same way about the "Mandelbrot set" and the beautiful fractal forms it produces. One mathematician commented that "much more comes out of the structure (which produces fractals) than is put in it in the first place. One may take the view that in such cases the mathematicians have stumbled upon 'works of God'" (Davis, p. 143).

The relationship of numbers and geometrical forms was worked out in elegant detail by the Pythagoreans and many Platonic philosophers after them. It is the geometric forms which have of late become such a fascination in my life, since I have been working with the eight planetary squares for quite some time. I have discovered that planetary squares hold many hidden references to the Tree of Life through their numeric symbolism (called in Qabalah, gematria). I stumbled upon the amazing technique of creating "flashing color tablets" (to be explained in due course) of the planetary seals made from magical squares (or kameas) which have been used in the magical tradition since the Renaissance.

Many of the Renaissance scientists and philosophers have not been given proper credit for the depth of their perception of reality. Kepler's analysis of the solar system was heavily influenced by his perception of the mystical influence of number, often describing God in geometrical terms. William Blake's famous etching, *The Ancient of Days* (a title of the God Name *Kether,* or Number One, on the Tree of Life), shows God leaning down from heaven to measure earth with dividers, giving the impression of a master artisan at work.

God the Geometer is still busy at work (or play), and Her artwork is evidenced all around us as we continually discover the symmetry of fresh snowflakes on a wintry day or the rich harmony and perfection of a new flower. In today's modern physics there is still the basic assumption that mathematics plays an underlying role in the rational ordering of the universe.

In modern mathematics, however, there is a number known as Omega, a random number which is thought to be uncomputable—or, in mystical language, unknowable except through revelation. It has even been compared to number mysticism by a leading scientist, Charles Bennett, who says, "Omega is, in many senses, a cabalistic number. It can be known of, but not known, through human reason. To know it in detail, one would have to accept its uncomputable digit sequence on faith, like words of a sacred text" (Davis, p. 134).

Although we could never hope to understand the Great Mystery of Being with our rational minds, Qabalah gives us a most effective and yet challenging way to relate to the Godhead and all of Its attributes or particular vibrations (we could call them planetary chakras or rays), starting with the most primordial archetypal forms, number, and geometry. The most practical way to integrate this number mysticism is through an understanding of magical squares and talismans. In the second of his *Three Books of Occult Philosophy*, Cornelius Agrippa said that mathematics and magic are so intimately connected that nothing successful could ever be achieved by the magician without a thorough understanding of numbers. The neo-Platonic reasoning of his day intuited that numbers were the direct thoughts of a governing Creator and geometry was the means whereby the true essences of number were first made manifest. This may have been the reason why the planetary squares were themselves considered talismans.

A magic planetary square is an array of numbers arranged so that the sum of any row is equal to the sum of any column. They have been esteemed for their magical and mathematical properties for thousands of years in other traditions besides hermeticism, in places such as China, India, and the Middle East. The planetary spirit of the magic square is viewed as a guiding, inspiring, or informing entity, and many planetary talismans of the Middle Ages have their planetary seals and squares engraved in the talisman dedicated to the mythic figure represented by the planet, *e.g.*, Mercury (number eight) or Mars (number five). The Mars square has twenty-five cells (5x5), and the sum of any row equals sixty-five. The "theosophic extension" of the square is the addition of all the numbers from one through sixty-five, which in this case is 325. These are the sacred numbers of Mars.

According to John Michell, who has done perhaps the most comprehensive modern analysis of ancient sacred sites in his many excellent works, magical squares were regarded as "numerical illustrations of cosmic laws. Every (ancient) structure was laid out according to one of the patterns which magic squares reveal" (1969, p. 110). We will look briefly at some illustrations of this idea in later chapters. If this thesis is correct, then magical planetary squares date back very far indeed. This important revelation— that geometry is related to the numbers in the planetary squares—was also noted by the great occultist, Eliphas Levi, who said more than a century ago that they may have been influential in the construction of the ancient wonders of the world. These geometric forms are the basis of all talismanic magical work.

Modern advances in physics continue to give credibility to ancient beliefs, sometimes in amazing ways. One theory implies that in the origin of the universe, there may have been perfect symmetries: matter froze out of energy like ice crystals in a congealing body of water. The breaking of this absolute symmetry was the creation of the universe itself. This is called the *Vacuum Genesis* theory. Out of nothingness could have come the spark of Genesis. Perhaps the darkness held the first original geometric forms, and matter was coaxed into releasing its endless complexity out of these primordial forms which are themselves unmoving and unchanging.

These Platonic Ideal Forms are not just a philosophical fancy of the past. Numerous scientists today find themselves solidly in the Platonic camp, since it is still the most viable theory to explain how nature is so rationally intelligible. One such scientist, Roger Penrose, explains how such ideas also make communication so fluid between mathematicians, or people of like minds. It is worth quoting at length since so much of what we will explore here is based on this very premise:

> Whenever the mind perceives a mathematical idea it makes contact with Plato's world of mathematical concepts. . . When one "sees" a mathematical truth, one's consciousness breaks through into the world of ideas and makes direct contact with it. . . The mental images that each (person) has, when making this Platonic contact, might be rather different in each case, but communication is possible because each is directly in contact with the same eternally existing Platonic world (Davis, p. 144).

These Platonic Ideal Forms are not only basic to the numerical mysticism of Qabalah through its long historical development; through talismanic art, particularly geometric art, and Qabalah's mystical number squares, new revelations await us. These particular revelations may or may not have been known to the ancient Qabalists, but they were nonetheless there, waiting to be discovered. Some of the geometrical forms that my colleagues and I have discovered have truly astonished us, and with the advent of computer technology there is almost no end to what we may discover in the future. Yet this is nothing we have invented; it is only one application of an ancient system which, in my mind, is the most profound esoteric tradition of Revelation ever known to humankind: the Mystical Qabalah.

Chapter 1

QABALISTIC TALISMANS:
How Do They Work?

But perhaps there is a pattern set up in the heavens for one who
desires to see it, and having seen it, to find one in himself.

—Plato

D o talismans have power independently of the person who designed them? Some
think that a consecrated or charged talisman does; in ages past it was believed
that one had only to wear a talisman or amulet made by someone else to benefit from it, without understanding its special symbols and signatures. Others, like
Paracelsus, explained their magical power in psychological terms, and many modern
interpretations claim that if anything is charged, it is the mind of the believer; the talisman's primary purpose is simply to act as a reminder of the ceremony of making it. But
if this is the case, it leaves the talisman itself with very little power and the principal benefit would be for the maker and not the wearer.

I will leave these vexing questions for the reader to ponder; like the age-old debate concerning any kind of magical phenomenon, one can never prove one's theory in either case.
The problem centers on whether one believes there are actually spirits out there who work
through the charged talisman, or whether these forces are primarily projections. Both
approaches are incorporated in this book, and the reader will find this discussion moving
in different directions, depending on context. If we are talking about *invocation*, we will
identify ourselves squarely in the Golden Dawn tradition, believing that an actual force
is being summoned, and this energy can be very personal, including the taking of a physical form. For the most part, however, we will follow the interpretations of the great

Qabalist and master of gematria, Dr. Paul Foster Case, whose orientation is primarily psychological. At any rate, the talismans in this book are not meant to be worn, but rather to be meditated upon.

Most modern magicians agree that talismanic power, however it is used, resides primarily in the vehicle of *symbol*. Symbol has the strange ability to act as a magnet, drawing to us those things which we conceptualize with a directed will and which are empowered with greatest affect, or emotion. The basic idea of talismanic magic is simply that *images attract the forces they represent.* For example, any five-pointed image, such as a pentagram or a pentagon, attracts the energy known as Geburah (identified with Mars) on the Tree of Life (See figure 1–A). The student needs a good understanding of these primary Tree correspondences, which can be discovered in a plethora of books available today. Only rough outlines in the form of charts and graphs are given here, but they should enable the sincere student to begin making some very creative and useful talismans.

The first thing we notice about the above example (*e.g.*, that a geometric figure with five points relates us to the fifth Sephira on the Tree) is that *number* is very important in talisman making. Number is, in fact, based on the Sephiroth, which are the ten emanations of the God-energy on the Tree of Life. There are many other correspondences as well, but number is primary. Despite what you believe about how talismans work, the three most important ideas connected to making successful talismans are correspondences, intention, and will. In addition, the symbols we choose in creating a talisman need to have some emotional energy connected to them in our own subconscious mind; we all know that some symbols excite us more than others. Some have no charge at all. Some repel us. Talismans work best when we use symbol to suggest something to the subconscious that has a charge emotionally. The same idea holds with visualization, affirmation, etc. The famous Qabalistic teacher Israel Regardie used to repeat the old maxim: "Enflame thyself with prayer." Our spiritual life or our magical life is most effective when it comes from the heart, from the soul, even from the guts.

We have said that symbol has this wonderful ability to attract the energy of the image it represents. In Case's interpretation, the image makes a suggestion to subconsciousness, whereupon you have set up a relationship between consciousness and subconsciousness. This is a basic Jungian concept now used in a variety of ways, *e.g.*, active imagination. It is also the principle upon which all magic is based—an intricate system of correspondences represented through symbol.

Working with an image and having a discussion through it with the subconscious can be confusing because symbols can stand for a lot of things. In order for consciousness to have a relation with subconsciousness, which is fluid and efficacious, we want to be as clear as possible, from the consciousness side, about what we are making the talisman for. The first task is to simply state our intention. Intentions for talisman making are many, but for our purposes they fall into two broad categories: to align oneself to a certain energy one is attracted to, and to compensate for some kind of energy which feels unbalanced. In other words, modern talismans—especially when used as mandala-like images for meditation—are used principally for psychological reasons, although in the

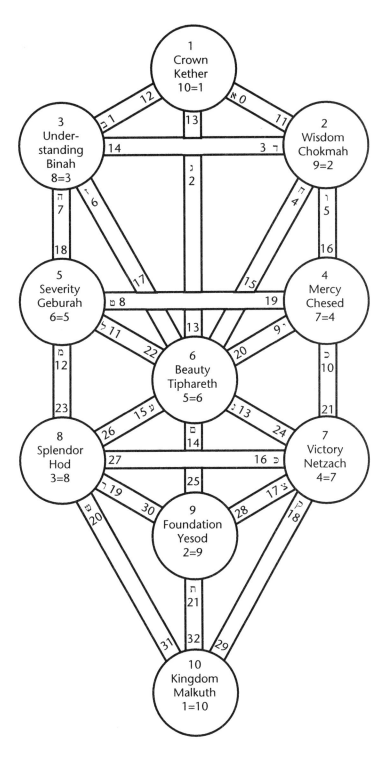

Figure 1–A:
The Tree of Life

Qabalistic tradition they can also act as astral doorways (a fancy word, which for our purposes means working in the realm of the imagination) or for manifesting desires. Sometimes the lines between these categories are not at all clear-cut. It may be that we have a desire to manifest a particular kind of job, say for a newspaper firm. We would then want to work on that part of our personality that will elicit dynamic communication abilities, as this job would involve both verbal and written communications. We may do this through designing a talisman with a lot of Mercurial correspondences, and also do some creative work with the active imagination through meditating on the completed mandala, which will connect us to Mercury or Hod, the 8th Sphere on the Tree of Life.

Symbols are very archetypal, but they can also be very personal. You probably have certain kinds of symbols which may mean something to you that no-one else understands. However, the archetypal symbols have great power in talisman making *because they have a tradition*—these are images that have been built up in the ether, or akasha, for thousands of years and that have direct correspondences to certain ideas, so they come already invested with the power to speak in a certain way. This in no way means that the archetypal image is limited, for it speaks to us all in distinctly individual ways.

This is so even when symbols represent archetypal entities such as Michael the Archangel. I probably have a different relationship with this entity than you do, even though the correspondences around his image would be relatively the same for both of us—fire, power, and so on. The beautiful thing about relationships with these Divine Forces is that they can be distinctly personal. In one relationship, Michael may infuse one with energy to be very bold; for another Michael may be the benevolent but powerful protector. So we draw on that tremendous storehouse of energy to come to our aid in specific ways.

If one examines many talismans of the Middle Ages (when times were bad, indeed) or in the ancient world, one can sometimes go through a lot of trouble (as I have on a number of occasions) deciphering a lot of strange symbols, including sigils (or angelic signatures) and seals, and decoding words in some esoteric script—including Hebrew, which is considered an esoteric or sacred language—only to discover that the talisman was made for what would appear to be a very mundane reason. Love, power, and riches seem to be the strongest motivating factors for much of the amulet or talisman making of the past (although amulets have been primarily used for protection), and I dare say that human nature is slow to change. It is perhaps true that human beings need to have their basic needs met before they can content themselves with prayers, affirmations, and magical work, for spiritual purposes, but if personal desire is the extent of one's use of Qabalistic talismans, it would cut us short indeed.

There is probably no spiritual tradition richer in images to draw upon than Qabalah, and no end to the depth it possesses to aid one on the path to enlightenment, salvation, God-realization, or true gnosis (take your pick, but be committed). At any level from which you approach it, it has something to offer through its system of correspondences and through the ever-expanding consciousness it holds for those who study it in depth. Dr. Case emphatically believed that the magic of magical squares was not to align oneself with planetary energy to achieve a specific end—which is the more mundane interpretation of magic in many circles today— but to *act as a source of revelation.* Only the student who studies and works with magical squares consistently understands this. The word *talisman,* in fact, may be a derivative of the Arabic *tilsam,* which means *mystery,* pointing to its real inherent value—to unlock for us the mysteries of God and nature. If fascination with the powers which have been attributed to talismans over time eventually pulls you into a deeper study of Qabalah, it will be no small miracle, as you will see if you work with Qabalistic talismans long enough.

The end result of all true Qabalistic work is to draw closer to the God-energy known as Kether, the essence of the Tree. It is the real "crown" of magical work. All great Qabalistic magicians will testify to this, for it is what true magic in the western esoteric tradition is all about, although it has often been greatly misunderstood.

A word of caution is in order for those who simply want to experiment with talismans for the reasons mentioned above: for love (or sex), power (especially over someone else) or money (especially without work). There is nothing wrong with actualizing one's desires provided that they are *never* geared toward manipulating another person, and that they are used in a balanced way in one's own life. Besides the big three desires mentioned above—which seem to occupy so much of humanity's attempts to find meaning in life—there is a fourth very necessary leg of the table which constitutes life's banquet: *spiritual and emotional integration.* This is why most Golden Dawn magicians do some form of therapy in conjunction with their magical work. Israel Regardie once advised no less than 100 hours of any kind of therapeutic work for neophytes.

One of the dangers of using magic, and perhaps talismans in particular, is that in actualizing more mundane desires, psychic energy is robbed from another place in the system—one's spiritual path. This is one of the negative aspects of the New Age movement, which has a very materialistic side. It is vital for a Qabalist to remember this. If you are sure to devote as much time in your talismanic work to developing emotional wholeness and spiritual devotion as you do to other talismanic pursuits, you will be in no trouble. We must remember that we are in a global community, trying to survive in an ecosystem with finite resources. Americans have a disproportionate amount of these resources, and this may be an uncomfortable issue to face while doing affirmations for abundance.

On the one hand there is nothing wrong with using talismans to manifest goals in the world, because every time you do, it helps to strengthen and develop the will, and this is vital for a magician, but attempting to develop your will at the expense of another human being will certainly backfire, as all spiritual teachers and traditions have taught us. There is a difference between making a talisman to attract friendship and making one to entice your fantasy dream date over to dinner. Eliphas Levi (otherwise known as Abbe Louis Constant), who was a master of Rosicrucian and Qabalistic magic of the last century, said:

> It is well to observe here that every action promotes a reaction, and that in magnetizing others, or influencing them magically, we establish between them and ourselves a current of contrary but analogous influence which may subject us to them

instead of subjecting them to us, as happens frequently enough in those operations which have the sympathy of love for their object (Levi, 1972, p. 215).

It is important to think through what you are doing. The principal question you are faced with at the onset of any magical working of this kind is: Does this operation involve another person? If so, they should be made aware of your intentions and you should certainly have their permission—even in healings. *This is a cosmic law.*

First one must clarify one's intention in making the talisman. In the Qabalistic tradition, as in any true spiritual tradition, this intention should include a very important element: how can this desire incorporate in some way the element of service? If you think about this carefully, it will act as a safeguard to desires the ego may feel are paramount, but which may not benefit it so well in the end. This is because this intention incorporates work with your Higher Self.

If one's true goal is God (the kingdom of heaven) or simply the highest good, then all other things fall into place. This kind of goal is completely incompatible with using talismanic magic for manipulative or unethical ends. Your first affirmation should be that your magical working is not only for your own benefit but for the greater good of the universe.

Let us return to the problem of symbol for a moment. Many who have studied psychic sciences will have noticed that in any kind of psychic phenomenon, such as divination, visions, channeling, dreams, etc., there may occur a plethora of images which have multiple meanings and which are, in turn, frequently misunderstood, misinterpreted or misconstrued by the conscious mind. These problems can be more easily solved by calling upon the assistance of the Higher Self, or Holy Guardian Angel (a relationship we will devote considerable time to in Chapter Two), for greater understanding. Once this relationship is formed, it acts both as a filter and as a vehicle for transformation.

Symbols have many layers of meaning. One vision or dream symbol may have ten different kinds of interpretation. A classic visionary experience (such as Ezekiel or Revelation) may speak in symbolic language so dense it may be analyzed and interpreted for many generations to come. Symbols can be tricky. One trap is a simplistic or one-dimensional interpretation; this often leads to false divinations. It can also frequently lead to a reductionistic understanding of how an archetypal symbol is moving in our lives. The more we develop and strengthen the relationship between consciousness and the subconscious, the more readily will we be able to understand the level of meaning that is trying to make itself known.

This is the great contribution of archetypal techniques like active imagination and pathworking—we begin to bridge the gap between the conscious and subconscious mind; we begin to discover the common language with which the two halves of the personality can speak to each other. This takes practice. But with every practice session—every time you do work consciously with symbol—the process deepens and the communication becomes more fluid. It helps to congratulate one's subconscious occasionally to encourage further growth, and it is very useful to research symbols, especially if they come up in some kind of synchronistic way in one's life. This is certainly true when one is using them in any kind of correspondence work, such as talisman-making.

Just as there are potential problems with consciousness understanding the symbolic language of the unconscious mind, there can also be the reverse problem. We spoke earlier about the necessity of clarity of intent. It should be clear by now why this is so important. If consciousness is vague in intention, or uses too many symbols—especially in some kind of syncretic way, that is, from a variety of traditions—or, if it is haphazardly using a symbol it does not yet clearly understand, the subconscious may interpret it in quite a different way and yield results which are not in harmony with what the talisman-maker had actually hoped to set in motion. This is particularly true if the subconscious has been locked into patterns created by persistent or obsessive thoughts generated by consciousness. These kinds of patterns are dangerous because symbol then can act as a doorway to archetypal possession.

If a symbol could stand for ten different things, we need to understand what particular thing we want it to mean in a given situation, and draw boundaries around the other elements that it may attract. We refine this by adding more layers of symbolic meaning to the talisman to help clarify our intent and purpose. For example, the symbol of a triangle may mean fire or it may mean a trinity. If we add the name Michael in Hebrew we clarify our purpose by calling on the fiery energy of Michael; or if we include a planetary sigil of Mars, it will be a different kind of fiery energy. But if we add other images and God-names which identify it as Trinity, or as representing Binah on the Tree of Life, then the image of the triangle changes in psychic structure because we design it in accordance with specific conscious intention.

It can't be emphasized enough that it is important to develop a working language with the subconscious which is built on clear correspondences. Otherwise, subconsciousness may attach its own past associations of a symbol (which now may be consciously forgotten) and go out and try to energize that correspondence to make it work for us. Consciousness should make its *present* interpretation of the symbol clear to subconsciousness. For this reason every talisman is unique and very personal.

This is why it is difficult to decipher a seal or talisman made by someone in the distant past. This is also the reason, in my opinion, it is useless to copy or reproduce talismans from other magical books. Only by completely understanding the meaning of the symbols on the talisman will the magician get any results. Most books with pictures of seal, and sigils are of little value to us because we have no idea what was in the mind of the creator when the talisman was being made. Moreover, ancient seals could have been recopied many times before publication, resulting in many errors. Or some could have encoded information, (such as the arrangement of certain letters) that were an abbreviation or formula known only to the magician who made them. To attempt to reconstruct such a formula, even if one has a good working knowledge of Hebrew or Latin, may be of little avail; if the formula was intended for publication, the seals and sigils could well be *blinds* anyway. We will examine the problem of mistakes as well as blinds in magic squares and sigils in Chapter Three.

In the Qabalistic tradition there is a certain sense of correctness: One does not just formulate a desire and put things together. It should be clear by now that one needs a set of correspondences which, because it has the backbone of tradition, has certain built-in rules. One would not put the mark or seal of the planet Mars on a talisman for healing, along with an angel or Intelligence from the Sphere of the Moon. One uses Mars for other purposes; healing would belong to the Sphere of the Sun (or, in some cases, Mercury); and in neither case would you use the Intelligence of the Moon. This is an example of combining three different energies that have little or nothing to do with one another. We don't put an angelic name on a talisman because we like the way it sounds, or even because of past associations from childhood. In Qabalah, talismanic images, symbols, or names are in no way arbitrary. If you don't know Qabalistic correspondences well, study the charts given here and choose carefully.

The tattwa images are less rigid in terms of categories, *i.e.*, they were incorporated into the Golden Dawn tradition late and have been used as symbols for the planets, Tarot keys, and elements, as well as elemental combinations, by different people with different variations in meaning. Correspondences relating to the Tree—which have a much longer history—will have a greater tendency to be interpreted by most Qabalists in the same way. Some seals and sigils (if they are not blinds or mistakes) can therefore be re-interpreted centuries after the fact by those who know what Sphere or planetary energy they represent. This is not to say we understand the intention in the mind of the person making the talisman. However, some symbols, (*i.e.*, planetary signs, the sigils, and Hebrew letters which spell the God-names, angels, etc.,) have remained the same in the Qabalistic tradition.

Tattwa combinations, on the other hand, are almost endless. As used in the Golden Dawn, they comprise twenty-five variants of the five principal elements, *i.e.*, earth, air, fire, water, and ether, represented by a square, a circle, a triangle, a moon shape, and an egg shape. They have been attributed to Tarot keys with some success. I have a number of students who use them regularly. But there are some inconsistencies and a number of different interpretations. Tattwa images and their possible uses can be found in the works of Mathers (1971) and Regardie (1984). Case attributes Tattwa images to zodiacal signs and the internal planetary chakras, which in turn relate specifically to color correspondences.

The latter were particularly important to Case, who felt that the Tattwa images served as mandalas for healing the emotional, physical and etheric bodies through meditation on their colors and accompanying tones. In his book *Tarot* (1947), Case gave these tones and colors in a somewhat veiled fashion, and they have been published in other books as well, such as *Archetypes on the Tree of Life* (1991) by Madonna Compton. Some sources, such as Emahmn's *The Book of Correspondences* (1991), have different attributions. (See bibliography for above books.) They are not as fixed in interpretation as are the talismans which are directly derived from the Tree of Life.

One single Tattwa image, for example a square (which is attributed to earth), could be added to many different kinds of talismans—it would go with different planetary energies for a variety of purposes. When added to one with Venus, or Netzach, it may refer to the need for grounding in a particular relationship; when added to one with Mercury, or Hod, it may make concrete certain aspirations for getting a teaching job. This will become more clear as we explore the tattwa and talisman correspondences in more depth.

For meditation images which lead one directly to an experience of the Intelligence of the path (or those belonging to the Tarot archetype), I suggest the Hebrew Letters themselves, which are rooted in the Tree tradition and are specific in intention. These should be done on flashing color tablets—that is, in colors which are complementary. If the ground is red, the image is green, etc. For more information on the Hebrew Letter relationship to the Intelligences, see Case's excellent *The Book of Tokens* or other books linking the Letters with the paths on the Tree. Tattwa images are frequently used for pathworking purposes, but it must be understood that their influence is more arbitrary. They are excellent for meditation mandalas because of their vibrant colors, and are useful when added to a talisman. They are also used for balancing energy, through Color and Sound healing (as will be explained in chapter fourteen), and are very accessible for contacting elemental energy.

For a number of years I have used a combination of basic tattwa symbols from the Golden Dawn and offshoot traditions as flashing color tablets to evoke both color healing and planetary energies in tattwa-like talismans, thus combining a variety of techniques. As I hope you will discover, by building on a solid Qabalistic tradition and incorporating newer experiments using tattwas and talismans as meditation mandalas, many amazing results can be achieved.

Chapter 2

✤

GETTING STARTED

For he hath given his angels charge over thee; to keep thee in all thy ways.

—Psalm 90:11

Before you embark on a serious talisman-making adventure, it is good to have a Guide. For our purposes, we will identify this Guide as the Higher Self or The Holy Guardian Angel, to distinguish it from what is commonly referred to as "spirit guides." I highly recommend that you pause and ask yourself if you have a relationship with your Holy Guardian Angel that is Qabalistically based. In other words, if you already have a clear sense of the name, colors, tones, and other correspondences connected with this Entity, fine. If not, you can learn how to do this through a very simple process.

✤ Getting a Guide

First, ask for a name to be revealed to you. It may come in a dream, or you may have an inspiration about it, or it may drop into your life unasked, perhaps through some kind of synchronistic event. You may choose some Biblical name (this is *not* the same as the Biblical character) or one mythologically based. At any rate, *get a magical name*, a name for your true Higher Self, who is guiding this whole process.

When you have decided upon a name, you may want to add the suffix AL, which is a God-name attributed to Chesed, the Merciful. It makes the entity angelic, it gives it wings (Aleph) and scales (Lamed). You may need to play with the name a bit before it sounds right. Then try to figure out how to spell it in Hebrew (see the chart in figure 2–A), and when you are comfortable with the spelling (you may want to check some gematria associations, if this is important to you), keep it for all your magical work. One of my students originally took the name Sarah, then, for magical workings, changed it to Sariel.

Hebrew	Pronounciation	Spelling	English	Number
א	Aleph	ALP	A	1
ב	Beth	BITh	B	2
ג	Gimel	GML	G	3
ד	Daleth	DLTh	D	4
ה	Heh	HH	H, E	5
ו	Vav	VV	V, U, W	6
ז	Zain	ZIN	Z	7
ח	Cheth	ChITh	Ch	8
ט	Teth	TTH	T	9
י	Yod	YVD	I, J, Y	10
כ	Kaph	KP	K, C	20
ל	Lamed	LMD	L	30
מ	Mem	MIM	M	40
נ	Nun	NVN	N	50
ס	Samekh	SMK	S	60
ע	Ayin	OIN	O	70
פ	Peh	PH	P, F, Ph	80
צ	Tzaddi	TzDI	Tz	90
ק	Qoph	QVP	Q	100
ר	Resh	RISh	R	200
ש	Shin	ShIN	Sh	300
ת	Tau	ThV	Th, T	400
ך			K (Final)	500
ם			M (Final)	600
ן			N (Final)	700
ף			P (Final)	800
ץ			Tz (Final)	900

Figure 2–A

You should also begin to use this name frequently in your prayers. Begin a real relationship with this Entity, who is the most lofty aspect of *your own aspirations and inspirations,* a radiant ray of the Lord's love, shining on you and through you, protecting, guiding, taking an interest in you. A famous magician of our century, Franz Bardon, says that the guide will eventually inform his protégé about the laws of the physical world, as well as guide him or her in the astral:

> (The Guardian's purpose) clearly shows how necessary it is that the magical development of a human being during his time in the physical world leads him towards perfection in order to be prepared for life in a higher sphere (1991, p. 84).

There are some general Qabalistic guidelines for a Guide or Holy Guardian Angel which we will look at in the next section.

When you begin to build a relationship with this wonderful Entity (which we will now refer to with the initials H.G.A.), It will likely start manifesting little signs for you, to assure you of Its presence. However, you should not have to ask for signs and wonders; it may be best to let It speak to you in Its own way. On the other hand, you can say anything you like to your H.G.A.—It is your closest Friend; just affirm in the beginning that It is directed toward your higher good and the good of all. It will then act as the right kind of filter, and soon you will begin to understand how to trust more in the process of letting It—and only It—be your true direction. This may seem like a kind of surrender, but it also strengthens the will, as you will see the more you work with developing this relationship. This may take time. If you don't already have a Holy Guardian Angel in your life, it may seem a bit superstitious, but what are you doing but having a relationship with your subconscious? You are trying to establish an archetypal encounter, and learn a common language.

This is part of the western occult tradition: get an H.G.A. from God, trust It, and begin to work with It. An ancient magical treatise known as *The Sacred Magic of Abramalin, the Mage* (translated by S. L. M. Mathers) advises the neophyte to live alone, concentrating on nothing but his or her H.G.A. for 6 months. Some Qabalists have actually attempted to do this; others have tried this meditation process on a smaller time scale, such as during an isolated retreat. Concentrating on one's H.G.A. most certainly focuses and strengthens the will and one's intention for magical workings.

If it is not possible to take any time off to begin to deepen your relationship with your H.G.A., then just do it through some simple but committed practice. Devote a certain amount of time in prayer, reflection, meditation—even if it is 5 or 10 minutes a day—to some spiritual practice that will purify you so that you will be a clear vessel for your H.G.A. We want to purify our vessels. The Middle Pillar exercise given in so many Golden Dawn publications is excellent for this, and once memorized can be visualized in its entirety in about 10 minutes. (This is not a full Middle Pillar Ritual, which involves bodily movements, chanting, etc.; it is a condensed form many practicing Qabalists can do in their imagination. See Bibliography for more on Regardie's excellent books on this.)

❖ Guidelines for the Holy Guardian Angel

There are some general Qabalistic guidelines outlined by many teachers in the western tradition; here we will give the principle ones outlined by Edwin Steinbrecher in his *Inner Guide Meditation*, and some hints from Dr. Paul Case, which are similar in many ways. Neither advise associating this kind of imaginative work with astral projection; we are not trying to get *out* of our bodies. Even when we use the tattwas and talismans as astral doorways, we mean a *conscious* excursion into the realm of the imagination. Neither are we trying to just enter some kind of daydream, unless we mean a *controlled daydream*. Fantasizing and daydreaming, in the western occult tradition, are the great thieves of the life energy. Doing *active pathworking* opens the door for the energy to manifest on the physical plane that is compatible with a full, rich life in harmony with the magician's intentions. As Steinbrecher explains:

> The Inner Guide Meditation is a way of working on inner planes that is a direct outgrowth. . . of the western Mystery Tradition. It is an action oriented method: you move, you utilize your ego and your senses, you ask questions. . . and barter, you insist, you explore, you discover, you laugh and you cry. It is the method of the Child in us all (p. 82).

In other words, it requires full participation and consciousness. Many trance states produce just the opposite effect, and this is one reason why these guide guidelines are also quite specific. They insist on the presence of consciousness and will, so important for the development of a magician. Let us examine some of these guidelines:

1. Your H.G.A. will not be dead, *i.e.*, a dead relative or historical figure. It is angelic. The former has a tendency to possess, albeit ever so subtly. Angels do not possess; they inform. Don't expect Joan of Arc, St. Germain, or your dead aunt. Spirit guides are not Guardian Angels.

2. Your H.G.A. will not volunteer any information, and will not invade your privacy; it should only manifest when called upon, *i.e.*, in the suggested meeting place determined by you or in pathwork, etc. You must ask (clarify your intention) for information, and give permission for an answer. In fact, you may need to give permission several times, and press for information, especially at first.

3. H.G.A.s that are true guides will not tell you what to do (*e.g.*, "my Guide told me to poison your dog"). Watch this one; it shows an immediate false guide. Your H.G.A. will never coerce or interfere with your free will. They do function as intuition, hunches or conscience. Sometimes (often) they speak in symbolic language, and leave it for you to interpret. They seldom make predictions(global or personal.)

4. The H.G.A. will not judge or flatter (*e.g.*, agree with you that someone is treating you badly; fluff up or demolish your ego, etc.). It will advise, if asked.

5. A Guide who is a real H.G.A. will never have a vibration of fear, only love. This is not a shadow figure; it is here to protect you.

6. Your H.G.A. will answer "yes" if asked "Are you my true Guide?" A false guide will avoid the question or disappear. *Test them.*

7. Steinbrecher says your Guide may also have the characteristics or features of your ninth house placement (Superconsciousness). I have not always found this to be the case, but you can check it out.

Dr. Case calls the H.G.A the Inner Voice, and identifies It with the Hierophant, or Inner Teacher, in the Tarot. The way to tune into this energy is through quiet listening.

In fact, a good way to determine if someone is actually having a relationship with their H.G.A. is to watch their outer behavior and see if they *listen*. Is he or she able to listen attentively to what other people have to say? Does the information he or she claims to receive from the Inner Teacher agree with ethics and good sense? Does the person show self-discipline or does he or she pester everybody with accounts of his or her incredible visions? These are some good criteria to test yourself and others.

❖ Building a Telesmatic Figure and Sigil

When you are building this beautiful relationship with your closest and most trust-worthy Friend, begin to discover clues about Its nature. Does your angel seem male or female? Does He or She glow with certain colors? You can determine what colors are actually associated with the letters of the Hebrew Name (which, ideally, should be 5–7 letters). Begin with the first letter. Find it in the color chart (see figure 2–B). You may need to compare the

Attributions of the Hebrew Letters

Color	Sign, Planet	Letter	Tarot #	Element
Yellow	Air	Aleph	0	Air
Yellow	Mercury	Beth	1	Air, Earth
Blue	Moon	Gimel	2	Water
Green	Venus	Daleth	3	Earth, Air
Red	Aries	Heh	4	Fire
Red-Orange	Taurus	Vav	5	Earth
Orange	Gemini	Zain	6	Air
Yellow-Orange	Cancer	Cheth	7	Water
Yellow	Leo	Teth	8	Fire
Yellow-Green	Virgo	Yod	9	Earth
Violet	Jupiter	Kaph	10	Fire, Water
Green	Libra	Lamed	11	Air
Blue	Water	Mem	12	Water
Blue-Green	Scorpio	Nun	13	Water
Blue	Sagittarius	Samekh	14	Fire
Indigo	Capricorn	Ayin	15	Earth
Red	Mars	Peh	16	Fire, Water
Violet	Aquarius	Tzaddi	17	Air
Violet-Red	Pisces	Qoph	18	Water
Orange	Sun	Resh	19	Fire
Red	Fire	Shin	20	Fire
Indigo	Saturn	Tau	21	Earth, Air

Figure 2–B

Hebrew Letters in this chart with the ones in figure 2–A to find the correct correspondences between the Letters. Imagine your H.G.A. with the first color emanating from His or Her head. If it is a dark color, like purple, imagine it a bit lighter, or more refined than dense. Any color can also be tinged with gold. Take the next color-letters for the neck, arms, torso, and clothing, in the order in which the letters appear in the name. The last two letters (if it has an AL or El ending) are the yellow wings (A) and the green shoes and scales (L).

Begin to build this image through artwork, meditation, practice and dialogue. You may perceive your H.G.A. to be predominately one sex or the other, and this could change over time. However, sexuality is primarily only an attribution humans attach to angelic entities in order to make our visualization more relatable. Next, learn Its sigil and use it on all your talismans. The sigil is your special seal of protection.

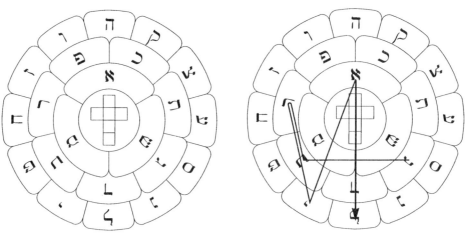

Figure 2–C   Figure 2–D

The way of doing this, and the traditional way of creating many sacred and angelic sigils or signatures in the Golden Dawn tradition, is to take the letters of the Name, for instance Gabriel (GBRIAL), and trace them in order onto the Golden Dawn Rose glyph (see figure 2–C) through a thin sheet of paper. It is best to use a ruler. The usual way of making a sigil is to indicate its opening with a circle and close with a small line. In our lodge we usually close with an arrow, so Gabriel looks like figure 2–D.

What have you just done? You have made a glyph or visual image of an angelic name or vibration. Here we have a western technique wherein the image or visual representation is another method of communicating to an entity whose word or name we are calling upon verbally and mentally, similar to the yantra/mantra concept in the East.

We could color it according to the Letter associations just mentioned, that is, make the first part of the line blue (G, Gimel); then yellow (B, Beth); orange (R, Resh); yellow-green (I, Yod); yellow or golden (A, Aleph); and emerald green (L, Lamed). Once again,

Hebrew Letters and Corresponding Incenses and Tones

Letter	Incense	Tone
A–Aleph	Adamant, Acacia, **Galbanum**, Lavender, **Gum Arabic**, Sage	E
B–Beth	Fenugreek, Horehound, **Mastic, Storax**	E
G–Gimel	**Camphor**, Aloes, **Jasmine**, Pennyroyal	A–flat
D–Daleth	Myrtle, **Sandlewood, Rose**	F–sharp
E, H–Heh	**Dragon's Blood**, Geranium, Tiger Lily	C
V, W–Vay	Borage, Mallow, Periwinkle, **Storax**	C–sharp
Z–Zain	Orchid, **Wormwood**	D
Ch–Cheth	Anise, **Camphor, Lotus**, Onycha	D–sharp
T–Teth	Catnip, **Frankincense**, Cinnamon	B
I, J, Y–Yod	Lily, **Narcissis**	F
K, C–Kaph	**Cedar**, Hyssop, Saffron	A–sharp
L–Lamed	**Amber**, Hyacinth, **Galbanum**	F–sharp
M–Mem	Fern, **Lotus**, Violet, **Myrrh**	A–flat
N–Nun	**Benzoin**, Pine, **Opoponax**	G
S–Samech	Aloes, Dill, **Heliotrope, Iris**	A–flat
O–Ayin	**Civit**, Hemp, **Musk**, Thistle	A
P, F–Peh	Capsium, **Dragon's Blood**, Eyebright, **Rue**	C
Tz, Ts–Tzaddi	Cloves, **Galbanum**, Olive	B–flat
Q–Qoph	**Ambrigris**, Hibiscus, Mugwort, **Poppy**	B
R–Resh	**Cinnamon, Heliotrope**, Laurel, Sunflower	D
Sh–Shin	**Copol**, Frankincense	C
T, Th–Tau	**Cypress**, Lovage, Nightshade, **Storax**	A

Figure 2–E
Note: The most important incenses, Qabalistically, are in bold type.

you should understand that if you decide to use this name, it is *not* the same entity as the archangel Gabriel, only the same name. (Not everyone named John is the same person.)

One could then proceed to find the tones connected to the various letters in the name (see th chart in figure 2–E) and compose a little personalized mantra of the Magical Name. It could be incorporated into one's magical workings, along with other prayers, affirmations, Divine Names, etc., or simply used whenever you want to call upon your H.G.A. You may also make an incense compound from the letter correspondences (also in E). This is a very powerful method for connecting the neophyte with the corresponding vibrations of the H.G.A., since it is literally infused into one's body cells through inhalation. There are many variations on these themes that can be utilized by the creative student. The principal point is to establish relationship. Steinbrecher pointed out that of all the archetypal entities encountered, connecting with one's H.G.A. should be the first and most important archetypal relationship. This idea has counterparts in many aspects of Jungian work as well. It is the most valuable kind of Guide in any kind of active imagination, pathwork or visualization. Jung himself had a primary "archetypal friend" whose name was Philamon.

If you work with the Tarot, begin meditating on the 14th Arcana, (which pictures an angel) for inspiration. An excellent treatise on the H.G.A. is given in the book, *Meditations on the Tarot* (1991) by Valentin Tomberg (who here calls himself Anonymous), in his reflection on the Temperance Key (#14). It is truly an inspirational chapter where he explains, from a hermetic point of view, the functions of the H.G.A.: to guard, cherish, protect, visit and defend.

There are many other excellent books on angels available today that can deepen the aspirant's relationship with his or her H.G.A. This is an age in which humankind is being visited by angelic beings in a way perhaps never known in recorded history.

These techniques for forming a telesmatic image of an angelic figure can be successfully used with any angel or archangel. Although there are other color scales— in the Golden Dawn tradition there are four, which correspond to the four worlds—we are using what is known as the King scale, which Case advises for the Tarot keys, zodiacal signs and corresponding Hebrew Letters (*i.e.*, the tree paths). The Sephiroth or planetary color scales are from what is known as the Queen scale. What is most important is consistency and knowing the correct complementary color scales to make flashing color tablets (see the table in figure 2–F).

Complementary Colors

Complementary Colors
Red—Green
Blue—Orange
Yellow—Violet
Red-Orange—Blue-Green
Yellow-Orange—Blue-Violet (Indigo)
Yellow-Green—Red-Violet

Figure 2–F

Note: There are many hues or shades the student can experiment with; for example the Golden Dawn complementary chart is a bit more complicated than this one, but I have found the best results to come from personal experimentation.

❖ A Practice Flashing Tablet

Historical writers in the beginning of the Christian era recorded the belief that the stones of the breastplate of the High Priest were so highly magnetized by their particular angelic rulers that they responded to questions and gave directions in flashing color language. How this manifested exactly is shrouded in mystery, but the flashing color tablets have always been an important part of the western magical tradition. In this book they are a vital part of talismanic art and the student should experiment with the possibilities outlined here. To get a sense of how powerful yet simple this technique is, I suggest you attempt to make your first flashing color tablet by using the simple design in figure 2–G,

Figure 2–G

a triangle within another triangle within a circle, in the flashing colors of green, red, green (red background). This symbol evokes the vibrant energy of fire. Make this design in colors as bright as possible. You may use paint or magic markers, or even construction paper. The whole diagram should be about the size of a regular 8-1/2x11 inch sheet of paper when finished, and mounted a few feet away, at eye level, to meditate upon. The technique is to stare with unbroken eye contact for a full three to five minutes. You may find your eyes tiring, but try to remain focused on the figure at one point, rather than moving your eyes around.

Then shut your eyes and see if an after-image occurs (in the opposite color). This usually happens, even on the first attempt. If it doesn't, try again. You may need to move the image closer. You will also probably see a very bright glowing color right behind the figure you are meditating on, which may also begin to have a flashing or darting effect. The point is to try and remain focused despite these rather beautiful optical illusions. (What you are actually seeing are the true astral colors, which are much more brilliant.)

When you shut your eyes, try to hold the image as long as you can and, if possible, bring it close enough so that it actually appears to encompass you, or you seem to pass through it. Then you will be in the magical or imaginative landscape of the energy evoked by the telesmatic figure. You may then choose to just observe. (But try not to become too passive.) Or you may want to dialogue with whatever kind of figure emerges.

Any talismanic design could be used for this purpose (for example, our lodge came up with the idea of using the planetary seals), although the flashing tablet effect works best if used with one or two pairs of complementary colors. You could start with simple designs such as this one, provided you are clear about the energy you are evoking. (See Chapter Three for description of the basic types of tattwa images and other correspondences.) These could later be incorporated into a larger, more comprehensive talisman, which may end up being a much more intricate design. It is good to keep in mind that we are making mandala-like talismans primarily for meditation, so the more geometrical or symmetrical the whole talisman is, the better.

In my opinion, this is a far more powerful technique than simply making the talisman and compressing it (often mauling it in the process) into some kind of locket to wear. In the latter case it is soon forgotten, and in any event the image would need to be removed to be seen again. Meditation talismans continue to elicit suggestions to the subconscious, which is aroused at every meditation session. I do recommend that you shield the talisman from mundane eyes. It was created by you and it is meant for your eyes only. It is a good idea to hang it behind a thin silk screen, then take it out whenever you want to use it.

As with all talismans, you should release it when it has fulfilled its purpose. This does not necessarily mean destroying it, as is often recommended for talismans or amulets. It just needs to be discharged (a simple affirmation or ritual created by you would suffice for this) and put away. You could keep it in your magical diary, along with a description about the purpose for which it was designed and other magical notes to remind you of what it was employed for in the past. It should, however, be put out of your mind once used and no longer needed.

❖ Correspondences and Timing

Before attempting to create a talisman, one should have studied the correspondence tables and made sketches of the symbols and names one wishes to use. You may also make yourself sympathetic to the celestial influences you wish to contact through working with all of the senses. Agrippa said in the first of his *Three Books of Occult Philosophy*:

> One Operative Virtue that is diffused through all kinds of things: by which virtue, indeed, as manifest things are produced out of occult causes, so a magician doth make use of things manifest to draw forth things that are occult, *viz*, through the rays of the Stars, through fumes, lights, sounds, and natural things which are agreeable to those celestial, in which. . . there is a kind of reason, sense and harmony, and incorporeal and divine measures and orders (p 121).

In addition to having some clear ideas about the associated symbols to be used in the talisman one was going to make to invoke Venusian energy, for example, one could also prepare a Venusian incense, burn a green candle or work under a green light. As many correspondences as possible should be employed to evoke a sense of the numinous.

Before your magical working it is good to be aware of astrological timing. If working with planetary squares and symbols derived from the Tree, one can take various courses, such as attempting to make the talisman from beginning to end on the particular day attributed to that planet/sphere, *e.g.*, Sunday for the Sun, Monday for the Moon, etc. This could even be further subdivided into *planetary hours* and their ruling angelic forces (see next chapter). Generally, the first hour is calculated by the moment the sun rises on that particular day, and therefore the hours vary in length, according to whether the days are long or short. For many modern magicians (who have schedules as busy as anyone else), these minute time speculations may be too cumbersome. Other planetary influences may then be examined for the most auspicious timing.

If the talisman is to be Mercurial in character, you may ask: is the planet astrologically favored at the time the talisman is being made? One should attempt it at a time when the Sun is in Gemini or Virgo, for example, or when one of these signs is conjunct the Moon. You do not need to be an adept astrologer to discover some basic positive correspondences for the best times to make your particular talisman. The moon should also be on the increase (unless trying to diminish something). Failing all else, it is nearly always permissible to create any talisman on a Wednesday, because one of the things Mercury rules is the making of seals and pentacles.

❖ Prayers and Intention

Following the Qabalistic tradition, the neophyte should do some form of preparation, such as the Qabalistic Cross and Banishing ritual given in much of the Golden Dawn literature (see bibliography), or one could simply pause and say a prayer for a blessing of the work. Here are two ancient benedictions given in the *Of Occult Philosophy, Book 4* (p. 62–3), attributed to Agrippa, but probably written by one of his students:

1. After the casting of the circle of protection, repeat the Biblical phrase: "Thou shalt purge me with hyssop, O Lord and I shall be clean; Thou shalt wash me and I shall be whiter than snow."

2. Then light the incense attributed to the sphere or planetary energy being invoked and say: "The God of Abraham, God of Isaac, God of Jacob, bless here the creatures of these kinds, that they may fill up the power and virtue of their odors, so that neither the enemy, nor any false imagination, may be able to enter into them, through our Lord Jesus Christ."

Numerous other prayers and affirmations may be used in keeping with the student's own personal inclinations, but these should be studied, at least for the implications suggested, both psychologically and magically. Purification and intention—so frequently stressed—are vital at this point in the working. The medieval mystic Arnold of Villanova felt that although talismans were a blessing for those who were struggling on the spiritual path, they would only benefit those who had been purified in both mind and heart. Setting aside a time of prayerful reflection is a very important part of beginning. Regardie offers a number of other traditional Qabalistic prayers at the end of his wonderful treatise, *The Tree of Life*.

This is also the time to state your intention—out loud, and as clearly articulated as possible. If the student has these three principles firmly in hand: right dedication, right timing, and correct symbolism, he or she can proceed with confidence. You will also find that by repeated use of the same prayers, affirmations, or rituals, results can eventually be achieved with less effort. The operation will become fused with the magician's personal strength. This takes practice. Franz Bardon has estimated that about 462 repetitions are necessary for the influence of a true magician to be powerfully felt. But, with clarity and commitment, I would dare say that for our purposes here, you will be surprised at the results.

In creating a talisman, a great amount of versatility and creativity can be employed using the various symbols, numbers, and letters given in the charts in this book, but there are certain divine Names that should be on every talisman. The magician knows that these are symbolic designations of divine qualities and powers:

1. The words "In the Name of. . ." followed by one of the names of God, *i.e.*, by referring to the Sephira being invoked (see page 25). This could be written in English or abbreviated in the Hebrew form (MShB. . .). The sigil of the Divine Name taken from the Rose could also suffice. If the former method is used, the words could be written around the rim, leaving the inside blank for the rest of the design.

2. The name of the Archangel associated with the Sephira, and again, either the name or the sigil could be used.

3. The name or sigil of your H.G.A.

4. Other associations through number, symbol, etc. taken from the correspondence tables and the information given in the next chapter.

Chapter 3

CORRESPONDENCES

Current magical tradition follows these principles: after we clarify our intention, we proceed to concretize it through working with the Divine Names and Numbers. This alphabetical and numerical mysticism is at the heart of the ancient art of Qabalistic talisman-making, which is based on the mysteries of magical squares and the sigils derived from them.

In the first of his *Three Books of Occult Philosophy*, Agrippa says:

> The use of words and speech is to express the inwards of the mind, and from thence to draw forth the secrets of the thoughts, and to declare the will of the speaker. Now, writing is the last expression of the mind, and is the *number of speech and voice*. . . and therefore magicians command that in every work there be imprecations and inscriptions. . . (1971, p. 215).

Many other kinds of sacred correspondences are also included in talismans, and we will review these in this chapter. We will examine the squares and sigils, or signatures of the Divine Names, in the next chapter. The various sacred names or words which specify our particular intention, such as a Biblical verse or affirmation, are important parts of the talisman and should always be included.

Agrippa also wrote:

> The Scripture tells us that there are names written in heaven; why, it was said, should they be written there, if they be useless? Through the knowledge of such divine names, it is affirmed, Moses overcame the sorcerers of Egypt, Elias brought fire from heaven, Daniel closed the mouths of lions. . . By what secret to have power over this line of communication with superior worlds it is for practical cabalism to discover (1971, p. 242).

The celestial intelligences are, in practical Qabalistic magic, thought to be emanations of the Deity, and correspond to principles in the human microcosm. This is really an early and exceedingly perceptive psychology. Agrippa explains that:

> The more I dwell upon their qualities, the more I long for the divine, the more shall I be blessed by the reception of their rays. The more intensely I yearn heavenward, the more shall I bring down heaven to dwell in my soul (1971, p. 222).

Part of the process of tapping into the numinosity of these Intelligences is to become empowered by their attributes. Working with magical correspondences in this way is one means of purifying our vessels. As Regardie said in his *Tree of Life,* one's first task is to "perfect the immediate vehicle through which the Holy Guardian Angel is to manifest" (1972, p. 201).

To this end, the first goal should not be materializing desires for the satisfaction of the ego, but rather balancing psychic energy through compensatory magical workings. If the student finds him or herself hampered by poor concentration or burdened with a negative outlook on life, he or she should try and remedy these deficiencies. This could be done in a variety of ways in the Golden Dawn tradition, but for our purposes the means employed are limited to the uses of talismanic art. In examining the charts related to the planetary chakras, the student should seek out specific characteristics he or she feels would correspond to aspects of the personality that could be more properly balanced.

After several trial sessions of using talismanic art in this compensatory way, one should begin to sense a definite clearing in the mental and physical vehicles, as well as a strong feeling of grounding. Any session of using talismans for the purpose of working on aspects of the personality should also include the invocation of one's H.G.A. As Regardie explains:

> The attainment is grounded upon a solid base, one not built on shifting sands that the merest breath of wind could overthrow; the Knowledge and Conversation (of the Holy Guardian Angel) is rooted in the very spirit and body of the whole being, and no danger is there at all of an illumination obsessing him with a fanatical idea, or overthrowing the balance of his mind (1972, p202–03).

When choosing the Divine Names to be placed on the talisman, the God-name is of utmost importance. (This is distinguished from the angelic names and names of Intelligences and spirits, which we will examine in more detail in later chapters.) This is because the Divine Name, which corresponds to pure Sphere energy, is itself a complete, absolute, harmonious Idea of the Godhead; all other names evoke semi-intelligent forces of Spirit which are not completely developed (therefore representing only a limited aspect of consciousness).

Review the chart in figure 3–A, which lists the Sephiroth and their corresponding Divine Names, before each magical session. The names of the archangels are useful for this purpose, since they represent the first manifestation in the outpouring of the God-energy. One will also note other God-names which specifically correspond to the kameas when we get to these individual sections. They will be marked with an asterisk (*). Note that plane-

No.	Sephira	Deity	Archangel	Planetary Angel	Planet
2	Chokmah	Yah or YHVH	Raziel		Zodiac
3	Binah	YHVH Elohim	Tzaphqiel	Cassiel	Saturn
4	Chesed	El	Tzadqiel	Sachiel	Jupiter
5	Geburah	Elohim Gibor	Kamael	Samael	Mars
6	Tiphareth	YHVH Eloah Ve Daath	Raphael	Michael	Sun
7	Netzach	YHVH Tzabaoth	Haniel	Anael	Venus
8	Hod	Elohim Tzabaoth	Michael	Raphael	Mercury
9	Yesod	Shaddai El Chai	Gabriel	Gabriel	Moon
10	Malkuth	Adonai Ha Aretz	Sandalphon	Elementals	Earth
11	Daath	Yah Elohim	Mesukiel	Urial	Pluto

Figure 3–A

tary angelic energy is not the same as archangelic Names, even though at times they may seem to coincide. The chart in figure 3–A also gives the list of both archangels and planetary angels. With practice, familiarity with these different kinds of angelic energy will become second-nature. In Qabalah it is important to understand these differences, since it is a system which is definitely hierarchal. Intelligences and spirits are stepped down from the Source. They are also more specific and quite useful in talisman-making.

The student may ask, "Are these entities actually outside floating around in planetary space, or inside, a part of my own consciousness?" Earlier we spoke of the subconscious; now we seem to be talking about planetary entities in a way which implies that they have some kind of metaphysical reality. As stated in chapter one, we will adopt both philosophies; most modern-day magicians integrate both philosophies fairly easily. In any event, the debate about whether such symbolic entities are objective or subjective is a philosophical discussion that far exceeds the scope of this book. We will simply quote Regardie, who has found a happy synthesis between the two:

> (By) employing such herbs, incenses, colors, seals, lights, forms, and divine names as are consonant and congruous to the traditional nature of Mercury, the magician is thus the more easily enabled to stimulate the creativity of the Imagination, and evoke either from his own mind or the Astral Light, the idea or spirit pertaining to that grade or hierarchy called Mercury (1972, p. 207).

All of these various correspondences (and the other planets as well) will be found in the charts in this and following chapters. The incenses which are connected to the planetary energies are a vital part of the magical art of talisman-making (see the chart in figure 3–B). They can be burned both in the process of actual construction as well as used for fumigating or consecrating the magical seal when it is finished. Remember, when working with any kind of name—your own, your H.G.A, an archangel, etc.—an incense compound can also be made from the Letter-correspondences (see figure 2–E on page

Sephiroth and Planetary Incenses

Binah	Civet, Myrrh	Saturn	Cassia, Cypress, Patchouli, Myrrh, Violet
Chesed	Cedar, Juniper	Jupiter	Clove, Hyssop, Nutmeg, Pine
Geburah	Tobacco	Mars	Basil, Dragon's Blood, Galangal, Mustard, Rue
Tiphareth	Frankincense, Olibanum	Sun	Bay, Cinnamon, Copal, Heliotrope, Frankincense, Sunflower
Netzach	Benzoin, Rose	Venus	Lemon Verbena, Rose Geranium, Sandalwood, Vanilla
Hod	Storax	Mercury	Lavendar, Lime, Mace, Mastic, Spikenard
Yesod	Jasmine	Moon	Camphor, Eucalyptus, Galbanum, Orris, Ylang-ylang
Daath		Pluto	Dittany, Dragon's Blood, Mandrake, Myrrh, Wormwood

Figure 3–B

17). This particular technique is also useful in an alternate method of talisman construction based on the name alone, which is given in chapter thirteen.

Consecration is an important part of talismanic art, to be performed at the beginning—with the voicing of one's intention— and at the end, when a more ritualistic kind of offering could be made. In *The Magus*, Francis Barret clearly tells us that any vow, oblation, or sacrifice has the power of consecration, so almost anything could be consecrated if it is considered sacred to the magician. For example, I have most certainly consecrated the writings in this book.

In consecrating planetary talismans, it is advisable to use invocations of the Names on the finished seal itself, along with other prayers or affirmations the magician deems fit. The chart in figure 3–C lists the Sufi (Islamic) God-names, should the student wish to incorporate any of these Names on the talisman. They, like the Hebrew God-names, come from the same Arabic source, and because they belong to the western tradition can be used just as easily. One will note that many of the ninety-nine attributes in the Islamic tradition contain the letters *AL*, which is a God-name in Hebrew as well.

The student may either follow the traditional method of incorporating a Biblical phrase, or another prayer or affirmation which expresses the talisman's principle purpose somewhere on the magical seal itself. This can be a whole sentence, or something as short and simple as "I communicate." It can be printed around the rim, or, if it is not too long, it can even be made into a sigil and traced onto a planetary kamea (see next chapter). However you choose to use the prayer or affirmation, it should serve as a reminder every time you use the talisman as a mandala to meditate upon. Even just a glance at the talisman in the morning could elicit a subconscious response, and the affirmation would

The 99 Islamic God-names

1. Ar-Rahman—The Merciful	33. Al-Azim—The Grand	67. As-Samad—The Eternal
2. Ar-Rahim—The Compassionate	34. Al-Ghafur—The Forgiving	68. Al-Kadir—The Powerful
3. Al-Makik—The King	35. Ash-Shakur—The Grateful	69. Al-Muktadir—The Prevailing
4. Al-Kuddus—The Holy	36. Al-Ali—The Exalted	70. Al-Mukaddim—The Bringer Forth
5. As-Salam—The Peace	37. Al-Kabir—The Great	71. Al-Khabir—The Aware
6. As-Sabur—The Patient	38. Al-Hafiz—The Guardian	72. Al-Latif—The Subtle
7. Ar-Rashid—The Director	39. Al-Mukit—The Strengthener	73. Al-Adl—The Just
8. Al-Warith—The Heir	40. Al-Hasib—The Reckoner	74. Al-Hakim—The Ruler
9. Al-Baki—The Enduring	41. Al-Jalil—The Majestic	75. Al-Basir—The Seer
10. Al-Badi—The Incomparable	42. Al-Karim—The Generous	76. As-Sami—The Hearer
11. Al-Hadi—The Guide	43. Ar-Rakib—The Watcher	77. Al-Muzil—The Destroyer
12. An-Nur—The Light	44. Al-Mujib—The Approver	78. Al-Mu'izz—The Honourer
13. An-Nafi—The Profiter	45. Al-Wasi—The Comprehensive	79. Ar-Rafi—The Exalter
14. Az-Zarr—The Distresser	46. Al-Hakim—The Wise	80. Al-Khafiz—The Abaser
15. Al-Mani—The Withholder	47. Al-Wadud—The Loving	81. Al-Basit—The Spreader
16. Al-Muti—The Giver	48. Al-Majid—The Glorious	82. Al-Kabiz—The Restrainer
17. Al-Mughni—The Enricher	49. Al-Bais—The Raiser	83. Al-Alim—The Knower
18. Al-Ghani—The Independent	50. Ash-Shadid—The Witness	84. Al-Fattah—The Opener
19. Al-Jami—The Collector	51. Al-Hakk—The Truth	85. Al-Razzah—The Provider
20. Al-Muksit—The Equitable	52. Al-Wakil—The Advocate	86. Al-Wahhab—The Bestower
21. Dhu'l-Jalah wa'l Ikram—The Lord of Majesty and Liberality	53. Al-Kawi—The Strong	87. Al-Kahhar—The Dominant
	54. Al-Matin—The Firm	88. Al-Ghaffa—The Forgiver
22. Malik ul-Mulk—The Ruler of the Kingdom	55. Al-Wali—The Patron	89. Al-Musawwir—The Fashioner
	56. Al-Hamid—The Laudable	90. Al-Bari—The Maker
23. Ar-Ra'uf—The Kind	57. Al-Mushi—The Counter	91. Al-Khalik—The Creator
24. Al-Afuw—The Pardoner	58. Al-Mubdi—The Beginner	92. Al-Mutakabbir---The Great
25. Al-Muntakim—The Avenger	59. Al-Mu'id—The Restorer	93. Al-Jabbar—The Repairer
26. At-Tawwab—The Acceptor of Repentance	60. Al-Muhyi—The Quickener	94. Al-Aziz—The Mighty
	61. Al-Mumit—The Killer	95. Al-Muhaimim—The Protector
27. Al-Barr—The Righteous	62. Al-Hayy—The Living	96. Al-Mu'min—The Faithful
28. Al-Wali—The Governor	63. Al-Kaiyum—The Subsisting	97. Al-Awwal—The First
29. Al-Batin—The Hidden	64. Al-Wajid—The Finder	98. Al-Mu'akhkhir—The Deferrer
30. Az-Zahir—The Evident	65. Al-Majid—The Glorious	99. Al-Muta'ali—The Exalted
31. Al-Akhir—The Last	66. Al- Wahid—The One	
32. Al-Halim—The Clement		

Figure 3–C

be linked to the symbols on the talisman more with each use, imprinting an automatic psychic reaction. These kinds of suggestions to the subconscious are always more powerful if accompanied by visual symbols, which is the language the subconscious understands anyway.

If there are Divine Names on the talisman, these too can be memorized and chanted frequently throughout the day, or at least during the period of meditation. Paul Case felt that five focused minutes of concentration (with unbroken eye contact) was far more fruitful than hours of aimless passive meditation. (At five minutes, something seems to register in the subconscious.) If the talisman is serving as an astral doorway or vehicle for pathworking, one should be sure to remain actively engaged during this process, as explained earlier, rather than slipping into a state of passivity. What follows is a brief overview of the basic correspondences necessary for the art of Qabalistic talisman construction.

❖ Numbers

The first set of associations we will examine are based on number, which is the most primordial archetypal Idea. Numbers are much more than lines and circles on a page. In Qabalah, numbers *are* the Sephiroth, the initial Emanations of the God-head. They are specific energies which carry similar ideas in many metaphysical traditions, from the ancient Pythagorean numerical mysticism to modern-day numerology.

A good understanding of the primary ideas associated with the first nine numbers (as well as eleven, which will be used in this book) are crucial concepts to be employed in a variety of ways in magical work. Hebrew letters are also numbers—names have a particular numerical vibration. So do Biblical phrases or affirmations. Here is a brief review of numerical symbolism based primarily on the Qabalistic interpretations of Eliphas Levi and Paul Case.

1. One represents unity, the initial impulse, or sum of all existing things. On the Tree of Life, this is symbolized by Kether, the crown. It has no planetary association and is beyond conceptualization in terms of mythological or zodiacal correspondence. It is represented simply by a point; it has no basic form yet, such as we begin to see in number three with the primordial geometrical shape of a triangle. Modern physics tells us that one can draw a line an inch long and it will contain an infinite number of points. We can also draw a line a mile long or as long as the earth itself, and it will still contain an infinite number of points. This is because a point is a "distinct entity" in physics. The symbol of a dot within a circle connotes the center of infinity, but also the first cause; in alchemy, the *prima materia*. Although it is not employed as a means of contacting planetary energy, it can be represented by the letter Aleph (one) or Yod (which is the starting point of all of the Hebrew letters) and incorporated into any talisman for the purpose of including energy which represents initiation, inception, opening, unity, activity, and will.

2. Two symbolizes the initial impulse to create resulting in a binary relationship. Two ones represent duplication. One is active, two is passive. It is duality, the one having

extended itself. In Qabalah, this is visualized in terms of the two sexes, or a pairing of anything. It is particularly related to the two halves of the personality: one represents consciousness and will; two represents subconsciousness and memory. Two represents continuation, prolongation, or lengthening in space or time, and is symbolized by a line, or a point which has extended itself, but which is not yet capable of any definite form. On the Tree of Life it is attributed to Chokmah, Wisdom, to which belongs the Sphere of the entire Zodiac and every conceivable archetypal memory. Memory and the subconscious is characterized in the Tarot by the High Priestess. When employed in talismanic art, two draws energy which is related to reconciliation, union, memory, duplication, repetition, analogy, rhythm and periodicity.

3. When the primordial Idea of Unity is added to the Idea of a binary, what results is a ternary. It draws us out from the absolutism of dualism. It is the synthesis after experiencing thesis and anti-thesis: the creative third force. Three is the number of creation, the cause of everything comprehensible. It represents both adaptation and transmutation. It is Binah, the Holy Spirit or third Person of the Trinity on the Tree. It is characterized by the first geometrical shape, the triangle. The *triangle of art* in the western magical tradition is where materializations occur when doing evocations. As the number and Sphere of the first creative force actualizing itself in Binah, the Mother, it gives birth to all of the remaining Sephiroth on the Tree, and to it is attributed the planet Saturn. Aristotle noted that of two things we can say both but not all. Three is the first number which we can use to refer to the all. In the Tarot, this idea is represented by the fruitful creativity of the Empress. When invoking the power of three in a talisman, one should always include a triangle. Its powers express as creativity, materialization, concrete action, self-expression, and imagination.

4. Following the archetypal idea of the ternary is the quaternary, represented by a square or a cross. It characterizes the created, extended world of natural forms. The cross is a coordinate which defines and limits a plane. It again represents the duality of the physical plane: light and dark, spirit and matter. The Tau cross in Qabalah is the special seal or sign of redemption, the spirit crucified to matter and transforming it. Four symbolizes the unity of the higher and lower worlds, integration and equilibrium. It finds expression in the four elements, the four directions, and the four seasons. In Qabalah it is a very sacred number because the most holy Name of God, IHVH, or the Tetragrammaton is composed of four letters. On the Tree it corresponds to Chesed, or Jupiter, the mundane chakra. Four is the number of justice and reciprocity, echoed in the expression, "a square deal." It represents structure and foundation of creative existence, as well as order, affirmation, and happiness by attainment.

5. Five implies action, force, and power. It is represented by the planet Mars, the mundane chakra attributed to Geburah, the fifth Sphere on the Tree. It is also attributed to anthropomorphism in general, and one often sees the representation of a man with extended limbs in the shape of a pentagram or five-pointed star in medieval magical literature. Humans have five senses and understand the universe through its five elements (earth,

air, fire, water, and ether). Levi says it is the number of magic and enchantment. The five-pointed star is a symbol used both to invoke and to banish spirits. Five symbolizes the transcendence of spirit over nature. It signifies versatility and adventure as well as mediation and intuition.

6. Six is represented on the Tree by Beauty and Harmony, called Tiphareth. It is the number of perfect equilibrium and divine order through harmony. To it is attributed the Sun, which keeps the rest of the planetary Spheres in balance. It's symbolic form is represented by the six-pointed star or Seal of Solomon. The latter symbol is frequently described by the hermetic maxim, "As above, so below," or the analogical union of the macrocosm and microcosm. Its energy is loving, tolerant, compassionate, and harmonizing.

7. Seven is composed of the ternary and the quaternary and is considered sacred in many mystical traditions. It has endless correspondences: the seven planets, the seven notes on the scale, the seven virtues, the seven sacraments, the seven metals, the seven days of the week, etc. It is attributed to the Sphere on the Tree known as Netzach or Victory. It's mundane chakra is Venus. It is considered reserved, dignified, and affectionate. It is also related to ideas of mastery, conquest, and fulfillment of desire. The magical symbol of the heptagram will be examined later.

8. Eight represents realization. The eight-pointed star or eight-spoked wheel is a symbol of Christ, as well as Mercury. On the Tree, it is attributed to Hod, or the Sphere of Splendor. Its mercurial connections imply knowledge and truth-seeking, especially in magical work. It symbolizes concrete form wherein the force of Netzach finds expression. As a duplication of four, it also represents alteration and vibration. Levi relates it to the Astral Light, or magical agent wherein all vibrations exist. It also symbolizes culture, education, and evolution.

9. Nine represents fullness or completion. The numbers find their fullest expression in nine; after that, they start repeating and rearranging themselves. It is the number of divine reflection and on the Tree is represented by Yesod, the foundation. Yesod is often considered to be the reflection of the Sun, Tiphareth, and to it is attributed the Moon. It signifies goal, adeptship, conclusion, union of all elements, as well as innocence and spiritual virginity. In this aspect, the Moon is the *Anima Mundi*, the soul of the world.

11. Eleven is the duplication of one, only on a higher level. The eleventh Sphere on the Tree is sometimes conceived to be Daath, the great unknown. It is not truly considered to be one of the Sephiroth, however, because its form is as yet unrevealed. We are including it only because the time is appropriate for the release of certain Daath energies for those who are ready. I do not recommend working with this Sphere in any way, however, until all other planetary/Sphere energies have been well integrated. To Daath is attributed Pluto, rebirth, and the great abyss. Eleven is considered to be a master number in numerology and relates to the avant-garde and great visionaries. In the Tarot it is represented by the Magician acting through him or herself to produce Justice. Take this as a cue. If you use the eleventh kamea, apply it with great care.

❖ Shapes

The shapes given on pages 43–51 are suggested outlines for your talisman based on the number/Sphere which you are working with. The triangle within a circle is to be used for three—Binah/Saturn; the cube is for four—Chesed/Jupiter, etc. One only needs to count the sides to know which numerical vibration is being called upon. (Some have more than one shape). We have made full-page planetary shapes so the student can photocopy them and use them immediately. Other shapes incorporated into the talisman (circles, smaller triangles, squares, etc.) should be carefully drawn with a compass and a ruler.

❖ Planetary Relationships

Very early in its evolution, human consciousness deduced that there was some occult connection between the seven planets, metals, and days of the week. As each of the seven days of the week was considered to be under the auspices of specific spirits in the heavens, so did Mother Nature generate in her womb a concrete expression of that star in the form of the seven principle metals. Talismans were often made of the specific planetary metals and then worn. The science of alchemy seeks to release the spirit from the metal in the process of transmutation. We can visualize the same process happening within us, and much of the psychological interpretation of Carl Jung uses alchemical allegories.

Herbs, too, are rooted in ancient lore and are connected to planetary correspondences. Many of the charts and correspondence tables have the seven planetary spirits at their center. The ancients did not know about the three other planets which astrologers use today, although the empty space on the Tree for the hidden Sphere of Daath was integrated into Qabalah at a very early stage and incorporates much of what we now recognize as Plutonian energy. The more ancient understanding of the twelve signs and their planetary rulers is demonstrated in figure 3–D, which shows how the whole scheme was viewed within the concept of the cycle of the seasons.

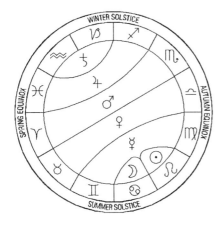

Figure 3–D

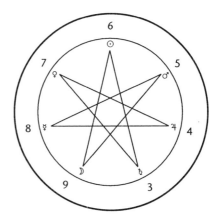

Figure 3–E

The seven-pointed star known as the heptagram or septagram is the classic representation of the seven planets of the ancients (See figure 3–E). It represents Binah (Saturn) and her six children on the Tree: starting at the bottom right is Saturn (three), then
Jupiter (four), Mars (five), Sun (six), Venus (seven), Mercury (eight), and the Moon
(nine). This is quite an astonishing little glyph, for it has another harmonious relationship. Besides the ordered numeration of the Spheres on the Tree, the days of the week can
be traced in correct order if one starts at the Sun and goes downward toward the Moon
and around the lines marked by the figure of the Star.

Even more amazing has been the discovery of the atomic weights, which in order of
density are: lead (Saturn), mercury (Mercury), gold (Sun), tin (Jupiter), silver (Moon),
copper (Venus) and iron (Mars). This can also be incorporated into the figure in a symmetrical pattern with every other one going clockwise. It has been calculated that the
mathematical probability of these kinds of symmetrical patterns are about 119 to one. The
ancient Chaladeans who gave us the order of the planets (which the Tree follows) could
not have known the atomic weights (or so it is postulated). This harmonious relationship
demonstrates the inherent beauty of the magical system which has been bequeathed to us.

❖ Planetary Associations

I have separated the planetary associations into four categories: attributes the student
may want to develop, trades or activities which belong to the various planetary deities,
desires or aspirations relating to their specific energy, and the body parts they rule.

The chart in figure 3–F shows the symbols of the planets, which the student may
want to draw on the talisman, along with their corresponding numbers and Spheres on
the Tree, as well as the associated Greek and Roman deities. The chart in figure 3–G
shows the planets, their association to the elements and their best placement (this helps
in determining timing for making a talisman). The planetary hours and their ruling

Symbols of Planets and Correspondences

No.	Sign	Greek	Roman	Sphere	Weekday	Planet
3	♄	Cronus	Saturn	Binah	Saturday	Saturn
4	♃	Zeus	Jupiter	Chesed	Thursday	Jupiter
5	♂	Ares	Mars	Geburah	Tuesday	Mars
6	☉	Apollo	Sol	Tiphareth	Sunday	Sun
7	♀	Aphrodite	Venus	Netzach	Friday	Venus
8	☿	Hermes	Mercury	Hod	Wednesday	Mercury
9	☽	Artemis	Diana	Yesod	Monday	Moon
10	⊕	Pan	Elementals	Malkuth	(none)	Earth
11	♇	Hades	Pluto	Daath	Nighttime	Pluto

Figure 3–F

Planet	Element	Best Place for Working
Sun	Fire	Leo, Aries, Sagittarius, Sunday
Moon	Water	Cancer, Taurus, Monday, Nighttime
Mars	Fire planet (also rules water sign)	Aries, Capricorn, Tuesday
Mercury	Air planet (also rules earth sign)	Gemini, Virgo, Wednesday
Jupiter	Fire planet (also rules water sign)	Sagittarius, Pisces, Cancer, Thursday
Venus	Earth planet (also rules air sign)	Taurus, Libra, Pisces, Friday
Saturn	Earth planet (also rules air sign)	Capricorn, Aquarius, Libra, Saturday
Pluto	Water (rules Scorpio, replacing Mars)	Scorpio, Aquarius, Capricorn, Nighttime

Figure G

angels are given in the charts in figure 3–H. This can be used for even more precise timing, but the student needs to determine the first hour by the moment of sunrise in the specific location of residency. To determine the length of a planetary hour, find out what time the sun rises and sets, and add together the total number of hours and minutes of the daylight in that day. (You should end up with a total number of minutes, *e.g.*, 780 minutes). Then divide that number by twelve to determine how many minutes are in each planetary hour (*e.g.*, Sixty-five minutes). If you don't finish the talisman within the hour, it is not so important as beginning it during the appropriate planetary hour.

❖ Planetary Attributes

SATURN: Positive: endurance, reserve. Strengthens capacity to carry out one's duties. Constriction, limitation, equilibrium. Use for grounding, stability, and making ideals concrete. Higher intuition. Patience. Negative: Hatred and discord. Impatience and coldness. Brooding, irksome, autocratic.

JUPITER: Positive: Good judgment, direction, honor. Benevolent power, expansion, contentment. Optimism. Spirituality and devotion. Mercy and generosity. Negative: Hypocrisy, pride, dogmatism. Smugness and greed. Exorbitant and self-righteous.

MARS: Positive: Dynamic action and energy. Ambition, physical strength, courage. Willpower, vitality, and anger (constructive). Enthusiasm, resolution, self-assurance. Efficient and valiant. Negative: Haste, aggression, hostility. Anger (destructive), cruelty, resentment, manipulation. Self-doubt.

	Day Hours												
Hour		Sunday		Monday		Tuesday		Wednesday		Thursday		Friday		Saturday
1	☉	Michael	☽	Gabriel	♂	Samael	☿	Raphael	♃	Sachiel	♀	Anael	♄	Cassiel
2	♀	Anael	♄	Cassiel	☉	Michael	☽	Gabriel	♂	Samael	☿	Raphael	♃	Sachiel
3	☿	Raphael	♃	Sachiel	♀	Anael	♄	Cassiel	☉	Michael	☽	Gabriel	♂	Samael
4	☽	Gabriel	♂	Samael	☿	Raphael	♃	Sachiel	♀	Anael	♄	Cassiel	☉	Michael
5	♄	Cassiel	☉	Michael	☽	Gabriel	♂	Samael	☿	Raphael	♃	Sachiel	♀	Anael
6	♃	Sachiel	♀	Anael	♄	Cassiel	☉	Michael	☽	Gabriel	♂	Samael	☿	Raphael
7	♂	Samael	☿	Raphael	♃	Sachiel	♀	Anael	♄	Cassiel	☉	Michael	☽	Gabriel
8	☉	Michael	☽	Gabriel	♂	Samael	☿	Raphael	♃	Sachiel	♀	Anael	♄	Cassiel
9	♀	Anael	♄	Cassiel	☉	Michael	☽	Gabriel	♂	Samael	☿	Raphael	♃	Sachiel
10	☿	Raphael	♃	Sachiel	♀	Anael	♄	Cassiel	☉	Michael	☽	Gabriel	♂	Samael
11	☽	Gabriel	♂	Samael	☿	Raphael	♃	Sachiel	♀	Anael	♄	Cassiel	☉	Michael
12	♄	Cassiel	☉	Michael	☽	Gabriel	♂	Samael	☿	Raphael	♃	Sachiel	♀	Anael

	Night Hours												
Hour		Sunday		Monday		Tuesday		Wednesday		Thursday		Friday		Saturday
1	♃	Sachiel	♀	Anael	♄	Cassiel	☉	Michael	☽	Gabriel	♂	Samael	☿	Raphael
2	♂	Samael	☿	Raphael	♃	Sachiel	♀	Anael	♄	Cassiel	☉	Michael	☽	Gabriel
3	☉	Michael	☽	Gabriel	♂	Samael	☿	Raphael	♃	Sachiel	♀	Anael	♄	Cassiel
4	♀	Anael	♄	Cassiel	☉	Michael	☽	Gabriel	♂	Samael	☿	Raphael	♃	Sachiel
5	☿	Raphael	♃	Sachiel	♀	Anael	♄	Cassiel	☉	Michael	☽	Gabriel	♂	Samael
6	☽	Gabriel	♂	Samael	☿	Raphael	♃	Sachiel	♀	Anael	♄	Cassiel	☉	Michael
7	♄	Cassiel	☉	Michael	☽	Gabriel	♂	Samael	☿	Raphael	♃	Sachiel	♀	Anael
8	♃	Sachiel	♀	Anael	♄	Cassiel	☉	Michael	☽	Gabriel	♂	Samael	☿	Raphael
9	♂	Samael	☿	Raphael	♃	Sachiel	♀	Anael	♄	Cassiel	☉	Michael	☽	Gabriel
10	☉	Michael	☽	Gabriel	♂	Samael	☿	Raphael	♃	Sachiel	♀	Anael	♄	Cassiel
11	♀	Anael	♄	Cassiel	☉	Michael	☽	Gabriel	♂	Samael	☿	Raphael	♃	Sachiel
12	☿	Raphael	♃	Sachiel	♀	Anael	♄	Cassiel	☉	Michael	☽	Gabriel	♂	Samael

Figure 3–H

SUN: Positive: Leadership, power and self-confidence. Harmony and illumination. Mental alertness and creativity. Open-hearted, loyal, equable, and compassionate. Negative: Arrogant, blaming, ego-oriented. Need for confirmation and control. Fearful.

VENUS: Positive: Gentleness, aesthetic beauty, affection, emotional sensitivity, kindness, and love. Reconciliation with others. Joyful, expressive, nurturing. Creativity. Negative: Self-indulgent, over-emotional, lustful. Superficial, possessive, jealous.

MERCURY: Positive: Adaptation and movement. Ingenuity, eloquence, precision, influence. Communication, intelligence, intuition. Skill and analysis. Good at making judgments. Negative: Craftiness, deceitful, impatient. Critical, aloof, divisive.

MOON: Positive: Dreaminess and imagination. Adventurous spirit. Spontaneous, alluring, psychic. Self-reconciliation. Negative: Impulsivity, instability and mental agitation. Mood-swings. Idleness. Obsession with psychic powers.

PLUTO: Positive: Transforming, rejuvenating, penetrating. Forces us to integrate our collective shadow. Negative: Baffling, sinister, depraved, fanatical, destructive.

❖ Planetary Trades and Activities

SATURN: Politics, business, agriculture, mining, clock-making, economics, masonry, plumbing, undertaking, tanning, occupations dealing with wills and real estate.

JUPITER: Philosophy, religion, government, banking, law, appraising, advising, finance, insurance, academia, civic leadership, work involving organizing, credit agencies, ministry.

MARS: Military, mechanics, surgery, engineering, iron and steel work, blacksmithing, fire-fighting, locksmithing, competitive sports, carpentry.

SUN: Acting, goldsmithing, royalty, anything involving executive or superior positions.

VENUS: Artistry, music, dance, decorations, designing, embroidery, lapidary, jewelry, ornamental gardening, social activities, ecology.

MERCURY: Teaching, lecturing, writing, communication in general, science, theater, contracts, business, bargaining, debating, commerce, advertising, postal work, jesting.

MOON: Farming, navigation by water, dream analysis, psychic work, child care and home affairs, fishing, nursing, obstetrics, silversmithing, nutrition.

PLUTO: Mass media, revolutions, new physics, atomic science, alchemy, psychoanalysis, anything involving transformation or rejuvenation.

❖ Planetary Aspirations and Desires

SATURN: Favorable for political activity, as an aid to study for exams, to acquire esoteric knowledge, for possessions and goods regarding business, events regarding the elderly, understanding death and dying, integrating limitation.

JUPITER: Good fortune in general, advancement, health, prosperity, successful career, to acquire worldly honors, to preserve health, spiritual visions.

MARS: For critical and confident decisions, for empowerment to change; use to destroy unwanted influences, to banish enemies, in exorcisms; brings favor in quarrels.

SUN: Promotes good health, abundance, peaceful environment, spiritual illumination, use to acquire mastery and supremacy, to obtain patronage, to recover lost property, to prevent war and promote friendship, harmonious relationships with superiors.

VENUS: Assists in matters of the heart, good for partnerships and social affairs, for anything to do with pleasure, the arts, traveling, relationships between younger people and women in general.

MERCURY: Aids in acquiring knowledge and intellectual friends, assists in communications, success in commerce, useful for magic, apparitions and divination, for obtaining information or making calculations, secures safety in travel.

MOON: Assists in smoothing domestic problems, growing of plants, insures safe journeys and acquisition of merchandise by water, successful embassies; connected with messages, dreams, cycles.

PLUTO: Seeks to change, to shatter old forms, to break completely new ground; aids in eliminating the outdated and no longer useful; assists in projects involving large numbers of people.

❖ Planetary Body Parts and Mental Health

SATURN: Skin, teeth, bones, gallbladder, pituitary glands (with Jupiter). Time passages: aging and dying; depression.

JUPITER: Liver, Pituitary glands, hormones. Growth of the human organism. Mental optimism.

MARS: Sex organs, muscles. Fevers. Strong magnetic aura.

SUN: Heart, spine, thymus. To maintain youthfulness; health in general. Helps to fight bacteria.

VENUS: Kidneys, throat, parathyroid. Calcium level in the body. Emotional balance.

MERCURY: Brain, nervous system, breathing. Mental alertness and concentration.

MOON: Breasts, pancreas, menstruation and conception. To achieve a reconciled heart. Work with cycles, fluctuations.

PLUTO: Antibodies, defense system, generational or inherited illnesses.

The Elements

△	Fire—hot and dry
△	Air—hot and moist
▽	Earth—cold and dry
▽	Water—cold and moist
⊛	Quintessance

Figure 3–I

Elemental Correspondences

Fire: Power, dominion, authority, prestige, expansion

Air: Health, sickness, disputations, intellect

Earth: Business, money, employment, practical affairs

Water: Pleasure, marriage, fertility, happiness, emotions

Quintessance: All matters spiritual

Figure 3–J

The Tattwas

△	Fire (Tejas)
○	Air (Vayu)
□	Earth (Prithivi)
◡	Water (Apas)
○	Ether (Akasha)

Figure 3–K

❖ Additional Correspondences

The symbols of the elements are given in the charts in figures 3–I, 3–J, and 3–K. 3–I is the more ancient alchemical formula; 3–K gives the elemental symbols according to the tattwa system, which will be explored in more depth in the section on Tattwas and Sound and Color healing. The Golden Dawn correspondences are included in J. These designs may be employed in any talisman to incorporate its specific elemental energy.

The geomantic symbols are some of the oldest designs used on talismans. Their origin is unknown, but they have been utilized in ancient seals as well as used as a method of divination from at least the middle ages. These symbols, which are related to the zodiacal signs, the planets, and the elements, are shown in the charts in figures 3–L, 3–M, 3–N, and 3–O. They can be easily incorporated into a talisman because of their simple designs, and are thought to increase or temper the particular force being evoked in the whole talismanic piece. It will be noted that there are a variety of creative designs that can be made from the simple series of dots, some of which are shown in figure 3–N.

The chart in figure 3–P lists symbols such as animals that can be hand-drawn and incorporated into the talisman to add a special personal touch. This chart lists the more basic symbols which are attributed to the Qabalistic Sephiroth, as well as other forms associated with the planetary spirits. See the chart on page twelve of chapter two for the Hebrew Letters attributions.

Following figure 3–P are some elemental shapes that can be used in creating personal talismans, as described on page 31.

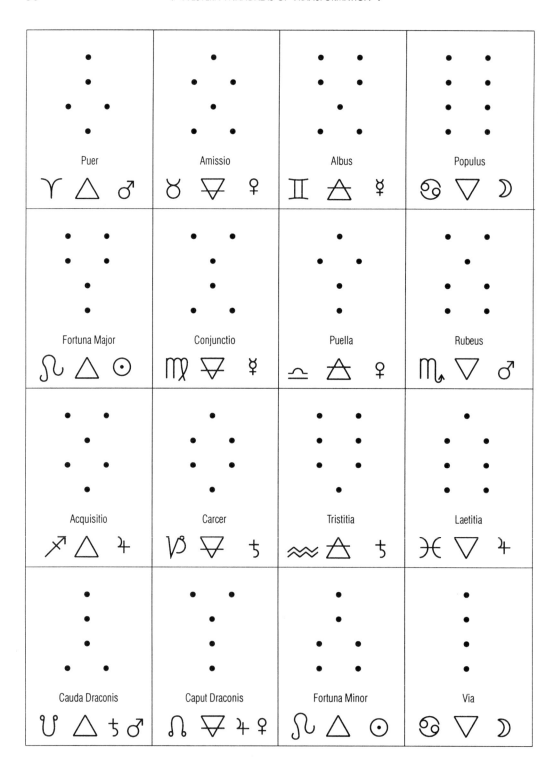

Figure 3–L

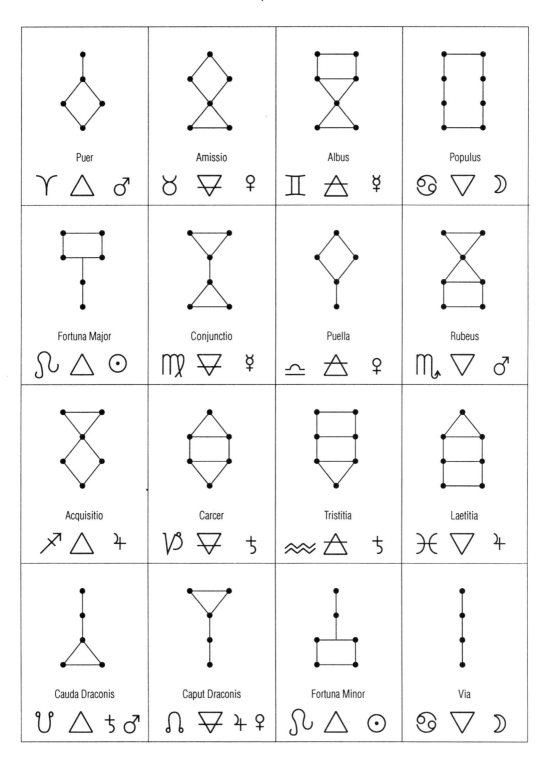

Figure 3–M

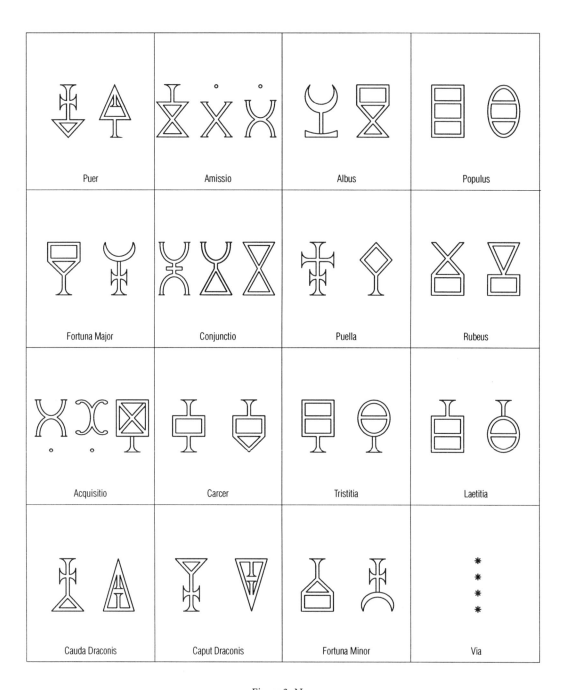

Figure 3–N

Geomantic Attributions

PUER: (Fire) Initial catalyst; active transmission

FORTUNE MAJOR: (Fire) Reflective, helping, fortunate for transition

ACQUISITIO: (Fire) Movement, pure intellect, expansive

CAUDA DRACONIS: (Fire) Life force going out with great energy

POPULUS: (Water) Psychic power, catalyst for uniting, gathering

RUBEUS: (Water) Joining of conscious with unconscious in violent kind of way—use with caution

LAETITIA: (Water) Intuitive, useful, outgoing

VIA: (Water) Conception, production

PUELLA: (Air) Feminine power and mediation; strength of will

TRISTITIA: (Air) Inspiration, analytical intuition, conscious understanding

ALBUS: (Air) Rushing thoughts, continuous motion

FORTUNA MINOR: (Fire) Concentration, controlled movement

CARCER: (Earth) Power and drive, but restrictive

AMISSIO: (Earth) Earthy emotion, control of flightiness

CONJUNCTIO: (Earth) Communication; understanding on the material plane

CAPUT DRACONIS: (Earth) Fixed matter, entering inward, centering

Figure 3–O

Basic Symbols of the Sephiroth

Sephiroth	Path	Sphere Intelligence	Titles	Symbols	Planet	Animal	Planetary Spirit	Intelligence—Spirit and Related Symbols
Kether	1	Hidden	Ancient of Days, Amen	Primal Point, Swastika	None	None	None	None
Chokmah	2	Illuminating	Abba, Supernal Father	Line, Phallus, Rod of Power	Zodiac	None	None	None
Binah	3	Sanctifying	Ama, Aima, Great Mother, Great Sea	Yoni, Cup, Triangle	Saturn	Crocodile, Crow	Zazel	Woman in a long black veil, King, Dragon, Crow
Chesed	4	Cohesive	Infinite Love, Divine Mercy	Pyramid, Cross, Wand	Jupiter	Bull, Eagle, Lion	Hismael	Unicorn, Peacock, Elderly bearded man
Geburah	5	Radical	Lord of Justice	Pentagram, 5-Petaled Rose, Spear	Mars	Horse, Wolf, Bear	Bartzabel	Man dressed in armor, Stag, King astride a lion, Horse, Sword
Tiphareth	6	Mediating	The Lesser Countenance, The Divine Child	Rosy-cross, Cube	Sun	Lion, Sparrow-hawk	Sorath	Phoenix, King holding a sceptre, Cockerel, Roaring Lion
Netzach	7	Occult	Lady Triumphant	Lamp, Girdle	Venus	Dove, Sparrow, Swan	Kedemel	Young girl, Dove, Camel, Lynx
Hod	8	Absolute	Vision of Splendor	Versicle, Apron	Mercury	Swallow, Ibis, Ape, Dog	Taphthar-tharath	Hermaphrodite, Magpie, Two Snakes
Yesod	9	Pure	Treasure-House of Images	Perfumes, Sandles	Moon	Dog	Chasmodai	Deer, Goose, Huntress with a bow and arrow
Malkuth	10	Resplendant	The Gate, Daughter, Bride	Circle, Equal-Arm Cross	Earth	None	None	None
Daath	11	None	The Upper Room, The Unrevealed Cosmic Mind	Silver Egg, Gate, Wheel, Chasm, Seed	Pluto	Dog	Vo-Baeb-anim	Tongues of Fire, Janus-Face, Star

Figure 3–P

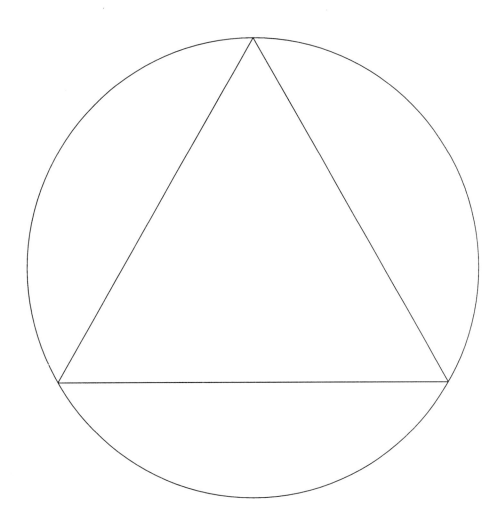

❖ **Three—Binah/Saturn** ❖

❖ Four—Chesed/Jupiter ❖

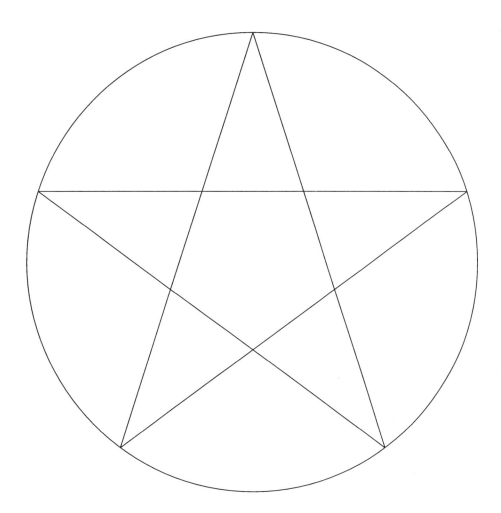

❖ **Five—Geburah/Mars** ❖

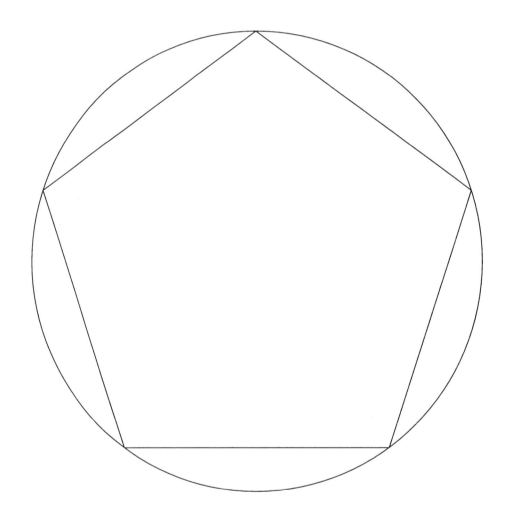

❖ Five—Geburah/Mars ❖

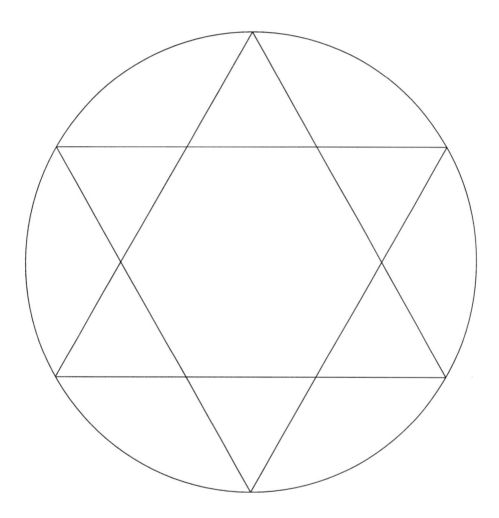

❖ Six—Tiphareth/Sun ❖

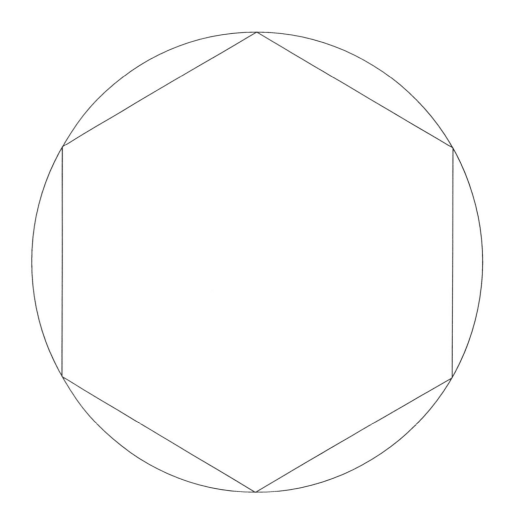

❖ Six—Tiphareth/Sun ❖

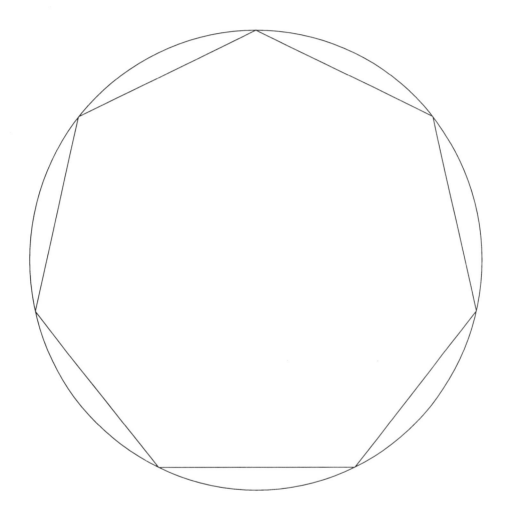

❖ **Seven—Netzach/Venus** ❖

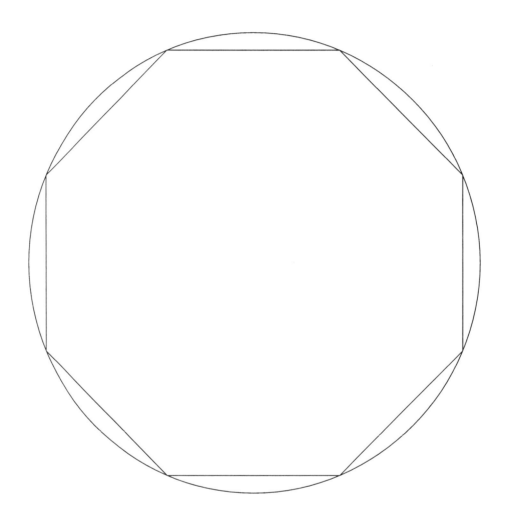

❖ Eight—Mercury/Hod ❖

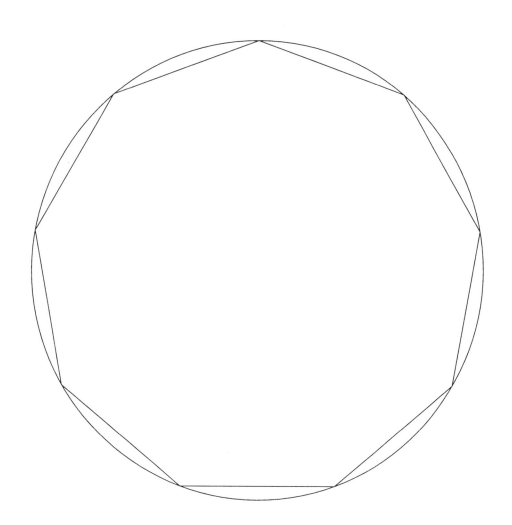

❖ Nine—Yesod/Moon ❖

Chapter 4

MAGICAL SQUARES
AND SIGILS

*There is no science that teaches the harmonies of nature more clearly
than mathematics, and the magic squares are like a magic mirror which
reflects a ray of the symmetry of the divine norm immanent in all things.*

—Paul Carus, *Magic Squares and Cubes*

Working with magical squares, sigils, telesmanic images, and talismanic mandalas can be some of the most fruitful and exciting of all magical work, but the student must first have a good understanding of the basics: how to construct a telesmanic image from the Hebrew Letters, how to create a sigil, and how to work with all elements derived from the magical squares in the correct way.

✥ Squares

Much misunderstanding and confusion surrounding magical squares and sigils has crept into the magical tradition and mistakes can be found all the way back to Agrippa, who was perhaps the first to publish them in their current format. Although they may be inscribed on a talisman with no additional adornments, magical squares, or kameas, are used primarily to create seals and sigils, or sacred signatures.

Numbers are the primary blueprint of the Sphere or planetary energy. When sigils are traced through a kamea, connecting specific planetary numbers, they draw out the particular planetary power being invoked. If one traces a sigil of one's own name (and one's magical name, or H.G.A.) on the kamea, one begins to instill the force behind the magical field of the planet in one's own aura. The correct way of tracing sigils is given in the next section.

It is not necessary to understand all of the anomalies and mistakes concerning magical squares that have crept up, intentionally or unintentionally, in the occult tradition which the Golden Dawn and its offshoots have adopted. All the student needs is the correct information, which I have tried to present in the examples and tables in this book. The advanced student will probably find the following discussion more helpful than someone just beginning to work with the squares and sigils, but in the long run it is important to understand the mechanics.

Regardie and others have noted that the early Golden Dawn chiefs did not incorporate this most important aspect of magical work because they felt that the real knowledge of how to use the magical squares had been lost, and also because they had noted some mistakes, which I will clarify momentarily. Let us first examine the correct way for a magical square, seal, and sigil to be constructed.

The magical square is called the *kamea*, which means *to bond*. It is the power grid of the planetary energy being called upon and is based entirely upon number. To each Sephira belongs a number and its corresponding planetary entities: God-name, Intelligence, angels, or spirits. These are drawn from the kamea that holds the key to the basic planetary numbers.

The numbers in the square are arranged so that the sum of any row, vertically, horizontally, or diagonally, are the same when added up. (This includes Mercury.) In mathematics, this is known as the Magic Constant of the square. If a square does not add up diagonally, it is called a *semi-magical square*.

The kamea reveals the planetary essence through the language of numbers, thus mapping out its individual energy. The first number relates to the Sephira itself: three, four, five, six, seven, eight, nine, or eleven. These are the square roots of the planetary kameas: the kamea of Binah, Saturn has three rows with three cells in each row, which when added up equal fifteen in any direction. When the number of the Sephira is multiplied by itself it equals the number of cells in the kamea (in this case, nine), and the theosophical extension (the addition of all the numbers when added together) is the total summation of the square; in this case, forty-five ($1+2+3+4+5+6+7+8+9=45$). A handy reference is given in the chart in figure 4–A.

The numbers three, nine, fifteen, and forty-five are critical in determining the relationship to the planetary entities, whose correspondences are related by the same numbers. Jupiter is related to the numbers four, sixteen (number of cells), thirty-four (the summation of any row), and 136 (theosophic extension). Four relates the planet to Chesed on the Tree of Life; sixteen is the numeration of the word hyssop in Hebrew, which is the planetary herb assigned to Jupiter; thirty-four is the number of El Ab, or God the Father, which is frequently the way that this emanation of God is imagined; it is also the number of tin in Hebrew, which is the metal associated with Jupiter; and the number 136 is the number of the Intelligence (Yophiel) and Spirit (Hismael) of the planet. Other numeric associations (called *gematria*) will be examined in more detail when we look at each kamea individually.

The magical seal of the kamea is a geometric pattern designed so that every cell in the square is touched when it is drawn. It represents the epitome of the entire kamea—it

Planetary Numbers

Sephira/Planet	Number	Number of Cells	Sum of Any Line	Total: Theosophic Extension
BINAH/SATURN	3	9	15	45
CHESED/JUPITER	4	16	34	136
GEBURAH/MARS	5	25	65	325
TIPHARETH/SUN	6	36	111	666
NETZACH/VENUS	7	49	175	1225
HOD/MERCURY	8	64	260	2080
YESOD/MOON	9	81	369	3321
DAATH/PLUTO	11	121	671	7381

Figure 4–A

carries every aspect of the magical square in its design. It is the power of the kamea transformed geometrically. There could be more than one design, and we will look at this in detail soon. The sigils are simply the signatures of the names (*e.g.*, Intelligence, spirit, angel, etcetera) when they are drawn on the kamea using numbers instead of letters. It is done the same way as tracing the Letters on the Rose. This, too, will be explained in greater detail when we get to the sections exploring sigils in more depth.

There are mistakes (where numbers clearly do not add up for the row to equal the number designated by the rest of the square) in numerous published kameas. In his Venus kamea, Francis Barrett, who published the kameas, seals, and sigils in 1801 and whose kameas have been copied many times in books on magical squares, had numerous mistakes in Hebrew, which makes the corresponding numbers wrong. Seldom have I seen a Venus kamea that does not still have these mistakes. The aware student can easily find this or any other error by adding up the numbers of each row. We find the same problem in the Moon kamea of Agrippa, and in numerous reprints of magical squares from other sources as well.

Regardie has commented on the dangers of this:

> It is not difficult to realize that if the object of the seal is to set up a strain in the Astral Light to which a corresponding entity hastens to respond, then a mistake in the textual inscription will cause a similar mistake in the type of astral strain. The result will be that the effect will be far different to that anticipated, even detrimental and dangerous (*Tree of Life*, 1972, p. 219).

I advise that you check the kamea you are copying at least twice, and be especially careful if doing it in Hebrew. The mistakes are not only in the older publications (*e.g.*, Francis Barrett), but in modern ones as well. I have found mistakes in Regardie's *How to Make and Use Talismans*, his *Golden Dawn* (1970 edition), the *Complete Golden Dawn System of Magic*, and Eliphas Levi's *Transcendental Magic*. The newest edition of Agrippa's *Three Books of Occult Philosophy*, edited by Donald Tyson (Llewellyn: 1993), has corrected all mistakes in the squares. Few published works are without mistakes. Even in some private Golden Dawn lessons I have found the same mistake in the Venus kamea. Errors are most often found in the Venus and Mercury kameas, but I have found mistakes in Saturn, Jupiter, and the Sun as well. I hope that pointing out these errors will help the student to identify the incorrect kameas and adjust his or her magical work accordingly. Correct versions are given here (in some cases two versions, if the kamea is radically different) in the separate sections dealing with each kamea.

The unorthodox kameas are what I call anomalies. They are rearrangements of the numbers which are not the same as those given by Cornelius Agrippa[1], but which are nonetheless correct numerically. Some of these anomalies are found in Paul Case's kameas of Mars and the Sun, and in others that I, along with some of my colleagues, have developed. There are numerous ways to set up kameas, which are still perfectly correct because the numerical pattern explained above is consistent.

The original mistakes found in Barrett were probably not blinds; they in no way affect the drawing of the sigil. Rather, they probably resulted from Barrett's somewhat limited knowledge of Hebrew, since most of the mistakes stem from a confusion of Hehs and Cheths (five and eight). These mistakes have been reprinted many times, following either Barrett or the Golden Dawn publications. If you are using a magical square on your talisman, use a correct one. There are no blinds or intentional mistakes in this book.

The magical squares are printed in both numbers and Hebrew letters, so the student can trace his seals and sigils on either type of kamea. Neither Barrett nor Agrippa give Hebrew magical squares as legible as those in *Kabbala Denudata*. Although this is a very old book (1684), this portion of Christian Knorr Rosenroth's text (the Hebrew lexicon) has never been translated into English. Parts of it are examined at various places in this book[2].

When the student has a correct magical square, he or she can then proceed to discover the seals and sigils. figure 4–B shows the traditional planetary seals as they have appeared in Agrippa and have been reproduced in nearly all books on talismans. Most books on magical squares tell you that the seal of the planet is formed by connecting every square or cell on the kamea. Regardie, Case, and Levi also stress that geometric symmetry is important. When pointing this out, you will invariably see that the Saturn kamea is given as the classic design. Bear this in mind, for we will return to it shortly.

If we look at the seals given in Agrippa and in the published Golden Dawn reproductions, we see that this rule is clearly not followed in every case. Any student who has worked with the squares will have noticed this. Mars and Venus, in particular, are clearly not geometrical, nor do they touch every cell in the kamea. Regardie and Levi encouraged the student to experiment with designs that are symmetrical and, although I believe that Case has

---

[1] It should be noted that some translations of Agrippa, (such as the John Freake translation) made deliberate changes in the magical squares which do not appear in the original manuscripts in the Vatican. I have worked primarily from the French translation edited by Gaboriau and the Vatican microfilms.

[2] The founding Golden Dawn teachers did translate the *Book of Concealed Mystery*, *The Greater and Lesser Holy Assembly* (Mathers), as well as *Aesch Metzareph (Sapere Aude)*, all found in Knorr Rosenroth's classic text.

ꔰ

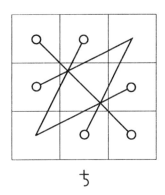

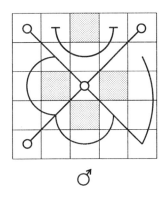

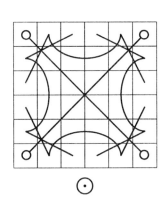

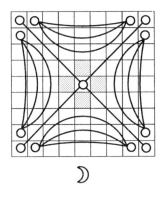

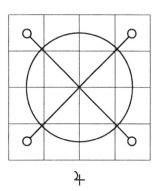

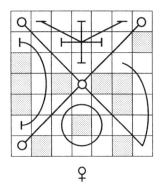

Figure 4–B

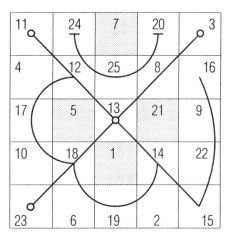

Figure 4–C

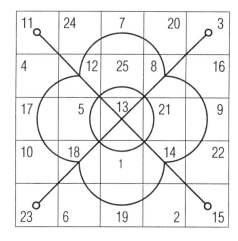

Figure 4–D

given us a big clue about the nature of planetary seals, I see nothing wrong with this. The important thing most teachers stress is consistency. In Qabalistic work, repetition builds power, because energy builds over time, and mixing too many elements or symbols weakens the whole operation.

Although a variety of designs that include all the squares can be formed on any given kamea, clues are given in Agrippa's original figures that lead the observant student to discover how a seal may easily be formed from the information given, if it is re-arranged. If we look at the irregular design in the Mars seal (see figure 4–C), we notice that it does not touch the darkened cells, but if we use one of the three designs given on the four sides of the Mars seal (the one repeated twice), and if we also expand the middle circle, we can see that it includes all the cells (see figure 4–D). We can do the same for the sickle design, if the center circle were expanded (see figure 4–E).

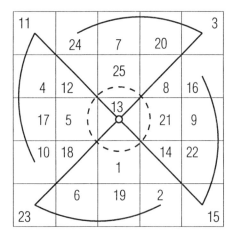

Figure 4–E

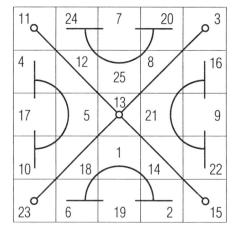

Figure 4–F

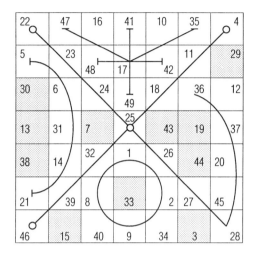

Figure 4–G

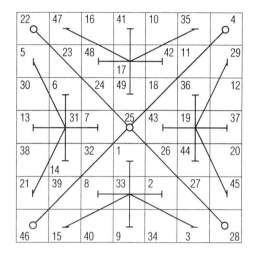

Figure 4–H

The side with the U symbol poses a problem: four cells are still left out. An additional refinement needs to be made and again a clue is given, on the very U shape itself, which has small lines on the ends. If these lines are extended slightly, they include the neighboring cells (see figure 4–F). With the three possibilities given in Agrippa's design, we see that three distinctly unique variations of a Mars seal can be formed without radically changing anything. Any of the three choices offered in the original seal will work if one studies the given possibilities. I personally find the sickle shaped one most Mars-like.

We could do the same with the original Venus seal as it appears in Agrippa (see figure 4–G). Unfortunately, the bar-line in the Y is missing in almost all later reproductions I have seen. If one uses the design as it originally appeared, one can see that it fills all the

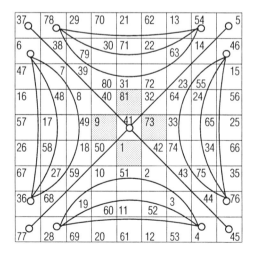

Figure 4–I

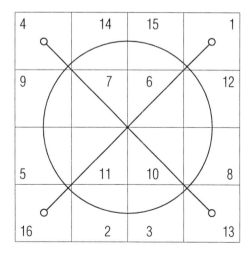

Figure 4–J

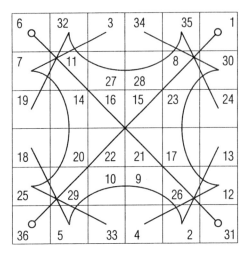

Figure 4–K

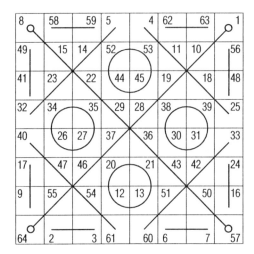

Figure 4–L

cells in that quarter of the kamea, and one can simply reproduce the design all the way around (see figure 4–H).

The larger the kamea, the more cells there are, and the more tricky it gets to include them all. The moon seal correctly includes all squares (eighty-one in all), except for the four in the center (see figure 4–I). This can be corrected by enlarging the center circle. The others work in the way they are generally given (see figures 4–J, 4–K, 4–L, and 4–M).

One can experiment with alternate designs on these kameas, provided that every cell is included. For example, I have used a very powerful symbol, which has come to be known as the Miraculous Medal, on the simplest of the planetary squares. This medal was revealed to St. Catherine Laboure (who has had an incorruptible body—now in an

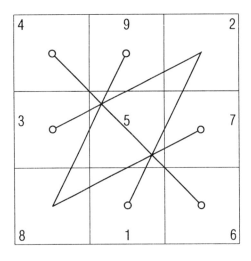

Figure 4–M

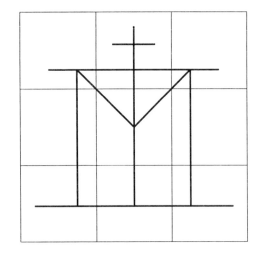

Figure 4–N

open casket in Paris—since her death in 1876), by the Virgin Mary in a vision, and has become a very potent miracle working talisman in the past 100 years.

It fits very nicely on the Saturn kamea (see figure 4–N). It is also appropriate there symbolically because *Mary* (Miriam),whose initial it is, means *bitter sea*, an attribution of Binah/Saturn, and she is said to be the universal mother. Qabalistic students will notice other similarities in the symbol, *e.g.*, the cross with three bars (which appeared in the original drawings of the vision but which are lacking on some of the current medals) symbolize the Hierophant, and the Supreme Initiation.

All of these planetary seals, along with the traditional (corrected) kameas, are pleasing and may be used by the student on their talismans to invoke specific planetary energy. The problem of defining what is a correct planetary seal gets even more intriguing—and opens up even more possibilities—when we examine the anomalies in the kameas discussed earlier. As we will discover (see chapters seven and eight, and compare the magical squares), Case's choice of kameas for both Mars and Sun differs radically from all others given, and he uses yet a different way to discover the planetary seal of the magical square.

Although he does not explain in detail how different seals are formed, they can be easily deduced by the aware student, if he or she follows the pattern revealed in the Saturn kamea (which is a correct magical square in all published accounts I have seen except one). The clue as to how to form a true planetary seal, one which uses all of the numbers of the kamea in order, is always revealed in the kamea of Saturn, the simplest design.

Let us re-examine the seal and kamea of Saturn, using two examples—the traditional one given by Agrippa and one that is given in *Aesch Mazareth*, an early Golden Dawn manuscript by Wynn Wescott. We should first note that we can test a kamea's seal-making abilities in another way—through theosophic extension, going from one to two to three, etc. until we get to the end and then see if the addition matches the magical number of the square. (In a kamea that does not have the correct number in every cell, it will not.)

This method of making a seal is hinted at (usually unknowingly) in all books that describe magical squares, but it is never explained in detail, and in the western occult tradition has never been followed through by anyone except Case. This is why Saturn is given as the first model. In 1949 Karl Nowotny explained this technique in an article written on Agrippa's seals, where he notes the consecutive numbering, but doesn't follow through on all the planetary squares. He also tells us that Agrippa distinguished between seals derived from the geometrical pattern of the distribution of numbers in the squares and other kinds of seals. We do not know if Agrippa was following an ancient tradition in doing this or not, or why he did not publish the other planetary seals done in this way.

If we make a seal using this method, we get an unbroken line that looks like figure 4–O. It looks like the original seal, only it does not contain three broken lines (compare with figure 4–M). If one follows this principle through all kameas, one can easily discover some elegant designs, but these have, as far as I know, never been published in books on magical squares. If we tried tracing the design in theosophic succession on the model given by Sapere Aude, it would not work, even though all the correct numbers are in the square

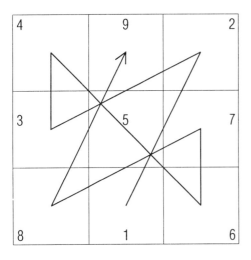

Figure 4–O

(see figure 4–P). They are not arranged in the proper cells. We have determined that, in this case at any rate, a pleasing geometric design which represents the seal or essence of the planet can only be made when the numbers are traced in theosophical extension and when the vertical, horizontal and diagonal rows all add up to 15. From this it can be seen that mistakes in the kameas—even though they may not make any difference in the sigil line, because the number is not included in the name—now become crucial. In many cases, an inharmonious or asymmetrical seal would be formed by following the numerical sequence; even one misplacement would cause a different seal.

Let us look at a correct Mercury kamea (Agrippa's original) and the beautiful design it makes when we use this method (see figure 4–Q). I suggest you compare this to one you can easily make by using this technique on a variety of other Mercury kameas (such as Barrett's or Levi's or those of anyone who has reprinted them). It is a good exercise to get a sense of how to test kameas given in other publications.

There are alternate ways of setting up the kameas numerically, and in the future more designs might emerge, but this method seems to suffice for the known magical squares of the last few centuries, with the possible exception of the Sun kamea. The principle point that emerges from studying planetary seals created with this method is that these seals reveal beautiful mandalas that, like tattwas, can act as powerful astral doorways when

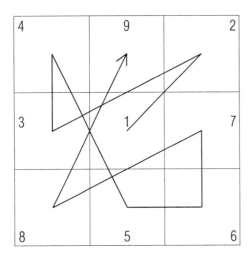

Figure 4–P

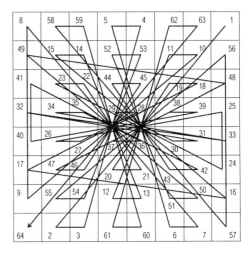

Figure 4–Q

meditated upon. Examples of some of these Qabalistic mandalas are given in later sections. These planetary seals are all drawn from Agrippa's kameas unless otherwise noted.

❖ SIGILS

Let us examine in more detail the art of sigil making. The sigil is the signature of the deity, angel, or energy (such as understanding, communication etc.) one is invoking when working with magical squares. In most cases, they are drawn from kameas that have the same numerical equivalents as the names themselves; the Intelligence and the Spirit of Jupiter/Chesod, for example, both equal 136, the theosophical extension of the kamea itself, (numbers one through sixteen).

When we examine each kamea individually, we see that Biblical quotations or other words used on the talisman may also have the same numerical equivalent. What does this mean? In Qabalah, there is an inherent identity between words or phrases that have the same numeration that reveals deeper layers of meaning when meditated upon. In all Neo-Platonic and esoteric philosophies which are constructed on the premise that number is truly an emanation of the God-energy, we look to number as a primary correspondence. We can therefore uncover this intimate sense of congruence between these emanations—the original archetypal forms—and the entities connected to them through an analysis of the correspondences of their names, which in Hebrew are also numbers.

This is done primarily through the technique of gematria, and numerous examples are given in later sections. We now begin to see why this aspect of Qabalistic work is not arbitrary. The Intelligence of Graphiel, which belongs to the Mars/Geburah kamea by virtue of numerical association (both equal 325), would never be used on a Jupiter kamea, unless one was specifically attempting to join these two kinds of energy. Here is where clarity of intention and knowing the correct correspondences both become crucial.

Unfortunately we encounter some of the same problems with mistaken, garbled, and confusing sigils as we have with planetary seals, so we need to address this issue briefly before examining some specific sigils. It is truly baffling that so many magical books give the same seals and sigils that have been available to the general public since the Agrippa and Barrett publications. On a number of occasions, Regardie clearly explains how to make a correct sigil, and just as emphatically emphasizes that the best results are achieved when the student figures them out him or herself. Yet books on talismans continue to be published with the same misinformation, showing the authors did not work them out for themselves. Some note that they do not seem to fit on the kamea, but reprint the sigils anyway. Many persons making talismans probably copy the sigils without bothering to question the full import of what they are doing. Some authors do not even give the information about how to make a true sigil, so the reader is left with no choice but to copy the ones he or she be-lieves are correct.

Let us look at an example of the correct way of tracing a sigil onto a kamea. The principal key the student needs is the chart frequently known as the Aiq Beker (see the table in figure 4–R), which has nine chambers, or a chart that refers the numerical equivalents to

Numerical Equivalents to the Sephiroth

300	30	3	200	20	2	100	10	1
ש	ל	ג	ר	כ	ב	ק	י	א
600	60	6	500	50	5	400	40	4
ם	ס	ו	ך	נ	ה	ת	מ	ד
900	90	9	800	80	8	700	70	7
ץ	צ	ט	ף	פ	ח	ן	ע	ז

Figure 4–R

the Sephiroth (see figure 4–S). These show the relationship of the numbers to the Hebrew letters, along with a method of reduction if the numerical value of the Letter is too great. For example: the letter Peh, which has a value of eighty, is often reduced to eight because no planetary kamea has the number eighty except the moon (which goes to eighty-one).

Let us look at the example of the Moon and her kamea. The lines all add up to 369, and the Spirit of the Moon, who is Chasmodai, also has a value of 369. In Hebrew, it is spelled ChShMVDAI (Ch=8, Sh=300, M=40, V=6, D=4, A=1, I=10). The 300 in this case, needs to be reduced to 30, as the number is not found on the kamea. It is frequently stressed that a number should not be reduced further than necessary. So, when traced on a correct Luna kamea, it looks like figure 4–T.

But when Agrippa's original sigil (see figure 4–U) is laid on the kamea, the horizontal line is off, because the letter Mem (M), which is forty, is missing.

The aware student will notice that there is no mark distinguishing the opening and the closing of the name—both have a line. It is irrelevant if one opens with a circle or a line, or opens with nothing at all, as long as it is somehow clear that there is a beginning and an ending. I usually indicate closing by an arrow. What is important is consistency.

Sephira	Number	Letter	Zodiac
Kether	1, 10, 100	A, I, Q	Air, Virgo, Pisces
Chokmah	2, 20, 200	B, K, R	Mercury, Jupiter, Sun
Binah	3, 30, 300	G, L, Sh	Moon, Libra, Fire
Chesed	4, 40, 400	D, M, T, Th	Venus, Water, Saturn
Geburah	5, 50	H, E, N	Aries, Scorpio
Tiphareth	6, 60	V, S	Taurus, Sagittarius
Netzach	7, 70	Z, O	Gemini, Capricorn
Hod	8, 80	Ch, P, F	Cancer, Mars
Yesod	9, 90	T, Tz	Leo, Aquarius

Figure 4–S

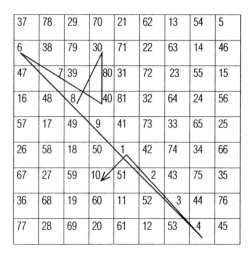

Figure 4–T

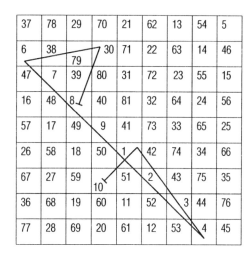

Figure 4–U

From just the sigil itself, one doesn't know where to begin the spelling of the name, but Agrippa gives the student the necessary magical information, because later in the chapter he reveals the correct Hebrew spelling of the names and he also gives the kameas in Hebrew, so anyone can figure out the correct sigil. By including the Hebrew spelling, both of the above problems are solved. I have seen a variety of other published moon sigils, which are also incorrect, but creating a correct sigil is very simple if one follows the spelling of the Hebrew Name. Although Case did not publish any sigil designs, he never had a single mistake in any of his kameas and he always gave his Hebrew spellings.

Published accounts frequently give the same kind of misleading information when they print certain sigils. Either there are two opening marks, or two closing marks, or they are occasionally reversed (which means you would spell the name backwards). Sometimes the whole sigil is reversed, as if held to a mirror, or drawn upside down or sideways. Some are given in a design that does not incorporate the full name, but rather some condensed version, leaving out certain Hebrew letters (which means the numerical equivalent would no longer be the same as the number of the kamea). Many of the problems of the sigils given in Agrippa's original designs stem from exchanging or combining the Aleph and the Yod, a fairly common cryptographic device used at the time.

Agrippa was concerned with the magician's responsibility to conceal his magical experiments, especially in regard to ceremonial magic. It makes sense to believe that he would not publish all the occult secrets of the period, when codes of secrecy were so strict; rather, he would only provide hints concealed in his glyphs and magical incantations.

In his excellent (but for the most part, non-Qabalistic) book *Practical Sigil Magic*, Frater U.D. comments that Agrippa made obvious mistakes to prevent any possible abuse. In today's world, magical information abounds, and if the student is foolish enough to practice magic for selfish and manipulative ends—not yet having integrated the law of Threefold Return—he or she can find books galore with spells, curses, and anything else imaginable. We no longer live in an age of censorship, and this forces the neophyte to take greater responsibility.

Because there are numerous books with drawings of sigils, the student can consult these if he wishes to simply copy them onto a talisman. I am not going to reproduce all the sigils of Divine Names, Intelligences, Spirits, or Angels here. All the necessary information for making correct sigils is given in this and the following chapters, along with numerous examples.

To clear up any confusion the student might have about sigils he or she may have seen in numerous Golden Dawn works, one should know that there is still an additional method for creating sigils, which can be used with any Name if translated into Hebrew. It is the famous Rose Cross (see figure 2–C on page 16) which we used for determining the sigil of our H.G.A. Sigils can be drawn from the Rose and then incorporated into the talisman.

This powerful little glyph has tremendous symbolic import for anyone with a Rosicrucian or Golden Dawn background and has been used successfully by many magicians in our century, but as Regardie noted, it is not rooted in antiquity. I personally always use the kameas for drawing the sigils of the Intelligences and Spirits and other numerical associations, but, like many others who have followed the Golden Dawn (and offshoot) traditions, I most often trace the Divine God Names pertaining to the Sephiroth on the Rose. Many of those sigils, such as those found in the excellent books on Golden Dawn rituals written and edited by Chic and Sandra Cicero, use Rose sigils, and this is why they are different from those used in this book. The student should not be confused about this—it is obvious that the sigil will change with every magical diagram it is traced upon. But the intelligent student should study and correct the many mistakes in the seals and sigils given in publications which are obviously incorrect—*i.e.*, sigils which are misspelled, done backwards, or other errors.

I highly recommend that the student use the Rose to discover the sigil of his or her Guardian Angel spirit and use this consistently on every talisman. I cannot stress the importance of this enough. Remember that the word *kamea* means *bond*. The Rose can be considered a type of kamea. You should have a very good bond with your Guardian Angel or Higher Self, before attempting to bond with these other entities, because they do have their trickster elements. Using the sigil and telesmatic images of your Angel in your magical workings ensures that you will have guidance and protection.

One can also cut a sigil (or geometric figure, such as a pentagram, etc.) in the air or ether. When doing so, one always uses the right hand with directed force. Make sure there is a definite beginning and ending of the sigil as you are drawing it. Any seal or design sympathetic to the magician's purpose can also be traced in the ether. Some seals and sigils are too complicated to be done in the air, so the simpler ones are easier for this purpose. More complicated designs can be used in other ways, such as for meditation mandalas, as we will see.

When one draws a seal or sigil, one should also see it in the mind's eye. This is the signature of an angelic force, and you are opening the door to let in its energy when you cut sigils. Do it with great care. I suggest that you have the sigil of certain powerful

Divine Names, such as IHShVH, or that of your Angel, imprinted deeply in your mind's eye as well, to instantly call upon if necessary.

These angelic sigils, whether cut in the ether or incorporated into a talisman, can be drawn from the Rose Cross or the planetary kameas themselves. In his book *How to Make and Use Talismans*, Regardie says that if the student takes time to try to understand the examples he gives, which are relatively simple, that the others should "not prove to be insuperable problems" (p. 56). It is vital for the committed magical student to spend time doing this, which is why I am not going to simply give charts to copy, although the sigils that are found here are correct and not given to mislead you.

The most important thing to remember is to use (and eventually learn) the correct spelling of the Hebrew Names (which are given in the various sections on the kameas) and use tables R and S to trace them onto a kamea. One of the most frequent mistakes in many sigils is that the A gets dropped in the angelic name. It may be arbitrary to leave out an A, since it is often taken as a vowel (*e.g.*, Bartzabel), but it is an important part of the name at the end because the Al (or EL) is that part of the angelic name which relates it to one of the sacred Hebrew Names of God. If, in forming a telesmatic image of an entity (for example, one's Guardian Angel, or one of the Archangels), one leaves out the A of the AL ending, it would be the same as leaving off the wings (Aleph)—an essential part of its angelic nature. It would also change the numerical spelling of the name. The student should keep this principle in mind. Sigils change if the pronunciation changes; if even one letter is omitted (with the possible exception of zero), it no longer has the same numerical value as the kamea and therefore loses its inherent identity with it, since the numbers of a true magical square are not arbitrary.

The wings are not just a fanciful visualization which is left over from medieval conceptualizations about angels. Many visionaries today are seeing and conversing with angels, and the vast majority report that angels do have wings. This may bring a smile to the lips of the intellectual who feels these are child-like projections, but from a hermetic point of view, wings are a powerful symbolic image. All organs of action are forms of crystallized will. As we use our legs to propel us forward on the horizontal plane, wings are projections of our will to rise vertically. In Qabalah, this is sometimes called "rising on the planes." To the Qabalist, wings are a concrete expression of the Qabalistic Cross, since they express the will for movement not only expanded outward, but elevated upward. (See Regardie's *Middle Pillar* for more on this technique.)

Let us look at one more example of sigil-making in detail before we proceed, so the student is very clear about the method given here. Graphiel (GRAPIAL) is said to be the Intelligence, or benevolent angel of Mars. Its sigil is frequently given as shown in figure 4–V. However, if we follow the traditional rules of not reducing further than necessary and using all the letters in the Name (and not some arbitrary condensed version which has a different nu-merical value, or produces a different spelling of the name), the correct sigil will look like figure 4–W.

The precise way the signature looks changes if the kamea changes (provided it is still a numerically correct kamea), as shown in the variant of the Mars kamea used by Case. On this kamea, Graphiel looks like figure 4–X. It still uses every letter of the name, but the sigil line is different. Your own name will also have a different sigil line on every kamea it

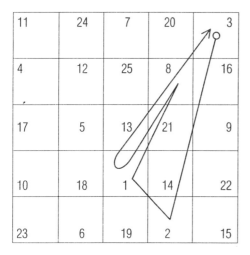

Figure 4–V

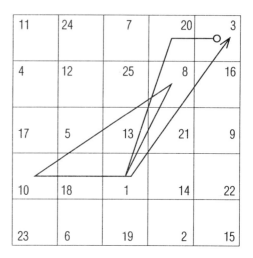

Figure 4–W

is drawn. One could be very imaginative with these figures when drawing them, such as turning the entire sigil into a geometric figure and coloring it to use as a flashing color tablet for meditation purposes (see figure 4–Y). The complementary colors for Mars are red and green.

I must say that I have never seen a correct sigil of Tiriel, the Intelligence of Mercury, in any published source. There are Golden Dawn lessons I have seen that use the same sigil as we do in our lodge, and it is published here. Taphthartharath, the spirit of Mercury, is correct in nearly all books I have seen, and to the unaware student, this could pose a danger, because one should never use the spirit or daimon without also including

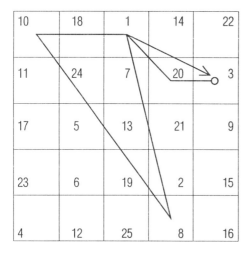

Figure 4–X

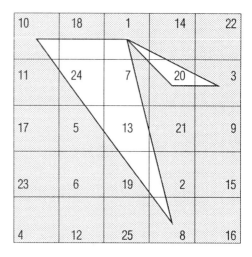

Figure 4–Y

the sigil of the Intelligence of the planet on the talisman as well. On the physical plane, it would be rather like a person who had a tremendous amount of energy (spirit) without knowing how to direct it (intelligence). Such a person may be active but mindless, like a chicken with its head cut off, to use an analogy that I find suits Taphthartharath quite well. Spirit needs direction, it needs Intelligence. A *little* knowledge, in the occult tradition, can do more harm than good.

Chapter 5

THE KAMEA OF
BINAH/SATURN

The magical numbers of the Saturn kamea are three, nine, fifteen, and forty-five. Let us explore some of these numerical associations and their sigils. There are only two Hebrew words that add up to three, and the first one is *AB, father*. The Father principle belongs more specifically to Chokmah, number two, on the Tree of Life. Why then is it attributed to Binah, the Mother? As mentioned in Chapter Three, the second Sephira has no geometrical form (except for a line, or plane) and no kamea, because as number two it has not yet come into full manifestation. In other words, fatherhood is just a possibility; it needs motherhood to become an actuality.

Kether is not the father principle on the Tree, as is the common attribution of the first Person in the Christian paradigm. In Qabalah, Kether is thought of as a whirling motion generated by Light which is concentrated at a point. It is then communicated to the Father principle, Chokmah, through the first Letter, Aleph, called the Fiery Intelligence. Case points out that the other Letter, Beth or B, is the Intelligence which forms the path to Binah. Chokmah possesses the latent potency of becoming Binah, just as two always points to three. Binah, the Mother, completes this first Qabalistic Trinity. Levi calls the Triad the universal dogma and the basis of magical doctrine.

The Father exists in *potentiality* in Chokmah, Wisdom, and as number two finds fulfillment in number three, Binah, Understanding. AB=3 demonstrates this relationship (1+2 =3). It is shown as an arrow going straight up when placed on a Saturn kamea (see figure 5–A). Fabre de 'Olivet, the great Hebrew language scholar, says that Ab is "the potential sign united to that of interior activity (that) produces a root whence comes all ideas of productive cause, efficient will, determining movement and generative force" (1921, p. 287).

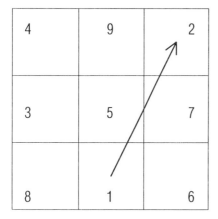

Figure 5–A: AB (3)

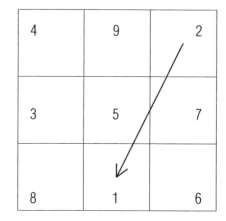

Figure 5–B: BA (3)

This concept of fatherhood, or the objective existence of a productive cause being only a potentiality also finds expression in modern physics. The uncertainty principle tells us that everything is possibility until it comes in contact with an observer—that is, it becomes real when it enters into relationship; it is where subjective and objective experience meets that what we like to call reality happens.

As the Third Sephira, Binah represents the origin of Trinitarian dogmas, because, as Levi explains, the universal way of thinking about relationship is grammatically: that which speaks, that which is spoken to, and that which is spoken about. In magic, this is origin, realization, and adaptation. In theology it supposes an intelligent cause, a mediation (the *Logos*), and a creative expression. Binah is the creative principle which in turn births the rest of the Sephiroth.

When we are dealing with only two-letter Hebrew combinations, there exists the possibility of reversal. We said that there were two words that add up to three. The first is *AB*, and the second is *BA* (Baw), which means to come, arrive, enter (Ben Yehuda). The root can be read either way. Here we see the beginnings of a fascinating topic that, although beyond the scope of this book, is vital for a Qabalist who is interested in studying Hebrew. It is the 231 Gates, which in Qabalah are all of the possible two-Letter combinations. I highly recommend de 'Olivet's book *The Hebrew Tongue Restored* to help decipher any of the two-letter Hebrew words or root combinations, because they all have great power.

Read the other way, de 'Olivet says that BA is "the sign of interior activity united to that of power (that) forms a root whence is drawn all ideas of progression, coming, passage, locomotion" (p. 301). It is demonstrated in the arrow-sigil which goes the other way (see figure 5–B). What this reversed gematria can tell us is that the cause of existence, often thought of as AB, Father, when reversed, implies another impulse—to find manifestation in the future. The Eternal God-Energy is beyond conceptualization of time, yet the changing of these two letters shows us that Spirit is not only the initial cause of our existence (or the existence prior to ours), but that Spirit has an evolutionary character and is manifesting in manifold ways through us as It appears to move into the future.

Let us look at some other words, which relate here in terms of their unity through gematria. 3x3=9, the number of cells in the kamea. Multiples of nine are prominent throughout the magical interpretations of numbers, and the first Hebrew word that points to this is *GAH* (number nine), a verb which means *to rise, to increase, to grow* (Ben Yehuda). On the squares, the simplest sigil designs (*i.e.*, of an arrow pointing in one direction or another) become slightly more com-

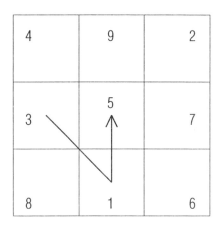

Figure 5–C: GHH (9)

plex with the addition of another line (see figure 5–C). Nine is, as we have noted, the last in the series of number extensions before repetitions. It is also the number of the Sephira called Yesod, linking the Mother Binah with Her ninth child on the Tree. Yesod is called the Foundation and is the building block of our physical world, Malkuth, number ten. Yesod is symbolized by the Moon and Saturn is symbolized by a sickle, showing a unity in their primary archetypal shapes.

Both shapes can be incorporated onto a talisman if one was working on unifying these two principles (see correspondence charts at the end of this chapter). A sample design incorporating the ideas we have examined so far can be made into a talismanic glyph that looks like figure 5–D. This is a talisman made by someone in my lodge and combines very simply and elegantly the primary ideas of bringing something into manifestation (three) and seeing it through to completion (nine). This is implied as well in the meaning of the sigil lines, which we have already discussed. It has the Divine Name *Yah* (IH) written in Hebrew at the top. This Name is also one of the multiples consistent with the kamea: fifteen (all columns add up to fifteen each way), so it is an appropriate correspondence.

The sigil of the H.G.A. and the statement of purpose were initialed on the back of this talisman, rather than incorporated into the actual design. Any of the Hebrew names

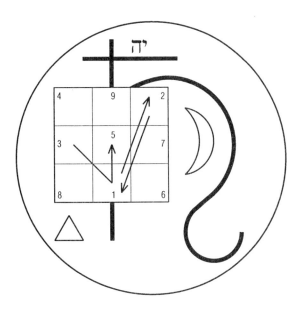

Figure 5–D

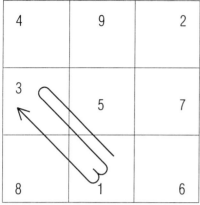

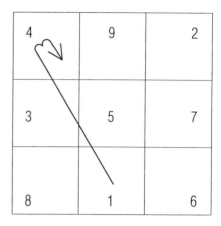

Figure 5–E: AGIEL (45)

Figure 5–F: ADM (45)

given in the correspondence tables in this and the forthcoming chapters can be used in this way. Drawn onto the kamea, they form their own sigils, just like the names of the Intelligences, spirits, etc. They communicate their particular energy when added to the talisman. Any word can be used, but those that have a numerical equivalent to the magical numbers of the kamea have a special added potency.

The Intelligence of this planet is Agiel, whose number is forty-five, the theosophic extension of the kamea (see figure 5–E). It is also the same as Adam, a Hebrew word which indicates the Life-force (Aleph, A) manifesting in the Life-blood (dam) of the microcosmic Human. Its sigil is pictured in figure 5–F. Either name can be spelled with a slight variation on the sigil line, and with the arrow (or any ending point) going either direction in the case of Adam (see 5–G and 5–H). Another name with the numerical vibration of forty-five is *hame* (HM), which means a *multitude, abundance,* and *themselves* (see figure 5–I). It is also one of the 231 Gates, because it is a two-lettered root.

Its opposite, *mah* (MH) is illustrated by a sigil line that is an arrow going the other direction (see figure 5–J). These arrows go in opposite diagonals from the first set of roots we examined and demonstrate that each of these signatures—even the most simple two-letter combinations—has its own specific energy. The arrow going up (HM) is from the root which means "the vital power of the universe" (de 'Olivet, p. 331), implying an outgoing, more masculine principle, while the MH root, signified by the arrow going down, means "female generation. . . essentially passive and creative. . . (it is) the element from which everything draws nourishment" (p. 387).

One will note from these simple examples that there are many complements, both in the Hebrew roots and in the Hebrew gematria. These are consistent themes in Qabalistic study of the kameas. We see this very principle of complementarity in the archetypal expression of Binah/Saturn herself, for this is traditionally thought of as a contracting, limiting, structuring energy, yet it is also connected to growth, agriculture, life, and other concepts (see correspondence charts at the end of this chapter), as is

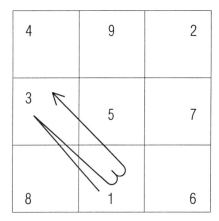

Figure 5–G: AGIEL (45)

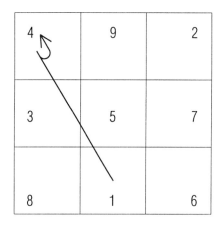

Figure 5–H: ADM (45)

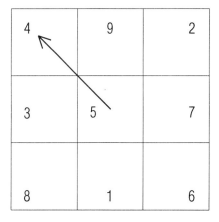

Figure 5–I: HM (45)

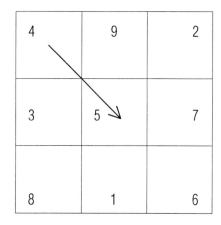

Figure 5–J: MH (45)

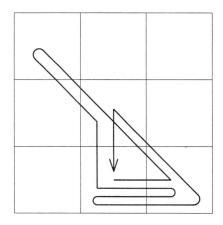

Figure 5–K: YHVH (45)

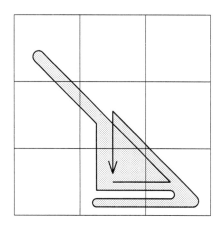

Figure 5–L: YHVH (45)

4	9	2
3	5	7
8	1	6

Figure 5–M

ד	ט	ב
ג	ה	ז
ח	א	ו

Figure 5–N

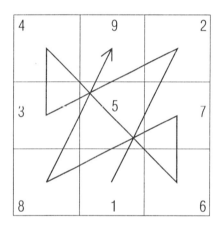

Figure 5–O

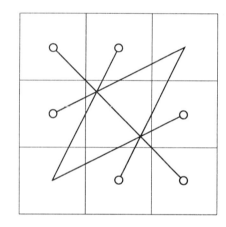

Figure 5–P

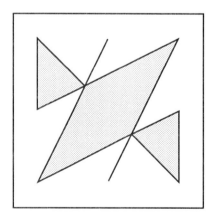

Figure 5–Q

demonstrated by some of the words we have examined here. Even though Saturn limits, it must be remembered that Binah is the powerful creative force on the Tree that brings all things into formation. In *Godwin's Cabalistic Encyclopedia* (an excellent gematria resource book that is a must for the serious student of kameas), the word *Mah* also means the secret name of the World of Formation; and the Tetragrammaton IHVH when spelled out, Yod-Ha-Vav-Ha (which also equals forty-five), is said to be the spelling of the Divine Name in Yetzirah, or the World of Formation. If all the letters are connected in a sigil, it looks like figure 5–K. Since it thus creates an enclosed geometric form, one could then color it and even make a flashing color tablet, as we did with the example of Graphiel in Chapter Four (See figure 5–L).

Figures 5–M and 5–N are the traditional kameas found in Agrippa, the latter in Hebrew. figure 5–O shows the seal made by connecting the numbers in theosophic extension, as explained earlier, and figure 5–P depicts the traditional seal used by both Agrippa and the Golden Dawn. figure 5–Q is the seal removed from the grid. Planetary seals will be included in each chapter, although later they will not look traditional.

Following are some of the other Letter correspondences which are identified with the kamea. Roots are not necessarily words found in a Hebrew dictionary. They do have a definite archetypal meaning, and so are included. All roots found at the end of each chapter are taken from de 'Olivet. Words marked with an asterisk (*) are God-Names.

It should be noted that in this chart the spirit of Saturn, Zazel, is spelled ZZAL by both Case and Crowley, and not ZAZL, as is commonly given.

Correspondences: Magical Names and Numbers of Binah/Saturn

❖ 3: Sephirah of Binah

*3: AB, ab: father
ROOT: productive cause, efficient will, generative force

3: BA, baw: coming, futurity, arriving
ROOT: progression, coming, passage, locomotion, happening

❖ 9: Divisions of Kamea

9: Sephirah of Yesod

9: GAH, gaah: to grow, increase; become powerful

9: ACh, ach: brother, kinsmen, friend
ROOT: equality, identity, fraternity; the common hearth

9: HD, hed: an echo, or shout
ROOT: the power of division

❖ 15: Sum of Rows in Kamea

*15: IH, Jah, Divine Name associated with Chokmah
ROOT: absolute Life, absolute being

15: HVD Hod, Splendor, the 8th Sephira

15: ZUB, zabe: to flow; menstrual flow

15: ABIB, abib: the first month of spring; month of Passover and Resurrection

15: GAVH: pride, exaltation

15: ABVHA, aboha, angel of Third decante of Sagittarius

15: GBHH: high

15: ZCh: to move, to impel
ROOT: movement made with effort; tenacious spirit

15: Number of the goddess GAIA in Greek

❖ 45: Theosophic Extension of Numbers in Kamea

45: ADM, adam: generic humanity

45: AGIAL, Agiel: Intelligence of Saturn

45: HM, hame: abundance, multitude, themselves
ROOT: universalized life, vital power of the universe

45: AMD, ahmad: to appraise, value, estimate

45: ZBVL, zebul: habitation, dwelling place

45: ZZAL, zazel: the spirit of Saturn

45: MAD, meode: strength, force, might

45: MH, mah: what? why?; secret nature of Yetzirah.
ROOT: female generation, root of all nourishment, passive and creative

*45: IVD-HA-VAV-HA, Yod-Heh-Vav-Heh: spelling of IHVH in Yetzirah, world of Formation

45: YLH, yelah: 44th name of Shem Hamphorash, associated with the 2nd quinance of Pisces

45: HVLD: begat

Chapter 6

THE KAMEA OF CHESED/JUPITER

The magical numbers connected to the Jupiter kamea are four, sixteen, thirty-four, and 136. We have noted in previous correspondence charts that four is connected to justice, reciprocity, governments, etcetera. It was noted by Theodore Parker, an American transcendentalist, that our own government has some interesting correspondences with the number four: the Fourth of July celebrates the Declaration of Independence; we have four branches of government; presidents have four-year terms.

Qabalistically, the number four represents perfect equilibrium and is often represented by a cross or a cubic stone. This stone, according to Levi, is the *keystone of the Temple*, or the structural foundation of masonry and occultism. On the tree, it is represented by the Sephirah of Chesed, often known as *Gedulah* (GDVLH), which means majesty or magnificence.

Gedulah has a numerical value of forty-eight, or 12x4, which suggests the multiplication of the powers of the four elements by the twelve signs of the zodiac. The Divine Name attributed to this Sephira, Al or El, is the ending of many angelic names. In her book *Archetypes on the Tree of Life*, which examines Case's interpretation of the Tarot keys, M. C. Compton writes:

> As a symbolic image, the letter Lamed (L) represents a serpent unfolding, or the wing of a bird which raises, extends and unfolds itself. . . we understand the Aleph-Lamed connection to represent the vital

4	14	15	1
9	7	6	12
5	11	10	8
16	2	3	13

Figure 6–A: Traditional Kamea of Jupiter

idea of the primal driving force being adjusted to suit our individual needs in terms of our relationship to this Energy. . . The might and power of God are being borne by the outstretched wing of Lamed, whose symbol is Libra, the scales. . . (pp. 154–55).

The underlying principle of this sacred Name is that of balance or equilibrium (Lamed, Justice) combined with the power of the Life-force (Aleph). This perfect equilibrium is represented by the number four, which is the value of AL when it is reduced (30+1=31=4). Another word which corresponds to four is *Abba* (ABA), which is often interpreted as father, but which actually corresponds more closely to the word *daddy*. It is the affectionate name which Jesus used to call his father and was considered slightly slang in the Aramaic of his day.

Another numerical correspondence is the root *bab* (BB), which means *hollow* or *vein* (Crowley); as a root it means, interior void or exterior swelling, as well as pupil of the eye (d 'Olivet). There is a hidden connection with this idea and *Ayin*, which is the Hebrew Letter that means eye, as well as surface appearance, and mammon or wealth. Another root word is *Gaa* (GA), which means proud or haughty, and is one of the negative characteristics of Jupiter. Pride is often associated with the power and authority of majesty (gedulah) on the physical plane. These correspondences are listed at the end of this chapter.

The Divine name attributed to Chesed is *Ab El*, a combination of the two Divine Names we have already examined in some detail. (See Chapter Five for the Name *Ab*). It's numerical summation is thirty-four, the magic number of the kamea, and it's meaning is God the Father. It's sigil on the Jupiter kamea is two arrows descending down (see figure 6–B), demonstrating the beneficent influence of Gedulah personified as God the Father pouring forth his majestic graces. One of the most powerful affirmations of Dr. Case was the one corresponding to Chesed on the Tree of Life, from his famous "Pattern on the Trestle board" (a complete copy of which can be found in his *True and Invisible Rosicrucian Order*, p. 158):

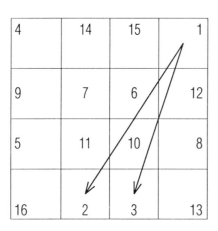

Figure 6–B: AB–EL

4	14	15	1
9	7	6	12
5	11	10	8
16	2	3	13

Figure 6–C: ZVG

> From the exhaustless riches of Its Limitless Substance, I draw all things needful, both spiritual and material.

This is a very valuable affirmation and would greatly enrich any sincere aspirant's life if it was said with devotion and concentration every day. It would also be a useful adjunct to any Jupiter talisman.

There are sixteen squares in the Jupiter kamea and there are also sixteen geomantic figures (see correspondence charts at the end of this chapter). The sixteenth path on the Tree of Life between Chokmah and Chesed corresponds to the Letter *Vav*, to which is attributed the Hierophant, often known as the Pope, which in Italian also means father. This demonstrates the relationship of the paternal power descending from Chokmah to find concrete expression in Chesed.

We have noted that the word hyssop in Hebrew also equals sixteen and this is one of the plants sacred to Jupiter. Another word valuable to use on a talisman is *ZVG*, which also has a value of sixteen and which means like or equal to (Crowley) or to pair or match (Ben Yehuda). It can be used to draw out an affinity with the forces being evoked in the talisman. It forms a perfect right angle (see figure 6–C), which, because it is open on the third side, is also a magical symbol of Masonry, according to Levi. It is the tool called a square which is used by masons and carpenters even today. I have found this signature to be an extremely effective sigil line, as well as others which form perfect right angles.

The Intelligence of Jupiter is Yophiel and its sigil is demonstrated in figure 6–D. One may also use more than one sigil on a kamea, if their energies are sufficiently compatible. For example, the spirit of Jupiter, Hismael, which is generally correctly given in most books on magical squares, can be combined with Yophiel to produce figure 6–E. Their names both have a numerical value of 136, the theosophic extension of the kamea. Another very valuable affirmation that also has the numeric equivalent of 136 is; "I will give thanks unto the Tetragrammaton with all my heart" from Psalm 9:2 (see figure 6–F for Hebrew spelling). This could be made into a sigil, or it could also be an effective inscription written around the edge of the talisman.

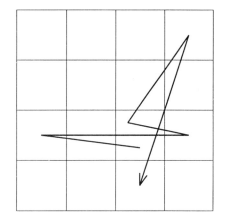

Figure 6–D: YOPHIEL–136

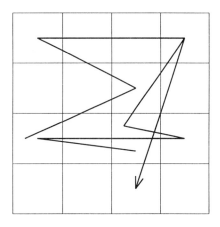

Figure 6–E: YHPIAL–Yophial
HSML–Hismeal

ד	יד	טו	א
ט	ז	ו	יב
ה	יא	י	ח
טז	ב	ג	יג

Figure 6–F: Traditional Kamea in
Hebrew

Another powerful motto with the value of 136, taken from Latin rather than Hebrew, is: "The undefiled glory of God" (*Dei gloria intacta*), which was said to be engraved in a circle on the vault of the legendary founder of the Rosicrucian order, Brother C.R.C. It was written around the figure of a man's head, which Case said represented Aquarius. Case's interpretation of the motto is that:

> (It) refers to the occult conception that the real Inner Man is identical with and inseparable from the pure essence of the Life Power. That essence is correctly associated with the element of air, to which the sign Aquarius (the Man) is referred, because Spirit and Breath are correlated in all ancient philosophies. Furthermore, the adjective *intacta*, which I have translated as undefiled, means even more than this. The Inner Glory that is the essence of the real Man is not only untouched by the action of its outer vehicle of personality. It is truly untouchable. It can never be defiled (*True and Invisible Rosicrucian Order*, p. 126).

The full realization of this symbol, however, belongs to the Age of Aquarius, into which we are just entering.

Another important correspondence that belongs to this kamea is the magical word *Qol* (QVL), which also has a value of 136. This is really the Voice of Intuition, or the Higher Self, or H.G.A. In Case's interpretation, it is represented by the Hierophant, which is, as we have noted, the sixteenth path. This path belongs to the Grade of Magus, or the Exempt Adept who has "so perfected the organization of his vehicles of consciousness that there is no obstruction between him and his communication with that One Teacher" (*ibid*, p. 286).

Qol forms a simple sigil line and can be joined to almost any name (*e.g.*, the Voice of Yophiel, Tzadqiel, Jeheshuah, etc.). It also has a correspondence to the root-word *ChaCh*, which Godwin notes means hook or ring (p.226). Hook or nail is the meaning of *Vav*, the Hierophant. d'Olivet says ChCh "expresses force as anything pointed or hooked, hence. . . to penetrate, to go deeply into." (p. 349) Its value is sixteen.

Mysteriously, Agrippa gives another word with the value of sixteen, *HVH*, but gives no meaning. It is ambivalent, its various definitions depending on vowel points, like so many Hebrew words. It means "mischief," "ruin or calamity," as well as "to be," "to exist," and "to form or constitute" (Ben Yehuda). Agrippa also gives *AHI*, which means "where?" Both of these words, it must be noted, are Names of God if one letter is added (*AHIH* and *IHVH*), one at the beginning and one at the end. There are numerous mysteries to ponder here, and Qabalists who have studied the Jewish Qabalistic texts will see the similarities between these words and the Divine Names to which they are related.

We said earlier that the simplest but most well-concealed secret of forming the magical planetary seals is to follow the hint given in the

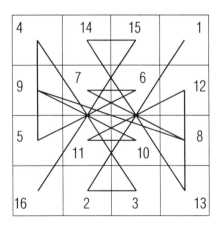

Figure 6–G: Agrippa's Kamea

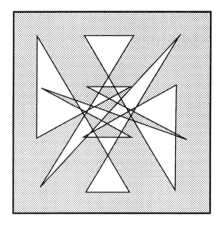

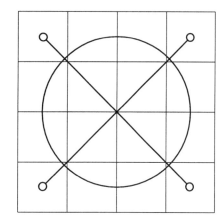

Figure 6–H

Figure 6–I

Saturn kamea (see Saturn figures in Chapter Five). This technique is as easy as connecting the dots in a young child's drawing book. If we connect the sixteen numbers, in order, on the Jupiter kamea, we get the design in figure 6–G. We can make a flashing color tablet in this design using the complementary colors of blue and orange that looks like figure 6–H (compare to the traditional Seal of Jupiter in figure 6–I).

It amazes me that, to my knowledge, no one in the Golden Dawn tradition has previously published these planetary seals; they are far more powerful as meditation mandalas than most any other talismanic figures I have ever worked with. Even some unpublished Golden Dawn lessons I have read did not reveal these seals, yet they are exceptionally easy to discover when attention is paid to the design on the Saturn kamea. The Islamic magicians were most certainly aware of them, and many of their magical designs have been incorporated in beautiful mandala-like Islamic carpets and artwork. We will examine this in more detail in Chapter Nine.

Information about how to make seals of the planets from the same planetary kameas as we have in the Golden Dawn tradition is available in the book *Islamic Patterns: An Analytical and Cosmological Approach*, in the chapter on magic squares. Dr. Case did not invent this method of seal-formation; as previously mentioned, it has been suggested that Agrippa himself knew about these seals but did not publish them. As far as I know Case was the only one to use them in the modern magical tradition. Our lodge now uses a number of different designs (some drawn from magical squares we have discovered) as flashing color tablets, and it works exceptionally well as an entry point for contacting the specific planetary energy. The student can experiment with them, coloring them in a variety of ways, but should retain the proper color scheme.

Correspondences: Magical Names and Numbers of Chesed/Jupiter

Aserisks (*) denote God-names

❖ 4: Sephirah of Chesed

4: ABA, abba: father, daddy

4: GA, gaw: proud, conceited, haughty
ROOT: the organic sign of Gimel united to the potential Aleph constitutes a root which is attached to all ideas of aggrandizement, augmentation, and magnitude

4: BB, bub: Hollow, vein
ROOT: every idea of interior void, of exterior swelling; pupil of the eye

❖ 16: Divisions of Kamea

16: 16th path between Chesed and Chokmah, Vav

16: AVDH: I will thank

16: AChZ: percent

16: ChBV, chebo: 68th name of Shem Hamphorash, associated with 2nd quinance of Cancer

16: ChCh, chach: hook, ring
ROOT: expresses force as anything pointed or hooked, hence. . . to penetrate, to go deeply into

16: HVH: to be, to exist, mischief, ruin

16: AHI: where?

16: ZVG: to pair or match

❖ 34: Sum of Rows in Kamea

*34: AL AB, El ab: God the father

34: BLB, ve-laib: the heart

34: ChHVYH, Chahaviah: angel of 6th quinance of Scorpio

34: LD
ROOT: expresses every idea of generation, propagation, of any extension whatso-
ever given to being. . . to make manifest, to put forward

34: DL, dal: a pauper
ROOT: every idea of extraction, or removal. . . of exhaustion and weakness

❖ 136: Theosophic Extension of Numbers in Kamea

136: Mystic number of 16th path, Vav

136: KPVL: double

136: HSMAL, Hismael: spirit of Jupiter

136: YHPYAL, Yophiel: Intelligence of Jupiter

136: MMVN, mammon: wealth, money, financing, fines

136: MTzAH: ability, means, to be supplied with

136: QVL, Qol: Voice, call, cry, thunder

136: AVDH IHVH BKL-LBI: I will give thanks unto Jehovah with all my heart

136: *Dei Gloria intacta*: the untouchable glory of God

136: MPIV: out of his mouth (Numbers 30:3)

Chapter 7

THE KAMEA OF GEBURAH/MARS

The magical numbers of the Mars kamea are five, twenty-five, sixty-five, and 325. This is true regardless of how the kamea is set up. Mathematicians have discovered there are several thousand possible combinations of the Mars kamea that will produce these same numbers, although most do not make harmonious seals. These combinations have been known for a long time; a three-volume set of magical squares was published in 1837 by Violle (in French), giving many variants of the kameas, and Case chose a different kamea for Mars and the Sun than those that have been handed down in the western magical tradition adopted by the Golden Dawn and others. We do not know his reasons for doing this.

Certainly every different arrangement of numbers will produce different sigils lines and some produce different seals. There are some interesting comparisons in this regard that we will examine in this and following chapters. Many of the sigils the student will have to work out for him or herself. A few examples should demonstrate that planetary energies change somewhat with the introduction of different kameas.

One may well ask what makes a kamea magical if there are so many possible combinations? When mathematicians use examples of magical squares, they imply nothing esoteric by this term, but throughout history kameas have been considered numinous in all esoteric traditions, because, although modern scientist's scoff at this idea, numbers are Emanations of the Deity. The same relationship exists between astronomy and astrology.

Simply because we now have a rational science that can define the physical characteristics of the planets in no way hinders the journeys of today's magicians into inner space. The planetary spirits are just as numinous today as they were in the ancient world for those who have experienced their angelic energies directly. We know a lot more about the geography of the body and mind today than we did in the Middle Ages, yet we are no

11	24	7	20	3
4	12	25	8	16
17	5	13	21	9
10	18	1	14	22
23	6	19	2	15

Figure 7–A: Traditional

10	18	1	14	22
11	24	7	20	3
17	5	13	21	9
23	6	19	2	15
4	12	25	8	16

Figure 7–B: Alternate

closer to understanding the mystery of what constitutes *soul* through any kind of rational analysis.

Because we have discovered many alternate kameas since Agrippa does not diminish their fascination or their power. From my own experience with tracing seals on many different kameas, there are few that produce symmetry and still contain the same mystery that constitutes a magic square, *i.e.*, the specific numerical relationships we explained earlier. The numbers themselves are consistant: they are simply arranged in different ways.

Let us examine the two used by Agrippa (figure 7–A) and Case (figure 7–B), both of which are found in the book *Magic Squares and Cubes,* published in 1917 by W. S. Andrews. In both kameas the number thirteen lies at the center. Thirteen is the numeration of a Hebrew word meaning unity (achad). It is also related to Mars because *Peh*, the Hebrew Letter attributed to Mars, reduces to thirteen (85=8+5=13). This letter, when spelled out (PH) means mouth and points to the power inherent in words. More information about this relationship can be had from Case's interpretation of the Tarot and the Hebrew Letters (see bibliography).

In both kameas the numbers in any two cells that are equidistant from the center always add up to twenty-six, which is the number of *IHVH*, Tetragrammaton. There are twelve sets of these pairs and they represent the positive and negative aspects of the signs of the Zodiac, balanced by the unifying point at the center. This is reflected in the phrase "Together in unity," which equals sixty-five, the magic sum of the square of Mars.

The first principle number relating to Mars is five, which is Geburah on the Tree of Life. This is the special seat of will power on the Tree and its principle Divine name *Elohim Gibor*, means God of Strength. To Mars is attributed the Letter *Peh* and also *Heh* (5), to which is assigned Aries, and the Emperor. This path is called the "Constituting Intelligence." Five is also the numeration of *Ad*, mist or vapor, and in Hebrew mysticism this refers to the dark cloud or vapor that constitutes the substance of primordial creation,

Figure 7–C: Traditional

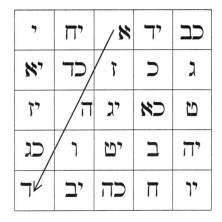

Figure 7–D: Alternate

and that hovered over the waters in Genesis. The root word *Gab* also equals five and refers to the vault or surface of heaven. The power of the Constituting Intelligence of Mars is further reflected in the magical phrase in Genesis: "Let there be," which has the numeration of twenty-five (*IHI*). This correspondence was noted as early as Agrippa.

We have noted that Case used a different Mars kamea than Agrippa (See 7–A and 7–B). If we refer to the simple sigil lines of the word *Ad* in figures 7–C and 7–D, we can see that they go in opposite directions, depending on which kamea they are placed on (*i.e.*, the traditional kamea used by Agrippa or the alternative kamea used by Case). The concept of hovering over the primal waters is more in keeping with the sigil in figure 7–D. We will also notice some of these same discrepancies in other seals and sigils drawn from these different squares, so the student should experiment and choose carefully the kamea that better suits his or her purpose.

This difference is particularly noticeable if one closely examines the different seals drawn from the kameas (see figures 7–E and 7–F). One ends with the arrow pointing

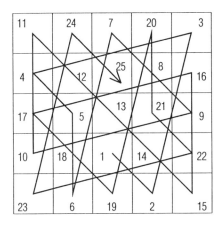

Figure 7–E: Traditional

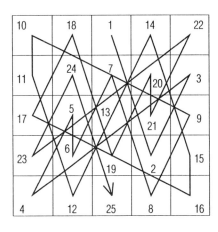

Figure 7–F: Alternate

Figure 7–G

outward, but in the traditional kamea, it ends inside the figure. Again, this does not seem befitting to the nature of Mars, which has a much more outgoing, even thrusting kind of nature (see correspondence charts in Chapter Three). It has an energetic, restless energy that resembles one of the symbols attributed to Peh, which is the lightening flash of the Tower in the tarot deck (see figure 7–G). The Mars seal also suggests this energy (see figure 7–F).

The sacred Name *Adonai* (ADNI) has a numeration of sixty-five. Graphiel, the Intelligence, and Bartzabel, the spirit of Mars, both equal 325, the theosophic extension of the line when all numbers are included. You may want to review chapter four for variations on the sigil of Graphiel.

Dr. Case never refers to sigils or their differences on the various kameas; he did, however, point out that the proportions in the angles created by the kamea in figure 7–F are in harmony with the number five. Look at the differences in the two seals made by drawing a line from one to twenty-five. figure 7–F contains two slanted rectangles (this is more clearly seen in figure 7–H) going in diagonals. Its symmetry is known as a *Root Five* rectangle. Agrippa's kamea, on the other hand, produces a seal which is more triangular. If one follows the points from number one to number five, the first image that emerges is an equilateral triangle shape (see figure 7–I). One can see these distinct variations by coloring or shading the seals, as is shown in figures 7–J, 7–K and 7–L. Again, these could be imaginatively painted in flashing color tablets, the primary colors being red and green.

The principle geometric form corresponding to five is the pentagon (see page 42). The pentagon divides a circle into five equal arcs, each of which contains seventy-two degrees. The number seventy-two is a magical number in Qabalah which refers to the Shem Hamphorash, or the seventy-two-lettered Name of God. It consists of seventy-two

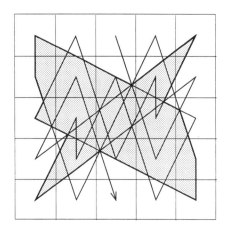

Figure 7–H: Alternate

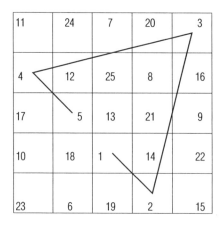

Figure 7–I: Traditional

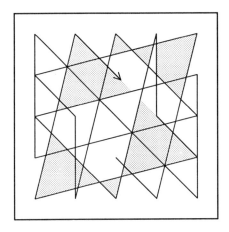

Figure 7–J: Traditional

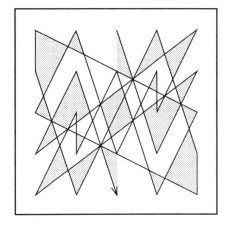

Figure 7–K: Alternate

Figure 7–L

three-letter roots to which are added either an AL or a IH ending, thus forming angelic attributions which correspond to one of the quinaries (divisions of five degrees) of the Zodiac. Furthermore, to each side of the pentagon is assigned one of the Letters of the Divine Name *Elohim* (ALHIM), which is attributed to both Binah (IHVH Elohim) and Geburah (Elohim Gibor).

The pentegram is a symbol of human dominion and is appropriately attributed to the power of Geburah. It is sometimes known as the star of the will.

Correspondences: Magical Names and Numbers of Geburah/Mars

Aserisks (*) denote God-names

❖ 5: Sephirah of Geburah

5: ABB, ahbah: to blossom or to bear fruit ("The whole universe is an expansion of my Primal Will to yield fruit," *Book of Tokens*, Meditation on Heh)

5: Heh (H), the number of the fifth Letter of the Hebrew alphabet, attributed to the Emperor and Aries

5: AD, ade: vapor, mist
ROOT: relative unity, an emanation

5: BBA, bahbah: door, gate

5: GB, bab: upper surface, vault, rim (of wheel)
ROOT: the idea of a thing placed under another thing, a protuberance, a knoll, everything convex

5: DA, dah: this, a talmudic word referring to man, the human, whose symbol is five
ROOT: the sign of natural abundance and division

❖ 25: Divisions in Kamea

25: IHI, yehi: Let there be

25: The twenty-fifth path between Tiphareth and Yesod, Samekh

25: HYY, hayeya: seventy-first name of Shem Hamphorash, associated with fifth quinance of Cancer

25: KH, koh: Thus, so; this way, that way ROOT: that which coincides with a point of space or time (This is a powerful sigil to use with IHI)

25: DKA, to break (Crowley)

❖ 65: Sum of Rows in Kamea

*65: ADNI, Adonai: The Lord

65: GDM IChD, gam yawkhad: together in unity

65: HIKL, haikal: Temple, meeting place for the Shekinah

65: SH, ROOT: that which is round in form: dome, moon

65: HS, ROOT: silence

65: LLH, Lelah : 6th name of Shem Hamphorash, associated with 6th quinance of Leo.

65: LUX: Latin for Light

❖ 325: Theosophic Extension of Numbers in Kamea

325: GRAPYAL, Graphiel: Intelligence of Mars

325: BRTzBAL, Bartzabel: Spirit of Mars

325: NYNDWHR, Nundahar: Angel of 2nd decanate of Scorpio

Chapter 8

THE KAMEA OF
TIPHARETH/SUN

The magical numbers of the Sun are six, thirty-six, 111, and 666. The first three numbers, six, thirty-six, and 111, when added together, equal 153, which is the number of fish mentioned in John 21:11. We know that Biblical authors did not use numbers arbitrarily, and in this story the catch of fish, which the early Christians saw as a symbol for Christ, represented the new Christian community, since these fish were caught after the Resurrection of Jesus. One may refer to David Fideler's *Jesus Christ Sun of God: Ancient Cosmology and Early Christian Symbolism* for other interesting associations of the number 153 with Pythagorean symbolism.

Eliphas Levi praises the Sephira of Tiphareth thus:

> Beauty, the luminous conception of equilibrium in forms, intermediary between the Crown and the Kingdom, mediating principle between Creator and creation—a sublime conception of poetry and its sovereign priesthood! (Transcendental Magic, 1972, p. 97).

To this Sphere is attributed the number six and the Seal of Solomon, or hexagram. This is the geometrical symbol which best illustrates the great maxim, "As above, so below," the joining of the microcosm with the macrocosm. According to the principle of analogy, whatever is in the Godhead is reflected in the human being. The three principles of Intelligence, Love, and Creativity find expression in the body through the three centers of the brain, the heart, and the sexual chakra, or seat of kundalini. As the "world is magnetized by the light of the sun, [so] we are magnetized by the Astral Light" (Levi, 1972, p. 72).

The function of mediation expressed in Tiphareth is reflected through gematria by the association, *agab* (AGB): "by means of, or through," which has a value of six. This is the great harmonizing Sphere of the Christ principle through which we are made aware of our own Divine nature. The word *Light* appears six times in John's Prologue to describe this perfected nature of Christ. Tiphareth is considered to be the pivot of the entire Tree, like the sun in our solar system. Many ancient peoples identified the sun with the Deity, yet the evolution of western religion advises us to express this identity with caution. Although the ancient Hebrews sang many hymns praising God's movement in nature, we know they distinguished themselves from the surrounding cultures which worshipped God in nature.

Moses himself inveighed against sun-worship, and the reason that Qabalah stresses the ineffable nature of God as distinct from as well as identified with the attributes on the Tree of Life (by postulating the unknowable Force called the Ain Soph) is because it is a materialization of our understanding of the God-energy to take the manifestation (the sun, the golden calf, gold, and others) for the Real Thing. This is the meaning of 666, according to Dr. Case, for this kind of materialism is the root of separated Ego-consciousness, since 666 is the number of a man in Revelation. It is the delusion of the materialist to think he has an autonomous ego, and to take the material world for the only real one. As Levi says:

> In all things the vulgar mind habitually takes shadow for reality, turns its back upon light and is reflected in the obscurity which it projects itself (1972, p. 72)

The mystery of 666, however, is that the very forces which bind us, when properly understood, also act as a source of liberation.

The theosophical extension of number six is 1+2 1 3. This points to an interesting relationship between Tiphareth and the Supernal Triangle. We know that Chokmah lies at the lower end of the path of Aleph (value 111, one of the magic numbers of the Sun). Binah lies at the end of the path of the second Letter, Beth. Because Tiphareth lies at the end of the third Letter, Gimel, Case points out that this Sephira was brought into manifestation before Chesed or Geburah, the fourth and fifth Sephiroth (see Tree Diagram on page 2).

The symbol of Tiphareth, the hexagram, is also called the Star of the Macrocosm because lines drawn from its center to its six points and intersections divides the circle into the twelve houses of heaven, and thus it is a symbolic map of the universe. When we use the Golden Dawn Banishing Ritual (see Regardie's *Middle Pillar*) and say the affirmation, "Behind me shines the six-rayed Star," we are implying that all powers represented by the hexagram are behind us, or backing us up.

It will be noticed that when the hexagram is laid on the Tree, it not only includes the mundane Spheres of Jupiter, Mars, Venus, Mercury and the Moon, but also Daath/Pluto, the hidden Sphere at its top point (See figure 8–A).

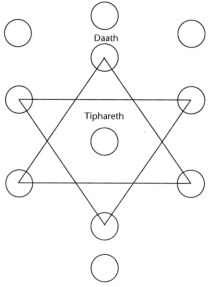

Figure 8–A

ו	לב	ג	לד	לה	א
ז	יא	כז	כח	ח	ל
יט	יד	יו	יה	כג	כד
יח	כ	כב	כא	יז	יג
כה	כט	י	ט	כו	יב
לו	ה	לג	ד	ב	לא

Figure 8–B: Traditional

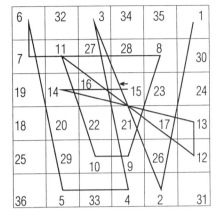

Figure 8–C: Agrippa's Kamea

Daath is separated from the Spheres below it since it resides in the Abyss. One of the words with the numerical vibration of six is *bid*, BD, which means something separated, isolated, or unique. We will look at Daath more in Chapter Twelve.

For now we note that the magical square of the Sun is also considered to be very unique—it does not follow the mathematical rules for forming a magical square that all others in the Decad do. I suggest that the student trace the kamea of Agrippa (see figure 8–B) to see the seal that it produces. Frankly, I don't believe it is a true magical seal of the Sun. If you trace it yourself, you will see that it does not really seem to be a pleasing line, not nearly as aesthetically beautiful or symmetrical as the others we have seen or will see in forthcoming chapters. It is not very easy to draw—there are lines that criss-cross all over the place, the seal goes backward on itself, tracing over several cells numerous times.

It is also difficult to paint, to find an inside and an outside, or a ground and a foreground. When tracing it across Agrippa's kamea, one notices that it begins to get chaotic at about cell 15 (This is where it turns back on itself, as can be seen in figure 8–C. When a seal is traced through theosophic extension on any correct planetary kamea and begins this kind of pattern, you can be pretty sure it is not going to produce a pleasing or symmetrical design.) Interestingly, this is the number of the Devil Key (see figure 8–D) in the Tarot (or the antithesis or shadow of the Sun). Case's design is somewhat more pleasing (see figure 8–E), but it is still not symmetrical. Both magical squares are given if the student wants to trace these seals.

For a long time I looked at alternate kameas of the Sun that were mathematically correct but could not find a symmetrical design. Then I discovered that a six-order square did not produce symmetry (a mathematician's definition).

Figure 8–D

3	2	1	36	35	34
31	32	33	4	5	6
15	13	23	19	20	21
22	24	14	18	17	16
12	11	10	27	26	25
28	29	30	7	8	9

Figure 8–E: Alternate

I presently use a design which traces a nice pattern (using the theosophic extension technique) as well as the traditional Sun seal. figure 8–F shows an alternate pattern I have used. figure 8–G is only a semi-magical square because the diagonals are off. It is nice, but is slightly asymmetrical.

While experimenting, I found a pleasing asymmetrical design for Venus as well, as can be seen in chapter nine. Some of the asymmetrical seals traced on certain kameas are quite unique and have a special kind of signature, although the vast majority produce erratic and chaotic designs that reveal their uselessness immediately. All of Agrippa's kameas produce beautiful geometrical patterns except for the sun.

Knorr Rosenroth changed the numbers of this kamea in the *Kabbala Denudata* completely—they do not even follow the principles by which a magical square is traditionally defined. (That is, the numerical qualifications which define the four basic numbers of the kamea—in this case, six, thirty-six, 111, and 666). We don't know the reasons why both Case and Knorr Rosenroth gave alternate kameas. Case chose one which can also be found in *Magic Squares and Cubes* by W. S. Andrews, printed in 1917. It is a correct kamea numerically, but the seal looks rather like a headless man. In the case of Knorr Rosenroth, it is usually taken as a blind, since it is such an obvious mistake, but one has to wonder why. It does not produce a geometrical seal; in fact the way it was created was to substitute numbers in the exact order as Agrippa's square; so the seal is the same. It does have some interesting numeric symbolism, since all lines add up to 216, which is the number of the lion in Hebrew, an obvious sun image (see figure 8–H).

Even though I have been told that mathematically a six-order square will never produce a harmonious or symmetrical design, I am not convinced. See the figure produced by the kamea in figure 8–F, which I stumbled upon quite by accident. It is a good kamea numerically and is quite symmetrical, although not as pleasing as some. I prefer to use figure 8–G for meditation (see colored plate) although the diagonals do not add up to 111.

There are thousands of kameas that are so difficult to find, they simply *haven't been*, but hypothetically they are supposed to exist. Whether they produce geometric patterns is unknown. We are in an age where our paradigms are shifting and other true kameas and seals may now be emerging, and may continue to unfold in the future. I am beginning to believe that as we are stepping up a level, the angelic energies will be speaking to us in more abstract language—that of pure geometric forms. This becomes more clear when one uses these kinds of seals for mandala-meditation purposes. Not only are they powerful catalysts for intuitive communication, but they give us a sense of how basic geometric forms connect everything. They are the building blocks of matter.

figure 8–I is an intriguing kamea. The numbers of the perimeter total 370, which is considered a sacred solar number to geomancers. The inside box of 4x4 squares also has

6	16	20	11	25	33
28	5	36	9	32	1
35	12	22	13	21	8
15	34	2	29	7	24
10	14	27	18	23	19
17	30	4	31	3	26

16	14	33	34	8	6
13	15	36	35	5	7
12	10	17	18	28	26
9	11	20	19	25	27
32	30	1	2	24	22
29	31	4	3	21	23

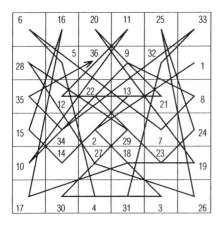

Figure 8–F: Alternate

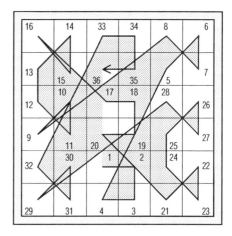

Figure 8–G: Semi-magical Square (compare with figure J)

11	63	5	67	69	1
13	21	53	55	15	59
37	27	31	29	45	47
35	39	43	41	33	25
49	57	19	17	51	23
71	9	65	7	3	61

Figure 8–H: Knorr Rosenroth's Kamea

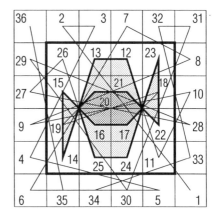

Figure 8–I

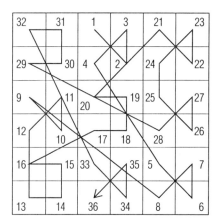

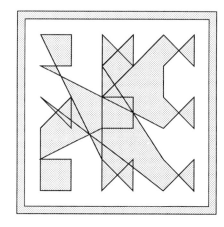

Figure 8–J: True Magic Square   *Figure 8–K: Seal Removed from Grid*

some interesting properties. Every line equals seventy-four in any direction and is therefore a magical square itself within the kamea of the sun.

Seventy-four is a factor of 666, since 74x9=666, the theosophic extension of the kamea. Although initially the theosophic line of this planetary seal seems to be chaotic, a definite figure emerges from the seal upon completion, one which looks rather like a UFO inside the center magical square.

I have puzzled over why the kamea of the Sun insists upon being so anomalous, but I am still experimenting, and I encourage the student to do likewise. The variants of the sun kamea given in figures 8–J and 8–K are some I have worked with, but there are others that can be discovered in the future. Many fascinating discoveries can be made by the student who wants to experiment with alternate kameas. You may certainly use the traditional seal of the sun for magical workings—it does connect all the cells, only not in order. The number of the line does not equal any of the magical numbers, as does a true planetary signature.

According to John Michell, Stonehenge was a solar structure, laid out according to the numbers of the square of the sun. Glastonbury Abbey likewise was built by Christian geomancers who constructed it according to the same solar design as Stonehenge. For example, the earliest outer bank of Stonehenge had the same measurements as the perimeter of the square of the sun, 370. One will note that many of the kameas found in this chapter and elsewhere also have a perimeter of 370.

Other measurements in the ground plan of both Stonehenge and Glastonbury correspond to other principal numbers in the kamea of the sun, such as the internal hexagon at Stonehenge, measuring 66600 square feet. The Abbey at Glastonbury is a rectangle shape which is 666 feet long and has an area of 66600 square cubits and can be shown to have been actually laid out on a magical grid of thirty-six squares. Michell concludes that "it is evident that the traditional reputation of this magic square for uniting and systematizing the principle cosmic ratios is by no means fanciful" (*View Over Atlantis,* p. 139).

THE FOOL.

Figure 8–L

6	32	3	34	35	1
7	11	27	28	8	30
19	14	16	15	23	24
18	20	22	21	17	13
25	29	10	9	26	12
36	5	33	4	2	31

*Figure 8–M: ShM IHShVH
Agrippa's Kamea*

Numerous sigil designs have been given in previous chapters, so we are only giving one in this chapter. However, one of the things the student will note in using the kameas of Agrippa (see figure 8–B) and Case (see figure 8–E) is that the direction of the current is reversed when the word Aleph (value 111) is traced on the square. (Aleph marks the beginning of the Hebrew Letters and is the Fool in the Tarot [see figure 8–L]. Reversed it is a mystical title of Kether.) The same holds true for the spirit of the planet, Sorath. As mentioned before, when using words or phrases for magical workings in this way, one should seriously consider the intentions in designing the talisman and analyze if the direction of the current is sympathetic to one's purpose.

We are giving the sigil of Shem Jeheshuah (see figure 8–M), which forms a perfect equilateral triangle on Agrippa's kamea. There are many wonderful magical names associated with the numerical vibrations of the Sun: six, thirty-six, 111 and 666. Number thirty-six is especially favorable for working with feminine energy.

Correspondences:Mystical Names
and Numbers of Tipareth/Sun

Asterisks (*) denote God-names

❖ 6: Sephira of Tiphareth

*6: ABBA: Father; title of Chokmah

6: BD, bid: separation; alone
ROOT: every object distinct and alone. . . whence issue ideas of isolation, solitude, individuality

6: GG, gawg: top of an altar
ROOT: that which stretches and expands without being disunited

6: HA, hah: to behold
ROOT: every evident, demonstrated, and determined existence

6: Vav: sixth letter of the Hebrew alphabet, attributed to the sixteenth path, the Hierophant

6: AGB, agab: by means of; through

❖ 36: Divisions of Kamea

*36: ALH, Elah, Goddess of Geburah; also oak terebinth

36: LAH, Leah, first wife of Jacob

36: AHL, Ohel: tabernacle ("And I heard a great voice out of heaven saying, Behold the tabernacle of God is with men, and he will dwell with them, and they shall be his people, and God himself shall be with them, and be their God," Rev 21:3). The tabernacle is also the meeting tent and dwelling place of the Shekinah (see Ex. 40: 34)

36: BKChV, Be-koakho: By Her Power

36: KBDI: my glory

36: Damcar: Latin for Blood of the Lamb

❖ 111: Magic Sum of Kamea

*111: AChD HVA ELHIM: The Lord is One

111: ALP, Letter name of Aleph, 11th path on the Tree: ox, family, clan

111: APhL, Ophel: darkness, obscurity

111: I TzVH: will command

111: KIPhA, kepha: Peter, the rock (Aramaic)

111: PLA, Mystical Name of Kether, the Wonder

111: NKYAL, Nachiel: Intelligence of the Sun

111: OVLA, avela: a sacrifice

111: OLVA, Olvah: Duke of Edom, a hidden reference to Daath ("And they call to me from Edom, Watchman, how much longer the night?" Is. 21:11)

111: MSVH: a veil, or face covering (Ex. 34:33)

❖ 666: Theosophic Number of the Magic Planetary Line

666: the square of the first 7 prime numbers

*666: ALHIKM, Elohikam: Your God

666: ASThHR, Isthar, the goddess Ishtar (Aramaic)

666: IHI MARTh, Yehi Meoroth: Let there be luminaries

666: SVRTh, Sorath: Spirit of the Sun

666: ShM IHShVH: The Name of Jesus

666: ShMSh IHVH, Shemash Tetragrammaton: Sun of Jehovah

666: Ho Seraphas: Greek for Serapis, Egyptian god

666: Euporia: Greek for material wealth, gold

666: The heart or soul in Greek

666: The number of the Beast in Rev. 13:18 (A certain wisdom is needed here; with a little ingenuity anyone can calculate the number of the beast)

666: ThSRV: you shall turn aside (G. G. Locks)

Chapter 9

THE KAMEA OF NETZACH/VENUS

The mystical numbers of the Venus kamea are seven, forty-nine, 175, 1225. We have examined the Star of Venus in chapter four. The vault of Brother C.R., the legendary founder of the Rosicrucian Order, was said to have seven sides and seven corners—the ground plan of a heptagon (figure 9–A). The Rosicrucian manuscript *Fama Fraternitatis* says the sides of this vault (which concealed his incorruptible body) measured five by eight feet. In his *True and Invisible Rosicrucian Order,* Case notes that these three numbers taken together (seven, five, eight) have the numeration of the word for copper, the metal of Venus (NChShTh).

The boundary of the ground plan for the vault was seven by four, and four is the number often attributed to Venus as Daleth, since it is the fourth letter in the alphabet. In Rosicrucian symbolism, it signifies not only the door which gives entrance to the vault of Brother C. R., but is an image

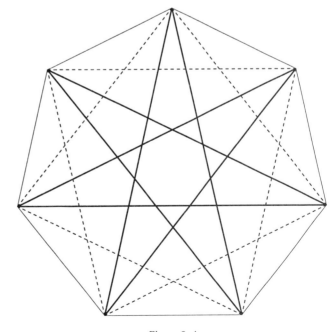

Figure 9–A

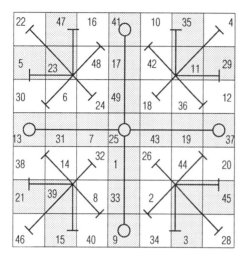

Figure 9–B

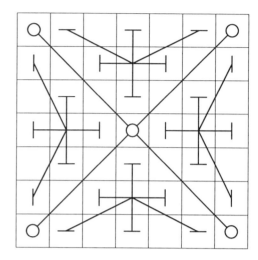

Figure 9–C

of the door to eternal life, Brother C. R. having conquered death. St. Paul once said that death was the last adversary, a motto Dr. Case was fond of quoting.

Seven multiplied by four is twenty-eight, the theosophic extension of seven, the planet Venus. The flower of Venus is the rose, and is the major symbol of both Rosicrucianism and the Golden Dawn. In the Islamic tradition, seven represented the planetary sphere of Venus as well as Universal Nature. Seven is a quarter division of the cycle of twenty-eight days and becomes the rhythm of a week. It is a particularly feminine planet in all cultures.

Magical squares were important to Islamic magicians, and Mulhammad himself once said, "Praise be God the Creator who has bestowed upon man the power to discover the significance of numbers." In the book *Islamic Patterns: An Analytical and Cosmological Approach*, (1983) Keith Critchlow notes that:

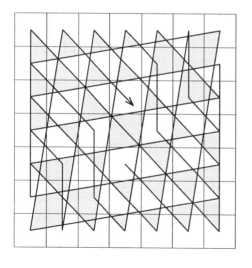

Figure 9–D

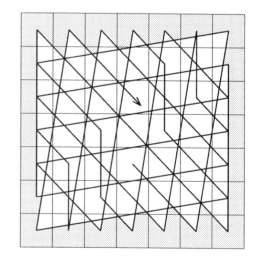

Figure 9–E

It is in the sense of finding the perfection of a "thing" that we might best understand both the pattern and effectiveness of a magic square. . . Far more significance than is normally realized outside Islam resides in the magical properties of the number patterns lying within the warp and weft of the great carpet tradition (p. 42).

Many of the elegant designs produced by these master weavers were determined by the symmetry of the numbers on the squares. For example, the Venus kamea in figure 9–B shows the arrangement of odd versus even numbers. It is interesting to note that the original design given by Agrippa fits quite well on this kamea, if the symmetry is repeated all around, and if the design is turned on its side. (Compare with figure 9–C.) From this symmetrical pattern alone many beautiful designs can emerge.

The seal that is created when we trace the line through theosophic extension of the numbers is represented in figures 9–D and 9–E, which can be done in more than one flashing color tablet using green and red. In this magic square (see figure 9–F), the cells that are geometrically opposite always total fifty, one of the secret numbers of Mother Binah and also the value of the letter Nun. The middle cell, which reduces to seven, is twenty-five, or the square of five, which is the number of Mars, the mythological complement of Venus. The student will note they also have complementary colors.

We are including alternate kameas of Venus in figures 9–G and 9–H, if the student is interested in tracing their seals. figure 9–G produces an interesting but asymmetrical seal that conceals a five-pointed star enclosed within the heart of the design, which, in Qabalah is the symbol for Mars, showing again their playful complementarity. I discovered quite by accident a design in *Waite's Book of Ceremonial Magic* (p. 204) called "The Seal of Astaroth," which looks remarkably like this seal (see figure 9–I). In fact, Astaroth, also called *Astarte* and *Ashtoreth* by the ancient Hebrews, was the same as the goddess Ishtar, the morning star, or Venus. She represented the spirit of sexuality and fertility.

22	47	16	41	10	35	4
5	23	48	17	42	11	29
30	6	24	49	18	36	12
13	31	7	25	43	19	37
38	14	32	1	26	44	20
21	39	8	33	2	27	45
46	15	40	9	34	3	28

Figure 9–F: Agrippa's Kamea

46	1	2	3	42	41	40
45	35	13	14	32	31	5
44	34	28	21	26	16	6
7	17	23	25	27	33	43
11	20	24	29	22	30	39
12	19	37	36	18	15	38
10	49	48	47	8	9	4

Figure 9–G: Alternate Kamea

30	39	48	1	10	19	28
38	47	7	9	18	27	29
46	6	8	17	26	35	37
5	14	16	25	34	36	45
13	15	24	33	42	44	4
21	23	32	41	43	3	12
22	31	40	49	2	11	20

Figure 9–H: Alternate Kamea

The keywords for seven are equilibrium and mastery. On the Tree of Life, Netzach means Victory. The pillars on the Tree, Jahkin-Boaz, which represent balanced equilibrium, have a value of 175, one of the magical numbers of the kamea, and the seventh card in most Tarot decks is the Chariot, or Victory (see figure 9–J). Furthermore, the sphinxs drawing the chariot, one black and the other white, symbolically point to the two pillars as well. The mythological figure of Venus is often represented as riding a chariot drawn by doves.

The ancient Pythagoreans attributed the number seven to Athene, a warrior goddess who also ruled craftsmanship. This number was thought to be important in the dynamic symmetry of art and in the actual structure of physical forms throughout the universe. One of the words that equals seven when the letters are added together is *bahdah* (BDA), which means to form, fashion, or produce something new.

Most students will know that Venus is most often associated with desire, often thought of in erotic terms. In Qabalah, the balance represented by the number seven is brought about by attaining mastery over the desire nature. This has nothing to do with

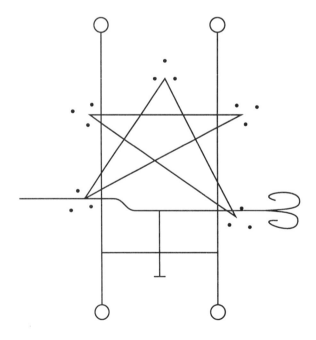

Figure 9–I

Figure 9–J

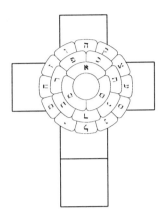

Figure 9–K

repression. It simply means that we control it, it doesn't control us. This lower desire nature, which is always hungry for things, is the object of many sublimation techniques, especially in eastern yogas. In the western tradition, the emphasis is on polarity. Dion Fortune once said that we cannot understand sex until we understand the principle of polarity, which is really an interchange of magnetism.

To really comprehend the Sphere of Nogah, or Venus, is to be empowered by the spiritual experience called *Vision of Beauty Triumphant*. It combines the ideas of power (Mars) with beauty (Venus), and hints at their proper relationship. The virtue which naturally results from this proper relationship is Unselfishness.

As we said earlier, the rose is a symbol of Venus, and when it is pictured as centered on a cross of six squares, formed by opening out a cube, it reveals the true emblem of the Rose-Cross (see figure 9–K). It is a symbol of the perfect coordination of desires (the rose) with the basic pattern of creation (the cross). The rose in the center represents equilibrium and balance of all the forces of nature. An ancient Rosicrucain motto was: "My victory is in the Rosy-Cross."

The figure of Brother C.R., because he represented true adeptship, or one who had conquered death (which is represented by the letter Nun in the Death key of the Tarot [see figure 9–L]), was often referred to as the *Lamb*. In the Book of Revelations, the Lamb with seven horns had the power to open the Book of seven seals. There have been many interpretations of this passage, but the most obvious one points to the seven seals that are connected to the seven planetary deities, over which the Lamb had authority.

The value in Latin for Lamb (*agnus*) is fifty-six, and this number is emphasized in Rosicrucian teaching as being the length, in feet, of the seven vertical lines bounding to the vault of Brother C.R. In the adaptation of the gematria to the German alphabet, often used in Rosicrucian texts, it stands for the word Alchimia, or Alchemy. In Latin gematria, the "gold of the philosophers" (*aurum philosophorum*) equals 231, which is the number of gates connected to the Sephiroth. This number also equals "dawn of the philosophers" (*aurora philosophorum*), a hidden reference to the true Golden Dawn. The 231 gates are all of the possible two-letter combinations of the Hebrew Letters, a hint that a practicing Qabalistic philosopher should perhaps explore these hidden gates.

Figure 9–L

Figure 9–M

We have mentioned that there is an intimate relationship between Venus, or Daleth, the Door (represented in Tarot by the Empress [see figure 9–M]), and Nun, which in the Qabalistic scheme is connected to Scorpio (ruled by Mars). Here is clothed one of the greatest secrets of occultism. It has to do with transmutation of the life force at the throat center, ruled by Venus. This transformation is allegorically portrayed in Tarot by Nun, Death, which, since it is connected to Scorpio, rules the sexual organs. In the image developed by Dr. Case, the skeleton figure in this Tarot key has a crook in his neck to represent the change in energy flow at the Venus chakra. Dr. Case tells us this mystery is also connected to the number 700, thought to be very sacred in the Zohar. This joining of the forces of Mars and Venus is the true nature of the alchemical Great Work.

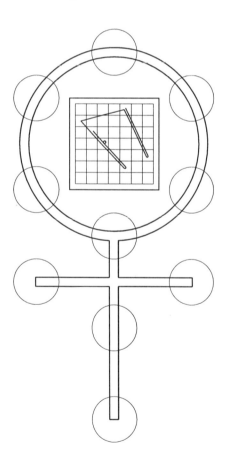

Figure 9–N: The Pillars

כב	מז	טז	מא	י	לה	ד
ה	כג	מח	יז	מב	יא	כט
ל	ו	כד	מט	יח	לו	יב
יג	לא	ז	כה	מג	יט	לז
לח	יד	לב	א	כו	מד	כ
כא	לט	ח	לג	ב	כז	מה
מו	טו	מ	ט	לד	ג	כח

Figure 9–O: Agrippa's Kamea in Hebrew

Correspondences:The Magical Names and Numbers of Netzach/Venus

Asterisks (*) denote God-names

❖ 7: Number of Sephira

7: the number of vertebrae in the human neck (Godwin)

*7: AHA, a name of God attributed to Nogah. Initials of Adonai ha Aretz

7: AV: desire
ROOT: the mysterious link which joins nothingness to being

7: GD, gad: Tribe of Israel; good fortune (Gen 30:11)
ROOT: the sign of abundance born of division

7: DBA, riches, power (Crowley)

7: DG, dag: fish
ROOT: that which is multiplies and is fruitful

7: BDA, bahda: to form, produce or invent

7: DAB, dahab: to faint, melt, pine away

7: BH: in her

❖ 49: Number of Cells in Kamea

*49: ChI-AL, The Living God

49: HYGAL, Hagiel: Intelligence of Venus

49: MVOB, Moab: from my father (Gen 19:37)

49: ChMA, chema: sun, heat, fever

49: MVG: solve, dissolve

49: ILDA: she bore

49: MT: The Rod of Aaron (Crowley) Ex. 7:10

49: DMH: her blood

❖ 175: Magic Sum of Kamea

175: QDMAL, Kadmael: Spirit of Venus

175: VIPGOV: and they met

175: LMINHM: after their kind

175: MKPLH: duplicity (Crowley)

175: INIQH: suction

175: LMOLH: on High ("And the cherubims shall stretch forth their wings on high, covering the mercy seat," Ex 25:20)

175: IKIN-BVOZ, Johkin-Boaz: The two pillars

175: HONN: The (Shekinah) Cloud (Gen 13:22)

❖ 1125: Theosophic Extension of Kamea

1225: OThIQA-DOThIQIM, Authiqa-de-Athiqin: The Ancient of Ancients

700: KPRTh: The Mercy-seat

700: Mystical number of sexuality in the Zohar

700: NUN final

*700: Chi Ro

Living from that Will, supported by its unfailing Wisdom and Understanding, mine is the Victorious Life (*Pattern on the Trestleboard*)

✧ Hexagram Laid on the Tree ✧

❖ Planetary Tattwas ❖

❖ Zodiacal Tattwas ❖

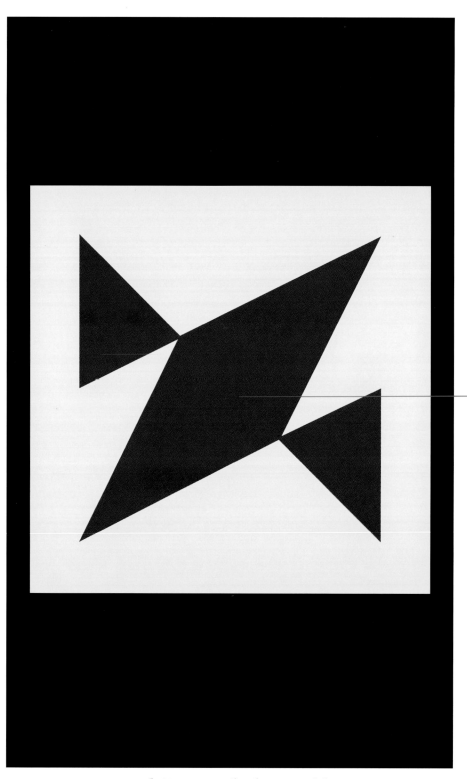

✢ Binah/Saturn Flashing Tablet ✢

❖ Chesed/Jupiter Flashing Tablet ❖

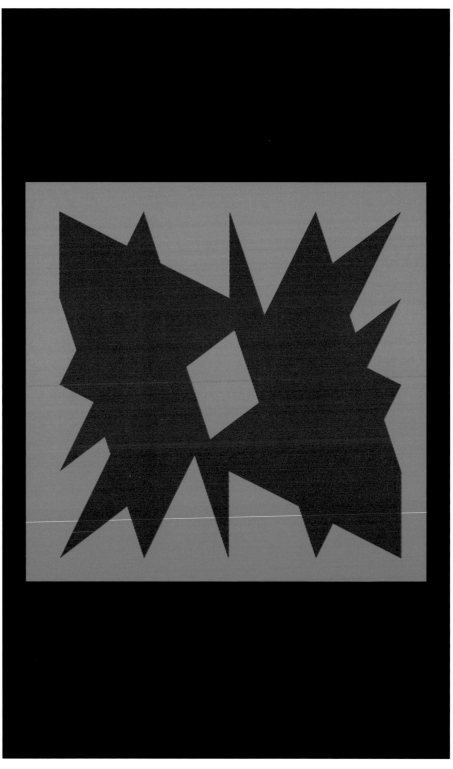

✤ Geburah/Mars Flashing Tablet ✤

❖ Tiphareth/Sun Flashing Tablet ❖

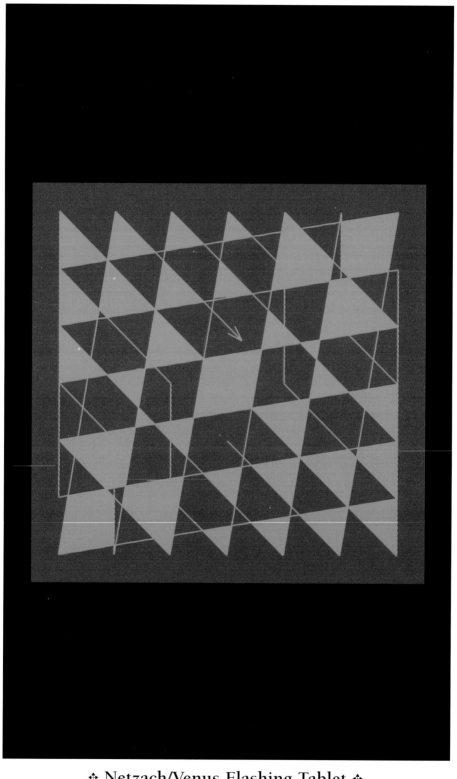

✣ Netzach/Venus Flashing Tablet ✣

✧ Hod/Mercury Flashing Tablet ✧

✣ Yesod/Moon Flashing Tablet ✣

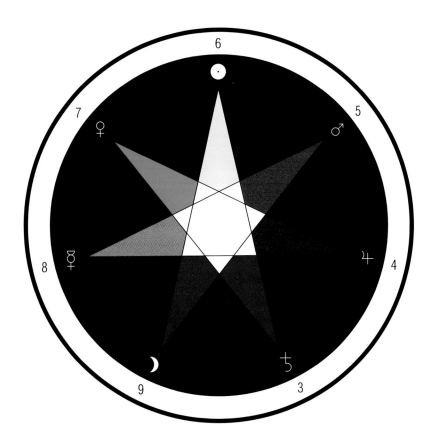

❖ Seven-Pointed Star with Planetary Sigils ❖

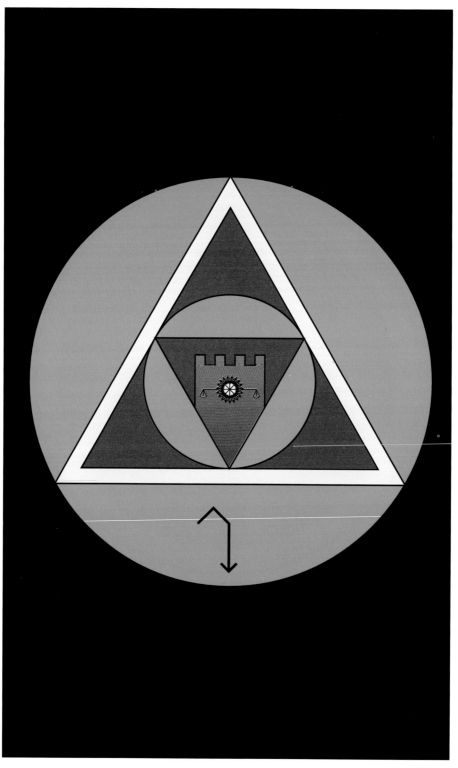

✧ Raphael (Combined) with Sigil ✧

✤ GShTh "The Bow" ✤

✤ The Rose Cross ✤

✧ Sample Talisman ✧

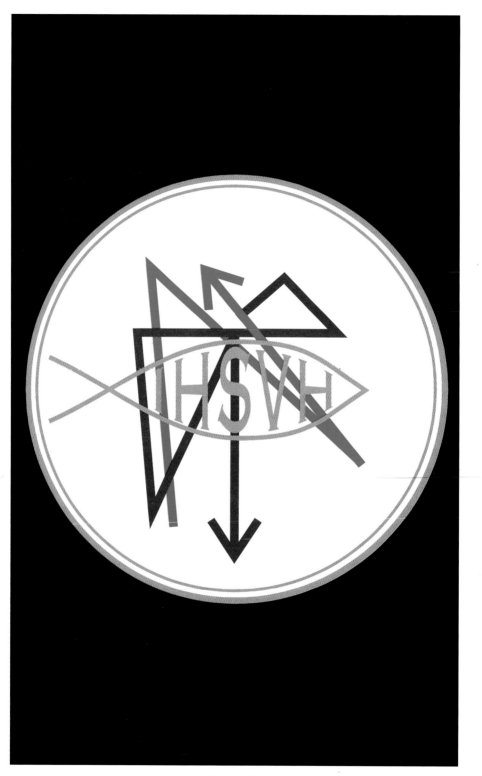

❖ Sample Talisman ❖

Chapter 10

✣

THE KAMEA OF HOD/MERCURY

The magical numbers of Mercury are eight, sixty-four, 260, and 2080. Mercury, the eighth Sephira, is known as the *ogdoad*. In it is concealed the mystery of the completion of the Great Work; and indeed, Mercury holds many alchemical secrets. Number eight was the number used to designate both Christ—often taken as the symbolic *Philosopher's Stone* to the Christian Qabalists—as well as Mercury. Dr. Case said:

> The real secret of this Stone is the real secret of the cross, which is the end and so the fulfillment of that whole dispensation that is represented symbolically by the twenty-two letters of the Hebrew alphabet (1985, p. 41).

The function of this magical principle represented by the Philosopher's Stone was synthesis. On the Tree, Mercury is the synthesized principle represented by the joining of the masculine and feminine polarities (Mars and Venus) on the twenty-seventh path, *Peh*.

One of the magical numbers of Mercury, 260, has several interesting words through gematria that point to this alchemical mystery: *Tzimtsen* (TzMTzM), which means to contract or draw together, and the plural of the Venus flower, roses (*veradim*). Likewise, the words *Adam-Eve*, when conjoined, equal sixty-four, another of Mercury's magical numbers (ADM-ChVH). This conjoined sigil looks like figure 10–A.

8	58	59	5	4	62	63	1
49	15	14	52	53	11	10	56
41	23	22	44	45	19	18	48
32	34	35	29	28	38	39	25
40	26	27	37	36	30	31	33
17	47	46	20	21	43	42	24
9	55	54	12	13	51	50	16
64	2	3	61	60	6	7	57

Figure 10–A: Adam–Eve

Figure 10–B

One of the things immediately apparent about this sigil is that it forms an X, which is a form of the Tau Cross. It actually resembles a figure eight lying on its side. One of the intriguing points of interest between the symbols of the Tau Cross (Christ) and the figure eight (Mercury) is that, when laid sideways—when the cross is a multiplication symbol (x)—it synthesizes with the lemniscate, or figure eight symbol, if the lines continue in an arc until they are connected (see figure 10–B). This is the Cross in the Sphere and the Mercurial wheel of nature, which Jacob Boehme spoke about. The number of Jesus, written in Greek, is 888; and Tau, the final Hebrew letter, doubled equals 800, which is Omega in Greek.

The curves in the number eight are reciprocal and alternating, expressing better than any other number the repetition of equal and complementary parts. Its key words are rhythm, alteration, and vibration, and its movement is marked by regular recurrence (see figure 10–C). We can see this idea of repetition of vibration in music as well, where the eighth note of the octave in the key-scale is produced by doubling the vibratory rate of the first tone of the scale.

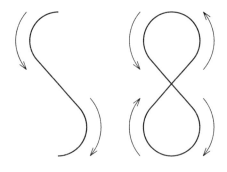

Figure 10–C

As a number, eight is composed of balanced parts: two fours, four twos, and eight ones. When drawn, it is the only number that may be repeated over again without lifting a pen from the paper. The lemniscate is also the symbol for infinity.

In the ogdoad, there is a special relationship between the Triad (three) and the Pentad (five), because to the alchemists the ogdoad represented the joining of the principles of Sulphur, Mercury, and Salt to the five Elements (including ether or Quintessence). Likewise, the third and fifth Sephiroth together equal Hod, which rests beneath them. The Great Pyramid, which both Eliphas Levi and John Michell believed is connected to Mercury, also has this three to five relationship because each face has three sides and the Pyramid itself has five corners, if the apex is included. This apex or cap-stone has been shrouded in mystery and written about by many intrigued by its meaning. This pinnacle stone is, according to Case, another symbol for Christ, the stone rejected by the builders.

This capstone is sometimes called the *Triangle of Fire,* "which is a stone emblem of the Eternal Flame" (Case, 1985, p. 83). John Michell tells us that the Pyramid has often been the scene of mysterious apparitions in the form of a light "which local Bedouins see at certain seasons hovering over its peak" (Michell, 1983, p. 160). This was also witnessed by a Mr. William Groff and other members of the Egyptian Institute, who saw a flame rising from the top, but could discover no rational explanation. The Pyramid has often been associated in hermetic folklore with revelation of the inner mysteries, and revelation of secrets is the domain of Mercury or Hermes. It is believed that initiation rites were once held within the dark pyramid chambers:

> Inspiration is Mercury, the messenger of the gods. Centres of the Mercurial influence, like the Great Pyramid, were places of initiation into the mysteries, for within their labyrinths could be found the spirit whom God had sent to speak directly with men. In the presence of Hermes, nothing was concealed except the person of God. . . The Pyramid was built as a meeting place for Mercury and for those who sought his instruction in the hidden secrets of creation (John Michell, *The View Over Atlantis*, 1969, p. 127).

We noted earlier that there is a strong hypothesis that the pyramid was constructed according to the magical square of Mercury, and one of the most astonishing features of magical squares is that so many of their numbers are found in the dimensions of sacred sites. John Michell goes on to say that the scientists of ages past understood these magical numbers so perfectly that they tapped into a source of power "which made all technological contrivances unnecessary" (ibid, p. 110). The magical number that is the theosophical extension of the Mercury kamea is 2080. Michell notes that in Greek this relates back to the fire connected to the apex, because by gematria, *the artificer's fire* equals 2080. In fact, the first three letters of *pyramid* (pyr) mean *fire*. Plato wrote:

> (The) solid which has taken the form of a pyramid shall be the element and seed of fire (ibid, p. 106).

Interestingly, the two words in Greek, *fire* and *light*, when added together, also equal 2080. Recall that the affirmation attributed to Hod on the *Pattern on the Trestleboard* is: "I look forward with confidence to the perfect realization of the Eternal Splendor of the Limitless Light."

It has been demonstrated that the dimensions of the pyramid show that the builders who constructed it had an accurate knowledge of the earth and its solar system, and those interested in this fascinating study should refer to the careful explanations of these measurements in John Michell's works.

Repeatedly we see that there are many parallels revealed by the magical numbers of Mercury that relate to Christ, both as the alchemical stone and also in reference to this pyramid shape. For example, see the figure produced by the sigil of the name Jesus on page 103. We see a similar phenomenon on the Mercury kamea in the sigil of Zauir Anpin, or the *Lesser Countenance*, a title attributed to Tiphareth. Again, the figure looks remarkably like a pyramid, or even a cap-stone, since the arrow pointing down indicates an energy flow beneath it (see figure 10–D).

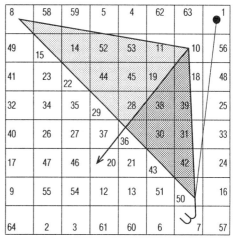

Figure 10–D: ZOIR ANPIN

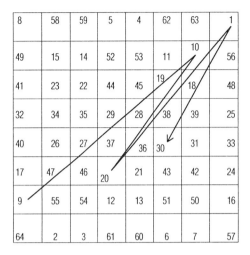

8	58	59	5	4	62	63	1
49	15	14	52	53	11	10	56
41	23	22	44	45	19	18	48
32	34	35	29	28	38	39	25
40	26	27	37	36	30	31	33
17	47	46	20	21	43	42	24
9	55	54	12	13	51	50	16
64	2	3	61	60	6	7	57

Figure 10–E

Since the holy name of Zauir Anpin is composed of two words, the triangle itself seems divided into two (implying more) equal sections. To make a flashing color meditation tablet of this or any designs drawn from the Mercury kamea, use the colors orange and blue. The initials for Zauir Anpin are ZA, which equals eight.

Dr. Case has noted that the spirit of Mercury, Taphthartharath, (whom he called the destructive spirit) also conceals the name of *Tiphareth*, (TPhARTh) minus the Aleph. Aleph is a very important letter, representing the initial Life-Power of creation. The name *A-dam*, we noted earlier, refers to the joining of this Life-force with the blood of humanity, since *dam* in Hebrew means blood. Furthermore, Aleph points to the inherent unity of God. We see this mystery hidden in the God-names of the Genesis text, because *Aleph*, which means one, is the fifteenth letter of Genesis, and the Divine Name, *Jah*, has a value of fifteen. It is also the twenty-sixth letter of Genesis, and *Yod-Heh-Vav-Heh* has a value of twenty-six; it is the thirty-first letter, which is the value of the God-name *Al*; and it is the eighty-sixth letter, which is the value of the name *Elohim*.

The sigil of Tiriel, the Intelligence of Mercury, is given in figure 10–E. This angelic name means encompassed about by God and reminds us of Paul's quote, "In him we move and breath and have our being." It is a beautiful name and Tiriel can be a wonderful friend. I have purposefully given the sigil of this Intelligence because rarely have I seen it correctly drawn.

The number 2080 is the extension of sixty-four, which is in turn the self-multiplication of number eight. The number sixty-four has many alchemical references by gematria, especially in Latin. It is the number of *Ve-Ha-Eben* (and this stone). *Din* (Justice), the highest attribution of the fifth Sephira, has a value of sixty-four, as well as its twin intelligence in Mercury, whose name is Doni. Sixty-four also equals *may zahab* (water of gold), as well as *mezahab* (mother of gold). In Latin, it equals *Sal Aqua* (salt-water or the *matrix corpus*); *solve*, which refers to the process known as dissolution; *sperma*, or the seed of the metal; and *virgo*, or the virgin matter.

The number 260 represents the multiplication of the power of the Sacred Tetragramatton (twenty-six) by the Sephiroth (ten). The Intelligence of Mercury, which also has a value of 260, designates the consciousness of the Divine Order which, when correctly applied, results in the human being's use of the objective mind as an instrument to link to superconscious powers.

Some of the powers generated by the different Sephiroth on the Tree refer to psychic powers, and we see hints of this in the gematria connected to Mercury, which is the figure

8	58	59	5	4	62	63	1
49	15	14	52	53	11	10	56
41	23	22	44	45	19	18	48
32	34	35	29	28	38	39	25
40	26	27	37	36	30	31	33
17	47	46	20	21	43	42	24
9	55	54	12	13	51	50	16
64	2	3	61	60	6	7	57

Figure 10–F

Figure 10–G

relating to divinations as well as to deceit, *i.e.*, the trickster element. The serious occult student should bear this relationship in mind.

The word for prophecy or prediction in Hebrew has a value of sixty-four and looks like figure 10–F, which resembles the Letter Beth, attributed to the Magician in the Tarot (see figure 10–G). The Magician is a figure that really synthesizes all of the powers of human self-consciousness by virtue of his concentration. The greatest powers of intuition come when we have perfected the art of inductive reasoning, or the ability to draw logical inferences from experience.

The number eight is the number representing rhythm and renewal, and because of its shape, is the lemniscate, or infinity sign as well. This symbol is placed about the head of both the Magician and the Virgin (see figure 10–H) in Key eight of most Tarot decks. The number has a hidden reference to the serpent-power that this virgin, who is also a magician, has control of. This picture hints at her ability to act as a time-binder, uniting past to present to future. The serpent is the most frequent symbolic mythological image attributed to Mercury. In astrology, the eighth sign is Scorpio, which rules the area of the body connected to the reproductive organs, often referred to as the seat of the serpent energy.

Figure 10–H

The number eight has many Biblical references, but we will only touch on a few. The Old Testament mentions that eight persons were saved in the ark, to people the world anew. In Christian hermeticism, this is taken as an allegory foreshadowing the resurrection, and the Bible records eight other resurrections besides that of Jesus. The references are: 1 Kings 17:22, 2 Kings 4:32, 2 Kings 13: 2, Luke 7:14; Mark 5:35, John 11, Acts 9:40 and Acts 20.

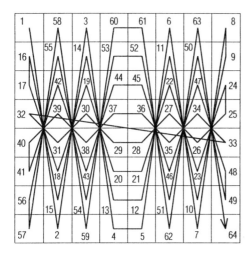

Figure 10–I

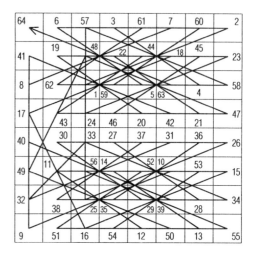

Figure 10–J

The Greek word for resurrection adds up to 971, which reduces to eight. In the spirit of this renewal, it is perhaps no coincidence that the Fama says that the Rosicrucian Order was founded by eight persons.

We mentioned earlier that a true magic square equals the same sum if any row is added up—including diagonally. Sometimes books on magic squares and seals state that Mercury does not do this, but a true Mercury kamea does. The one in Levi's *Transcendental Magic* does not (nor does anyone who has published his kamea—I have seen several), but it is because there is a mistake in his magical square. The original by Agrippa in Hebrew equals the same sum, as does the original in *Kabbala Denudata*. If it didn't add up correctly, it would not make the harmonious figure of the Mercury seal. I have tried it; I have traced every variation in all the magical sources I could find and none work to produce a symmetrical design except the original from Agrippa. I have discovered a few different ones in mathematical books on magical squares, and they are given in figures 10–I, 10–J, and 10–K. (The last one you can draw yourself). The kamea in figure 10–J is intriguing. It is called a *perfect* or *diabolic square*, because the sum of the numbers in each row equals 260, and if the whole kamea is quartered, each row of a four by four series of cells (or subsquare), including diagonals, equals 130, or one-half.

1	7	59	60	61	62	2	8
16	10	54	53	52	51	15	9
48	47	19	21	20	22	42	41
33	34	30	28	29	27	39	40
25	26	38	36	37	35	31	32
24	23	43	45	44	46	18	17
56	50	14	13	12	11	55	49
57	63	3	4	5	6	58	64

Figure 10–K

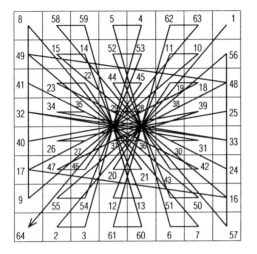

*Figure 10–L: Agrippa's Kamea
with Theosophic Extension*

*Figure 10–M: Agrippa's Kamea
(Removed from Grid)*

The planetary seal drawn from Agrippa's kamea is given in figure 10–L. Done correctly, it can make a stunning flashing color tablet for meditation (see figure 10–M). Use it with caution, for it has a tendency to jump off of the page.

ח	נח	נט	ה	ד	סב	סג	א
מט	יה	יד	נב	נג	יא	י	נו
מא	כג	כב	מד	מה	יט	יח	מח
לב	לד	לה	כט	כח	לח	לט	בה
מ	כו	כז	לז	לו	ל	לא	לג
יז	מז	מו	כ	כא	מג	מב	כד
ט	נה	נד	יב	יג	נא	נ	יו
סד	ב	ג	סא	ס	ו	ז	נז

Figure 10–N: Agrippa's Kamea (Hebrew)

Correspondences: Magical Names
and Numbers of Hod/Mercury
Asterisks (*) denote God-names

❖ 8: Sephira of Hod

8: The Ogdoad

*8: ZA Zauir Anpin (Notariqon)

8: ABH, abah: to will, to consent

8: AGD, ahgad: to bind, collect, tie together

8: AHB, ahab: to love; a lover, paramour, beloved

8: AZ, auz: there; in that place
ROOT: a fixed point in space or duration

8: BAH, bah: entrance, threshold

8: DBB, dabab: to go softly, to creep along; to slander

8: DD, dahd: breast of love; beloved (Deut 33:12)
ROOT: that which is divided in order to be propagated; effusion, affinity, sympathy

8: HBA, heba: bring

❖ 64: Divisions of Kamea

64: ADM-ChVH: Adam-Eve

64: DIN, Din: Justice and DNI, Doni, Twin Intelligence with Din

64: GBVAH, gebuah: prophecy

*64: HUA-BN (Hu-Kether and Ben, the Son) He is the Son (Mark 1:11)

64: HGVIM, he-goyim: the nations (the Hosts)

64: VHABN, ve-ha-eben: and this stone (Gen. 28:22)

64: YDIM, yadim: hands

64: IDID IHVH, Yediyd IHVH: Beloved of God (Deut. 33:12; John 13: 23)

64: MIZHB, mezahab: mother of gold

64: MI-ZHB, may zahab: golden waters

64: MIDI, midi: from my hand

64: NVGH, Nogah: Venus

64: SBB, sahbab: to revolve, turn, surround

64: *Sal Aqua,* (Latin): salt water, the matrix corpus

64: *Solve,* (Latin): dissolve

64: *Sperma* (Latin): seed

64: *Virgo* (Latin): Virgin

64: *Dictum* (Latin) : A saying, prediction, command

64: *Alethia* (Greek): Truth

❖ 260: Magic Sum of Kamea

260: TIRIAL: Intelligence of Mercury

260: GRZIM: Gerizim (Deut. 11:29; Josh. 8:33)

260: SR, sar: ill-humored (Godwin)
   ROOT: all ideas of disorder, contortion; also return, education, new direction

260: VRDIM, veradim: roses

260: KRM, kerem: vineyard

260: TzMTzM, tzimtsen: to contract or draw together

260: H-MRH, the Moriah: *i.e.*, Jerusalem (G. G. Locks). The land of Moriah was said to be the site of the sacrifice of Isaac, upon which the Temple of Solomon was later built (2 Chron. 3:1)

260: MONNIM, monnim: soothsayers

260: RKIL, rekil: talebearer

*260: Benedictus Dominus Noster: Our Blessed Lord

❖ 2080: Theosophic Extension of the Planetary Line

2080: ThPThRThRTh, Taphthartharath, Spirit of Mercury

2080: *Artificer's fire* (Greek) (John Michell)

2080: *Light* and *Fire* in Greek (Michell)

2080: *First-born* in Greek (Rev. 1:5)

Chapter 11

THE KAMEA OF
YESOD/MOON

The magical numbers of the Moon are nine, eighty-one, 369, and 3321. The moon is the ship and guide of the heavens, the numinous, ever-changing night light in the sky. It thus became the natural symbol in all early religious traditions for the transforming goddess, as did the symbols of the lotus and the lily—her moon-flowers. In the Jungian and alchemical traditions, she is the *anima mundi*, the soul of the world. In Latin, *anima mundi* has a value of eighty-one, one of the magical numbers of the moon.

She represents the unconscious wellspring, renewing all people, regardless of race, gender or religious affiliation with her intoxicating inspirations. As renewing and transforming anima, she immerses us in the bath of regeneration. She is the fecundating power of spirit. The moon is also the reservoir of memory. Occult philosophy tells us that subconscious memory is already perfect. We cannot improve it; we can only improve our ability to tap into its power. In Tarot, this occult power is represented by the High Priestess (see figure 11–A), who holds the etheric record of all experience on her lap, often called *etheric water* or *occult water*.

This is because in Yesod are manifested the fluidic energies of the astral light, often perceived as wave-like. Occultists know that this astral light is often associated in folklore with magic and sorcery. In gematria, we note the association in the word *ob* (AVB), which has a double meaning. It can be translated as necromancer or sorcerer,

Figure 11–A

as well as skin bag—*i.e.*, implying pregnancy. What this points to is that all the illusory forms of nature which become concretized in our physical world (Malkuth) have their origin in the form-building powers of Yesod. It is the raw material from which all imagery is formed and serves as the source of all astral visions, whether of ghosts or the gods. All are filtered through Yesod.

Levi explains how visions operate:

> All forms correspond to ideas and there is no idea which has not its proper and peculiar form. The primordial light which is the vehicle of all ideas is the mother of all forms, and transmits them from emanation to emanation. . . Hence the Astral Light, or terrestrial fluid, which we call the Great Magnetic Agent is saturated with all kinds of images or reflections. Now our soul can evoke these and subject them to Diaphane (*Transcendental Magic*, p. 66).

Figure 11–B

Diaphanous literally means translucid and by it Levi refers to the *plastic mediator,* which is the magnet that attracts particular visions from the Astral Light that correspond to the impetus of the will.

The Great Magical Agent in Qabalah is attributed to Saturn/Capricorn and corresponds in Tarot to the Devil key (see figure 11–B). Here we see a hint of the relationship between Saturn and Yesod. Binah/Saturn is the Great Sea, the Universal Unconscious, and Yesod controls the waters of the subconscious. The moon—the little mother—mimics Binah/Saturn, and we can see this represented in one of the alternative kameas of Yesod (see figure 11–C). This magical square contains nine small Saturn seals. I was truly astonished when I discovered it, since there are many other alternative nine-order kameas that produce no symmetry, and many that are fairly repetitive, like Agrippas (see figure 11–D).

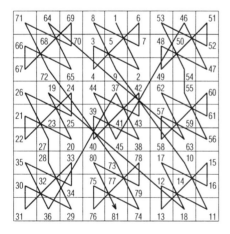

Figure 11–C: Alternate Kamea

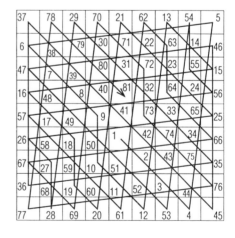

Figure 11–D: Agrippa's Kamea

This magical seal demonstrates the relationship between Binah and Yesod quite vividly. Binah is the will to form and Yesod is the storehouse of her images in visions and dreams. Like water, it is our first mirror. It is also the Foundation (which is the meaning of Yesod) for the forms in our physical world, which science now tells us are not really solid at all. All matter is composed of various forms of vibration.

Nine is one of the magical numbers of Saturn, since it is the total number of squares in the kamea, and nine is also the number of cells in any row of the Yesod kamea. Likewise, 3x3=9 and 9x9=81 (the number of cells in the Moon kamea). It is the squaring of the sphere of Saturn that brings forth the Moon sphere, from which our world comes into manifestation. Nine is the number of completion, manifestation and fulfillment; all numbers after nine repeat themselves. The Pythagoreans called the number nine the *Ripener and Perfecter.*

In Qabalah, we can see this demonstrated in the mystery of Kether's relationship to the Ain Soph Aur, the Limitless Light. Kether is produced by the nine Letters of the AIN SVP AVR, just as Malkuth is produced by the nine Sephiroth which culminate in Yesod. The word *gaah*, as we saw in chapter five, means to swell, rise, or increase. Nine is the number of months of gestation for humans, and relates to births of all kinds, both spiritual and physical. It is the number of self-multiplication and any number multiplied by nine will always have a product with digits that reduce to nine.

The goal or completion of the Great Work in Qabalah is really the manifestation of the Divine Name (IHVH),which is the complete expression and representation of all that the word signifies: "I am what was, what is, and what will be." Therefore the perfection of the creative process initiated in Binah is the manifestation of God's idea to God Herself. The "everlasting Kingdom" spoken of so often in the Bible implies the attainment of an objective which has been in the Universal Mind from the beginning or foundation of the world.

Another numerical example of this relationship is demonstrated in the equation 9x9=81. By gematria, this points to the fullness of this process at the level of individuation, because eighty-one is the numeration of the word *anoki*, which means *I*. It is only after the separation from the Mother, however, that this "I" can be born, and many myths reflect this archetypal individuation process in the hero stories of the slaying of the dragon or serpent, often said by Jungians to represent the mother.

The word *gev*, which means middle or interior, also has a value of nine. It really means "the center of things which preserves. . . and organizes" (d'Olivet, p. 312). This is perhaps one of the most important functions of Moon consciousness, according to Case. The Moon key in the Tarot (see figure 11–E) is called the Corporeal Intelligence (Qoph) because it organizes the millions of cells of the

Figure 11–E

37	78	29	70	21	62	13	54	5
6	38	79	30	71	22	63	14	46
47	7	39	80	31	72	23	55	15
16	48	8	40	81	32	64	24	56
57	17	49	9	41	73	33	65	25
26	58	18	50	1	42	74	34	66
67	27	59	10	51	2	43	75	35
36	68	19	60	11	52	3	44	76
77	28	69	20	61	12	53	4	45

Figure 11–F

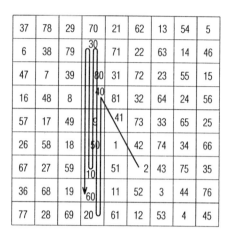

37	78	29	70	21	62	13	54	5
6	38	79	30	71	22	63	14	46
47	7	39	80	31	72	23	55	15
16	48	8	40	81	32	64	24	56
57	17	49	9	41	73	33	65	25
26	58	18	50	1	42	74	34	66
67	27	59	10	51	2	43	75	35
36	68	19	60	11	52	3	44	76
77	28	69	20	61	12	53	4	45

Figure 11–G

37	78	29	70	21	62	13	54	5
6	38	79	30	71	22	63	14	46
47	7	39	80	31	72	23	55	15
16	48	8	40	81	32	64	24	56
57	17	49	9	41	73	33	65	25
26	58	18	50	1	42	74	34	66
67	27	59	10	51	2	43	75	35
36	68	19	60	11	52	3	44	76
77	28	69	20	61	12	53	4	45

Figure 11–H

37	78	29	70	21	62	13	54	5
6	38	79	30	71	22	63	14	46
47	7	39	80	31	72	23	55	15
16	48	8	40	81	32	64	24	56
57	17	49	9	41	73	33	65	25
26	58	18	50	1	42	74	34	66
67	27	59	10	51	2	43	75	35
36	68	19	60	11	52	3	44	76
77	28	69	20	61	12	53	4	45

Figure 11–I

physical organism. It is related particularly to the medulla oblongata, which governs all the autonomic functions of the body and links the higher brain centers to the spinal cord and the rest of the body. Yesod is the vital seat or foundation of this autonomic consciousness which governs the functions by which we live, such as respiration and the heart.

The number 369 is the number of the addition of any row in the kamea and also the number of the spirit, Chasmodai. It is a name whose sigil is often misdrawn, as we saw in Chapter Four. The sigil of the Intelligence is given in figures 10–F, 10–G, 10–H, 10–I, and 10–J (drawn from Agrippa's kamea.) It is most easily done in five parts, but it can be combined (see figures 10–K and 10–L). Case noted that nearly all spellings of this phrase (which means "Queen among the Tarshishim forever, in the Spirit of the Dawning Ones") are corrupt. They are either misspelled, they don't add up numerically, or the words don't make any sense, if they do add up.

37	78	29	70	21	62	13	54	5
6	38	79	30	71	22	63	14	46
47	7	39	80	31	72	23	55	15
16	48	8	40	81	32	64	24	56
57	17	49	9	41	73	33	65	25
26	58	18	50	1	42	74	34	66
67	27	59	10	51	2	43	75	35
36	68	19	60	11	52	3	44	76
77	28	69	20	61	12	53	4	45

Figure 11–J

37	78	29	70	21	62	13	54	5
6	38	79	30	71	22	63	14	46
47	7	39	80	31	72	23	55	15
16	48	8	40	81	32	64	24	56
57	17	49	9	41	73	33	65	25
26	58	18	50	1	42	74	34	66
67	27	59	10	51	2	43	75	35
36	68	19	60	11	52	3	44	76
77	28	69	20	61	12	53	4	45

Figure 11–K

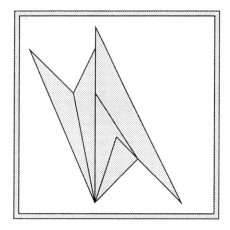

Figure 11–L: Combined Sigil of Intelligence

THE HERMIT.

Figure 11–M

The number 369 is also the value of *Olahm ha-Briah,* or the World of Creation. This world includes the Sephiroth Chesod and Geburah (whose colors combine to make purple, or Yesod's color on the Tree) as well as Tiphareth. This triangle represents the emanation of created forces, which in Qabalah are called Elohim. Their association with the Moon hints at the creative powers of reflection, and in this sense can be compared to the moon's reflection of the sun. There are many ancient Jewish Kabbalistic rituals which celebrate the joining of Sun and Moon, or Tiphareth and Yesod. In Hebrew The word for moon is *levanah,* which means beautiful heart (LB NH).

In Greek, the word *mathesis,* which means disciple, also has a numeration of 369. It has a particular reference here to adeptship, or the development of full discipleship in the

37	78	29	70	21	62	13	54	5
6	38	79	30	71	22	63	14	46
47	7	39	80	31	72	23	55	15
16	48	8	40	81	32	64	24	56
57	17	49	9	41	73	33	65	25
26	58	18	50	1	42	74	34	66
67	27	59	10	51	2	43	75	35
36	68	19	60	11	52	3	44	76
77	28	69	20	61	12	53	4	45

Figure 11–N   *Figure 11–O*

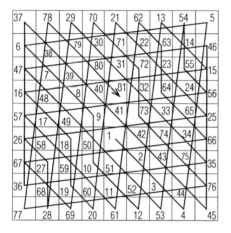

37	78	29	70	21	62	13	54	5
6	38	79	30	71	22	63	14	46
47	7	39	80	31	72	23	55	15
16	48	8	40	81	32	64	24	56
57	17	49	9	41	73	33	65	25
26	58	18	50	1	42	74	34	66
67	27	59	10	51	2	43	75	35
36	68	19	60	11	52	3	44	76
77	28	69	20	61	12	53	4	45

Figure 11–Q: "I will meet Gabriel"

Figure 11–P: Agrippa's Kamea
with Theosophic Extension

knowledge of the sacred sciences. Adeptship is represented by the ninth Tarot key, the Hermit (see figure 11–M), who acts as the hand of God.

To Yesod, as we will see in the next chapter, are attributed the Letters *Yod* and *Shin*, according to Knorr Rosenroth. Yod is contained in the word *Yesod* as well: YVD (YSVD). When combined with the *Shin*, it forms a root which means "of being," or "appearing like," and by its contraction come all ideas of "reality or substantiality," according to d'Olivet. (1921, p. 368)

The number 3321 is equal to the phrase "on earth as it is in heaven" in Greek, which, like the great Hermetic maxim, "as above, so below," points to the most perfect expression of the principle of reflection, brought to full manifestation in the sphere of the Moon. The number forty-one is the center of the kamea as given by Agrippa, and 41x81 (the number of cells) also equals 3321. His kameas and seal are given in figures 10–N, 10–O, and 10–P.

I am going to include one final example of sigil making using the techniques as outlined in the preceding chapters. Suppose you want to increase the power of memory, particularly in relationship to your dream life. If you want to remember your dreams, you would do the traditional things dream books recommend: keep pen and paper by the bed, and make suggestions to your dream-self before sleep. But you could also make a talisman to the moon and meditate on it for several minutes before your dream quest. Focusing on the talisman with unbroken eye contact for five minutes helps to register the image in your mind's eye as you drift off to sleep.

Depending on the nature of your dream quest, you could create a number of different designs, but in this case some appropriate sigils are *GAH* (increase), since you want to increase your capacity for dream recall; *AVB* (magic), through your visions and dreams; *VLILH* (in the night). Or you may choose to use another word or phrase, such as *AShIBNV* (I will bring back, value 369), *ob* (magic, value nine), *gev* (from the interior, value nine). The sigils from these affirmations may not be very elegant looking, but they nonetheless express one's exact purpose; moreover, they do so with the same numerical equivalents as the magical numbers of the Moon kamea from which they are drawn.

One may also use the phrase *AVOD* (I will meet, value eighty-one) and add the name Chasmodai, the spirit of the Moon, or Gabriel, the ruling archangel. An example of a conjoined sigil which says "I will meet Gabriel" is given in figure 11–Q.

For those who know little or nothing about gematria, these may seem like trivial or meaningless exercises, but the most effective magic is the most precise, and numbers have been at the core of the Qabalistic tradition since ancient times. You can use any kind of phrase to express your purpose and creativity, regardless of the numerical equivalents; we are only offering these examples as a particular way of tuning oneself to the planetary energies that have never been publicly revealed. Regardless of whether using correspondences through gematria is something you choose to do, I encourage the student to experiment with using words and phrases in your designs that are devised from sigils. Even though it may look like a child's scribbles (don't many ancient talismans look like scribbles to us today?), it makes a strong impression on your subconscious and that is what matters.

The moon also governs the cycles of women's bodies and has a particular relationship to motherhood, pregnancy, and birthing, of which there are also numerical references, as can be seen in the chart on the moon's magical numbers.

Correspondences: Magical Names and Numbers of Yesod/Moon

Asterisks (*) denote God-names

❖ 9: Sephirah of Yesod

9: The number of cells in Saturn kamea

9: AVB, ob: magic, ghost conjuror, sorcerer; skin-bag

9: ACh, ach: brother, kinsman, friend
ROOT: all ideas of equilibrium, equality, fraternity; the common hearth

9: BBH, babah: apple of the eye; pupil

9: BVA, bevah: to enter, alight, to come into; till one comes

9: BGD, beged: covering, garment, robe; concealment

9: GAH, gaah: to swell, rise or increase; elevated, exalted

9: HD, hed: shout of joy (Godwin)
ROOT: attached to all ideas of spiritual emanation; the effect of sound, voice, echo; the diffusion of a thing absolute in nature

9: GV, gev: middle, interior
ROOT: the center of things and that which preserves them; that which organizes and gives life to the organs

❖ 81: number of cells in kamea

81: ALIM, alim: rams

81: AVOD: I will meet (G.G. Locks)

81: BTNK, ve-tanek: your womb (Deut. 7:13)

81: ANKI, anoki: the personal pronoun, *I*

81: GChNK: your belly (Locks)

81: V-LILH, ve-layil: and night

81: L-AKL, le-achel: to be devoured, or consumed

81: L-HEDIL: to divide (Locks) "Let there be lights in the firmament of the heaven to divide the day from the night" (Gen. 1:14)

81: TBO, teba: nature

81: OBDH, abodah: divine service, work

81: KSA, kebe: time of the full moon

81: KSA, kibbe: Throne

81: H-MLAH, ha-melah: the fullness

81: *oculus* (Latin): eye

81: *Anima mundi* (Latin): soul of the world

❖ 369: sum of rows in kamea

369: ChShMVDAI, Chasmodai: Spirit of the Moon

369: ShHDNY, Shehadani: Angel of the second decanate of Gemini

369: NChVShH: brass (Job 28:2)

369: VHNChSh: now the serpent (Gen. 3:1)

369: AShIBNV: I will bring back (Locks)

369: B-MShKBH, be-miskba: her bed

369: H-ShVTMI: the Shuhamite (2 Kings 4:8)

369: HShMDK: you be destroyed (Locks). Destruction is the Foundation of Existence (*Book of Tokens*). That is: Peh=80=Yesod

❖ 3321: Theosophic Extension of the Planetary Line

3321: MLKA B-ThRShIShIM OD B-RVCh ShChRIM: Intelligence of the Moon: Queen of the Tarshishim forever, in the Spirit of the Dawning Ones. (The Tarshishim are a choir of angels assigned to Briah, the Creative World.) Mem finals equal 600

3321: On earth as it is in heaven (Greek)

Chapter 12

THE KAMEA OF DAATH/PLUTO

The magical numbers of the kamea of Daath/Pluto are eleven, 121, 671, and 7381. Gematria for these numbers is in the correspondence tables at the end of the chapter. Daath has seldom (if ever) been addressed as a planetary Sephira in treatises that deal with magical squares. Case does give some interesting correspondences through the numbers, and Knorr Rosenroth, in his *Kabbala Denudata*, gives us much fascinating material for reflection as well. Jewish Kabbalists seldom touch the subject of Daath (at least in their published writings) and when it is written about, we find opinions about its nature to be as diverse and complex as a philosophical treatise about the nature of God or the meaning of life. In other words, theories about Daath's mysterious nature vary.

William Gray considers its residence, the Abyss, to be frought with danger, for to fall into it is to never retrieve one's sanity (1968). The Abyss itself acts as a filter between the Divine triad and the rest of the Sephiroth and:

> . . . all the horrors, loathsomeness, abominations and evils that would be unthinkable in association with God. . . are swallowed up by the Abyss, where they exist in a state of completely insane chaos pending some ultimate disposal (p. 151).

One does not step off the edge of the Abyss lightly!

The Initiates of Knowledge (Daath) must possess unwavering concentration at the single point ahead to cross the Abyss successfully. Once one does jump, there is no turning back. The tools we use to cross are the Sword of Geburah (Mars) and the Rod of Chesed (Jupiter). The rod serves as a balancing force and the sword cuts away all useless material, which then falls into the garbage pit of the abyss. Mars, in this Qabalistic scheme, rules the north, the place of greatest darkness. The number eleven is sometimes thought to be associated with the *Qliphoth*, or Shells, whence dwell the dark or demonic forces that were, in essence, exorcised from the Tree.

Gareth Knight identifies Daath as the highest level of awareness of which the soul is capable, and says it is the "Sphere of the Upper Room at the descent of the Pentecostal Flames" (1965, p. 103). This is an apt analogy connecting it to Mars at a higher level, or the great unknown represented by Plutonian energy. The path on the Tree ruled by Mars is *Peh*, which means mouth and represents the vehicle by which the Word becomes known. Daath, we know, represents Knowledge, or the combined concrete expression of Wisdom and Understanding, its parents on the Tree, Chokmah and Binah. Allan Bennett, an early Golden Dawn member, made a penetrating analysis of Daath's nature in an Equinox article many years ago:

> When the fall had occurred and the Sephira Malkuth had been cut off from the Tree by the folds of the dragon, there was added unto the Tree Daath, the Knowledge, as the eleventh Sephira, to preserve intact the ten-ness of the Sephiroth. Showing how by that very eating of the Fruit of the Tree of Knowledge of Good and Evil should come the Saving of Mankind, for Daath is the priceless gift of Knowledge and Intellect whereby comes Salvation. Wherefore also is eleven the Key Number of the Great Savior's Name (IHShVH=326=11) (1972, p. 184).

He also noticed that eleven is the number in the Tarot of the "Wheel of the Great Law," or Kaph, called in Qabalah the Lord of the Forces of Life. The normal number of the Wheel (ROTA) is ten, but by this he meant that Kaph is the eleventh Letter of the Hebrew alphabet. As the perceptive student will notice in the chart in figure 12–A, a condensed form of the relationship of the Letters to the Sephiroth taken from Knorr Rosenroth's *Kabbala Denudata*, there is a special relationship between Kaph, the eleventh Letter and Tau, which means the Cross, which is the twenty-second Letter.

Let us briefly examine the particular way this pattern, revealed in the *Kabbala Denudata*, was devised. We spoke earlier about the 231 Gates and have touched upon some of them (the two-Letter combinations) in other chapters. These particular pairs, however, hold some very special secrets, because in essence, they mimic the Sephiroth.

Kether:	Aleph and Lamed	(value, 31)	AL
Chokmah:	Beth and Mem	(value, 42)	BM
Binah:	Gimel and Nun	(value, 53)	GN
Daath:	Daleth and Samekh	(value, 64)	DS
Chesed:	Heh and Ayin	(value, 75)	HO
Geburah:	Vav and Peh	(value, 86)	VP
Tiphareth:	Zain and Tzaddi	(value, 97)	ZTz
Netzach:	Cheth and Qoph	(value, 108)	ChQ
Hod:	Teth and Resh	(value, 209)	TR
Yesod:	Yod and Shin	(value, 310)	YSh
Malkuth:	Kaph and Tau	(value, 420)	KTh

Figure 12–A

In other words, Aleph (and its complement, Lamed) equals Kether, Beth (and its complement, Mem) equals Chokmah, etc. Those familiar with the technique of linking a Sephira with the first ten number-Letters will find this pairing one off, as indeed it should be, since most who have made this kind of comparison do not use Daath. Knorr Rosenroth has pointed out that it produces its own unique set of relationships.

I have to say to the sincere Qabalistic student that many mysteries are revealed by meditating on these eleven Gates, especially if one knows something about the Tarot. It is beyond the scope of this book to explore his very complicated glyph here, but one interesting phenomenon to be observed is that the very name of Daath is contained in Daleth, as is Yod in Yesod when the paths are linked to the Sephiroth in this way. Remember that these eleven pairs can be reversed, *i.e.*, every set of pairs can be read backwards, which gives us 22 sets of pairs, or the Sephiroth (including Daath) doubled. (For example, AL and LA belong to Kether.) Apparently in the Jewish Kabbalistic tradition that Knorr Rosenroth studied with great fervor there was a secret connected with these Gates that related to the highest grade, known as the last (fiftieth) Gate of Binah. Binah is here related to the Great Darkness (the first Sephira one contacts on the other side of the Abyss), and her last Gate is said to be the most difficult, and one that only adepts can attain. The way this is alluded to in the text is that this Gate is called *Nethib* (NThIB), the *narrow way* or *narrow gate*. It has a value of 462, or the 231 Letter arrangements doubled (reversed), as they are in this Alphabetic arrangement called AlBam.

One can begin to get clues of how to establish a relationship with these 231 gates by making flashing color tablets of these Letters and it would serve as a very useful meditation exercise. One can also substitute Tarot Keys, since in Case's interpretation they evoke the same energy. The revelations connected to these particular pairs of Gates are seldom written about because the aspirant needs to discover them him or herself. At the threshold, one must forge one's own tools.

It must be understood that Daath is not meant here to supplant Chesed as the fourth Sephira; it is simply an alternate method of pairing the Spheres with the Gates represented by the mystical combinations of the Letters. In the *Kabbala Denudata,* the Spheres have their own names using the Letters in this way (*e.g.*, Al, Bam, Gan, Das, etc.) as well as their own numerical associations. In the case of Daath, the numbers corresponding to Daleth and Samakh equal 64, which is one of the magical numbers of Hod/Mercury. This is a wonderful alchemical number. The student may want to check the gematria associations in chapter ten.

The way that Knorr Rosenroth illustrates the Gates is much more complicated than the simple scheme outlined above. He gives each of these twenty-two pairs a whole set of Hebrew Letters, thus an eleven by eleven square with 121 cells (with two Letters in each cell) and then a ten by eleven square the same way. The end result for both squares when added together is 231 combinations. So each Sephira has its own complete set of 231 gates. The sacred two-Letter combination represented by the particular pairing of the Hebrew Letters which correspond to the Sephira is always the bottom one on the right in the top eleven by eleven square. When each set of twenty-two is laid out in full (which

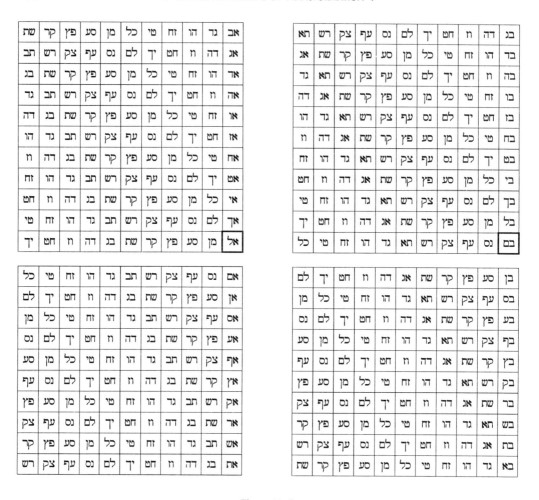

Figure 12–B

covers fifteen pages), a beautiful pattern emerges that would be impossible if one did not include Daath as a Sephira. Only the first two sets are included in figure 12–B, so the student can glimpse the inherent beauty of this arrangement.

For those who have this edition of *Kabbala Denudata*, there seems to be an anomaly in the second pairing, where Netzach is omitted and Daath is repeated twice. I cannot understand the reason for this and have come to the conclusion that it is probably a misprint. This entire series of Alphabetic permutations in the *Kabbala Denudata* (known as *the narrow way*) are called Albam (ALBM), (after the first pairings)—a method of *temura* (permutation) only mentioned in passing by S. L. Mathers in his introduction to *The Kabbalah Unveiled*. Yet Rosenroth refers to it repeatedly throughout other parts of the text. I realize some of you are thoroughly lost by now, but I have included this intriguing Qabalistic tangent for the sake of those who truly are interested in pursuing work with the Letters, and also because I welcome feedback from anyone else who has read parts of the untranslated *Kabbala Denudata* (Latin). The technique of translating the Letters to their archetypal meaning, to Tarot keys, or even to affirmations is a simple one and can be utilized by anyone with just the information in figure 12–A.

The value for Daath is 474, which is also the numeration for the phrase "you shall know," which refers to Knowledge itself, but it is used by the Jewish Kabbalist Gutman Locks in his excellent gematria of the Bible (1985) to refer to the phrase in Genesis 15:13, "And you shall know for certain that your descendants shall be aliens in a land not their own." This refers to the time that the Israelites would be in Egypt, but in an esoteric sense, it can be taken for the mysterious alien territory of Daath, about which we can only make strange guesses as to its real nature. It is interesting to note that Gareth Knight assigns the mundane chakra Sothis to Daath, as this was the deep esoteric mythology that most inspired the ancient Egyptians—it was said to be the home of Isis herself (Sirius). Isis is the High Priestess in the Tarot and this is the only path, it is said by the masters, that one can use to safely cross the Abyss.

Although some have placed Daath in the throat center (visualizing the Tree within one's body) or in the head, in this system, as we will see in the chapter on chakras, it is conceived as a silvery white light which emanates outside the body completely. As Mathers has noted, "Daath is the throne of Spiritual Consciousness and Spiritual Consciousness does not partake of the body but is the light which radiates" (1971, p. 133). Later on, in the technique we will give for meditation on the eight planetary chakras, Daath is conceived as a silvery white egg, within which swirl all of the colors of the rainbow, which are then distributed to the chakras as necessary. In this system it acts as the transmitter of the energies of the Life-Force, and is the Sun behind the Sun, since it resides behind Tiphareth in the Abyss. The number of Daath, 474, also adds up to six, which is the number of Tiphareth, the Sun Sphere on the Tree.

Properly visualized, it is not just the etheric egg surrounding the body, but the point of contact through which we are made aware of the Great Transformation. In Tantra, this concept is thought of as the *bindu point*, which, through great concentration, can release tremendous power. It is the chakra that will open up vast new areas of consciousness in the future. It is represented by Pluto because true Plutonian energy is transformative beyond the power of the ego to control. It is rather like the chain reaction of a nuclear bomb, which is beyond anyone's control once its effects are underway. Its power is released both from breakdowns (fission) and union (fusion). As the eighth planetary chakra it may be likened to the eighth heaven of the Gnostics.

It is this chakra that forms the gateway to other universes, and in this sense can be compared to the singularity of modern physics, a boundary point beyond which lies a different understanding of reality altogether. The astrological glyph of Pluto represents the universalized upreach of Soul embracing the circle of Spirit while resting on the Cross of Matter (see figure 12–C). At the singularity matter leaves the physical universe altogether and influences emanating from it are beyond the power of science to predict in any

Figure 12–C

way, even theoretically. It is the closest thing science has discovered to something akin to the supernatural. Yet it is this Wheel upon which turns all of the others. Jacob Boehme, the famous mystic, once said, "This wheel has seven wheels one in another, and one nave, and all seven wheels turn on that one nave."

If any Sephira can be compared to the Ain Soph, it is Daath, because both represent this unimagined territory, which religious philosophers of all traditions have said is the true nature of God. In Qabalah, the Ain Soph is not a part of the Tree at all, being beyond all attributes. It is Incomprehensible Nothingness, beyond and behind all manifestation, whose number is zero. Zero is the number of infinite space and time, and any number multiplied by it vanishes into its ocean of Infinity. However, from it proceeds all things. The Jewish Kabbalist ben Abraham ha-Lavan once said, "Nothingness is more existent than all the being of the world." And the Christian mystic Meister Eckhart echoed this thought when he said that "God's nichts fills the entire world; His something though is nowhere." This "nowhere" is often thought of in Qabalistic terms as the chaos from which the Divine Being created the world. God, it is thought, made the universe from Nothing.

The *Sepher Yetzirah* tells us that "He formed something actual out of chaos and made what is not into what is" (2:6). And the Gnostic Basilides said that the non-existent God made the cosmos out of the non-existent, casting down and planting a single seed containing within itself the whole seed-mass of the cosmos (Jonas, 1963). The Book of Proverbs tells us: "With wisdom God established the earth, with Understanding he established the heavens, and with his Knowledge, the depths (chaos) were broken up" (Prov 3:19, 20). It is through Daath (Knowledge) that the creative power of the Elohim (emanating from Binah) begins to manifest something from the chaotic nothing.

Although masculine language is used in Proverbs, in Qabalah, these depths are often referred to as the *Womb*, or *Ani* in Hebrew. This word is simply a rearrangement of the word *Ain*, or *Nothingness*, and therefore would have the same numerical value. This value is sixty-one, which is the number exactly in the center of the magical square of Daath, as can be seen in figure 12–D.

If we look at the kamea closely we can see a number of interesting properties. It just happens that this magical number *AIN*, or sixty-one, not only is the center point of the square but the numbers which form a cross on all four sides of it are one, eleven, 121, and 111. I discovered this quite by accident simply while meditating on the kamea itself. The student should be aware by now of associations relating to these numbers (two of them are the magical numbers of the Daath/Pluto kamea.) Meditation on these numerical associations yields some interesting fruit for a

56	117	46	107	36	97	26	87	16	77	6
7	57	118	47	108	37	98	27	88	17	67
68	8	58	119	48	109	38	99	28	78	18
19	69	9	59	120	49	110	39	89	29	79
80	20	70	10	60	121	50	100	40	90	30
31	81	21	71	11	61	111	51	101	41	91
92	32	82	22	72	1	62	112	52	102	42
43	93	33	83	12	73	2	63	113	53	103
104	44	94	23	84	13	74	3	64	114	54
55	105	34	95	24	85	14	75	4	65	115
116	45	106	35	96	25	86	15	76	5	66

Figure 12–D

Qabalistic mind and there are a number of techniques for working with the mysteries of the Hebrew-Letter Archetypes that have been revealed in the Golden Dawn and other Qabalistic schools. One is to translate the numbers into Letters, which then become names, mantras, sigils, or geometric figures as illustrated in various places in this book. Another, for those who associate the Letters with the Tarot keys, is to translate the number sequences into Archetypes and see what they reveal.

In this case we could first meditate on Kether, (number one), then move to eleven, 121, and 111. Eleven is made of two Hebrew Letters, Yod and Aleph (ten and one). These make the root *IA*, which means "the movements of the soul which spring from admiration and astonishment" (d'Olivet, p. 362). It gives rise to our modern expression *Oh!* which usually happens when we are completely awakened to a new level of understanding. Because this root is composed of vowel sounds that compose the Divine Names (IHVH and AHIH), it would be an appropriate mantra to chant or meditate on. It is the number of Daath itself, the kamea that is eleven by eleven. Translated into Tarot keys, it is the Magician (one) working through Justice (eleven). Or, one could work with the energies of the Hebrew Letters themselves—Aleph, the Primal Life-Force acting upon Yod, the primal point and the creative hand.

The next number, as we circle the points of the cross (clockwise), is 121. Besides the associations given at the end of this chapter, the Hebrew Letter Archetypes in this number are *Peh* (100) *Kaph* (twenty) and *Aleph* (one). Again, we can do a writing meditation exercise freely associating to what these Letter Archetypes mean in this particular relationship to one another; or use the foregoing method of working with the Tarot keys. It is useful to set the Tarot keys that spell the particular numerical vibration or word in front of you and meditate on them visually, making note of your impressions. Dr. Case said that many revelations will inspire the student who works with the keys in this way. Finally, we can finish our meditation on the mystical number of the Sun, 111, and record the whole operation in our journal, including any sigil designs or any other artwork that may emerge from our contemplations.

The magical number 671, which is the sum of any line, has many interesting correspondences. It is both the Intelligence, *Geburathekem* (GBURThKM) and the Spirits (VBABNIM). The *Vobe-ehbanim* is from a root which means vessels of stone. Both of these sigil lines follow exactly the same current when placed on the kamea together.

Six hundred seventy-one is also the number of the Gate, (*Throa*) which is an Aramaic title of Malkuth. Daath is also a Gate, the true Threshold to Higher Consciousness. Actually, as William Gray notes, there is not really a difference between Malkuth and Daath, since Daath was Malkuth before the Fall. Thus, Daath continues to be Malkuth after it has been perfected through experience. Then it is paradise regained, and we can see a numerical equivalent here because *paradise* in the Greek also has a value of 671. Another interesting association in this regard is that 121, the number of cells in this kamea, also is the value "of whirling motions" (Crowley), which refers to Kether. This is the Qabalistic term for the sum-total of the manifestation of the cosmic forces, which have their beginning in Kether and their fulfillment in Malkuth.

WHEEL of FORTUNE.

Figure 12–E

56	117	46	107	36	97	26	87	16	77	6
7	57	118	47	108	37	98	27	88	17	67
68	8	58	119	48	109	38	99	28	78	18
19	69	9	59	120	49	110	39	89	29	79
80	20	70	10	60	121	50	100	40	90	30
31	81	21	71	11	61	111	51	101	41	91
92	32	82	22	72	1	62	112	52	102	42
43	93	33	83	12	73	2	63	113	53	103
104	44	94	23	84	13	74	3	64	114	54
55	105	34	95	24	85	14	75	4	65	115
116	45	106	35	96	25	86	15	76	5	66

Figure 12–F

Case notes that the Wheel (ROTA) of the Tarot (TARO) (which are the words printed on the disk pictured in the Wheel of Fortune Key [see figure 12–E] when read clockwise), when translated into Hebrew, also have a value of 671. If one places the three sigil lines of the words Taro, Rota and Throa (mentioned above), it makes an extremely interesting design, forming a triangle with the current running in three directions (see figure 12–F). If one wanted to use the technique of making an affirmation based on the archetypal hints suggested by this design (which Case says is a very valuable way of working with the subconscious), it could read something like this: The Wheels (Rota) of Tarot descend through my Gate (Throa). Does this sound like nonsense? Perhaps to the conscious mind it does, but if you knew the symbolic language that was being spoken through these images, the subconscious would take off and go to work manifesting this affirmation based on the symbolic work you did in a talisman-making session. What it meant for me during an exercise I did once was simply that the destiny that the archetypes of the tarot reveal would pass through my Gate of Understanding. This is what the sigil lines meant for me at that time, and still do, for that matter. I am giving you concrete examples of how I have worked with the numerical values of the kameas so that you can begin to experiment and see for yourself how valuable this magical system can be.

It is foolish to think that one can make magic by simply drawing a line on a page and forgetting about it. There must be associations that mean something to subconsciousness, and there must be concentration, devotion, and practice for consciousness and will to become aligned with the work that the subconscious is activating via the symbol.

Correspondences: Mystical Names
and Numbers of Daath/Pluto

Asterisks (*) denote God-names

❖ 11: Mystical number of Daath

11: 11th path between Kether and Chokmah

11: There are 11 sets of pairs of the Hebrew Letters

11: AVD, ode: fire, firebrand; the fire of the magic of LVX ("that od force, which still from female fingertips burnt blue," E. B. Browning)

11: DHB, dehab,: gold (Crowley)

11: ChG, chag: a circularity of form or motion (Crowley); festival, tournement, carousal (ben Yehuda); Every turbulent movement; every transport of joy (d'Olivet)

11: IA, :Oh!
ROOT: all movements of the soul which spring from admiration and astonishment (d'Olivet)

11: AI; ROOT: where one acts, where one is

11: BBVA, ve-boa: the coming of

11: HBD, hebed: garment, covering

11: ChBA, chaba: to conceal

11: GDD, gedad: to cut off

❖ 121 Number of Divisions of Kamea

121: KSYAL, Cassiel

121: NYNVH, Nineveh (Luke 11:30)

121: AFM, apem: an end, extremity; fool for God; to cease, disappear

121: HGLGLIM: of whirling motions

121: ATzL, azal: emanated from

121: MLAIM, malaim: consecration

121: AIN-KM: you do not

121: ChZQV, chezka: be strong

❖ 671: Sum of Any Line

671: THORA, the Law

671: ThROA, the Gate

671: ROTA ("For our Rota takes her beginning from that day when God spake Fiat," *Fama Fraternatis*)

671: TARO

671: ASThIR: I will hide

671: GBVRThKM, Geburathekem: Intelligence

671: VBABNIM, Vo-baehbanim: Spirits

671: ARTz MTzRIM, Eretz Mizraim: Land of Egypt

671: OVShH PRI, Osh Periy: fruitbearing

671: Paradise in Greek

❖ 7381: Theosophic Extension of Kamea

7381: 7381=9=10=The One

Chapter 13

PERSONAL TALISMANS
OF THE NAME

There is an alternate method of talisman-making utilizing the tattwa elements and some symbolism from the Tarot that we have touched upon—here I would like to explain it in more detail. It is a very simple but powerful technique that can lend itself to an almost infinite variety of creative designs. It is done in a way similar to creating a telesmatic image; it is created entirely from a name. This can be one of the angelic or archangelic names, such as those found in Chapter Three (figure 3–A on page 25). You can use any name that is important in your life, such as one of the saints, or even one of the Sacred Names of the Sephiroth.

figure 13–A lists the Hebrew spelling of the Divine Names and the planetary chakras. This method can be employed using the word of a particular idea one wants to embody, and works especially well if one knows a little

NUMBER	SEPHIROTH	GOD NAME	ARCHANGEL	PLANET
2 ב	CHOKMAH חכמה	IH or IHVH יהוה יה	RTzIAL רציאל	- -
3 ג	BINAH בינה	IHVH ALHIM יהוה אלהים	TzPQIAL צפקיאל	ShBThAI (Saturn) שבתאי
4 ד	CHESED חסד	AL, EL אל	TzDQIAL צדקיאל	TzDQ (Jupiter) צדק
5 ה	GEBURAH גבורה	ALHIM GVBR אלהים גובר	KMAL כמאל	MADIM (Mars) מאדים
6 ו	TIPHARETH תפארת	IHVH ALVH VDOTh יהוה אלוה ודעת	RPhAL רפאל	ShMSh (SUN) שמש
7 ז	NETZACH נצח	IHVH TzBAVTh יהוה צבאות	HANIAL האניאל	NVGH (Venus) נוגה
8 ח	HOD הוד	ALHIM TzBAVTh אלהים צבאות	MIKAL מיכאל	KVKB (Mercury) כוכב
9 ט	YESOD יסוד	ShDI AL ChI שדי אל חי	GBRIAL גבריאל	LBNH (Moon) לבנה
11 יא	DAATH דעת	IH ALHIM יה אלהים	MSVKIAL מסוכיאל	OShIRM (Pluto) עשירם

Figure 13–A

Figure 13–B

rudimentary Hebrew. Let us first look at the example of Raphael. In Hebrew this is spelled RPhAL. If we examine the elemental shapes on pages 43–51, we see that this has elemental correspondences that can be related—or spelled symbolically—this way:

R—RESH—SUN—FIRE—TRIANGLE

P—PEH—MARS—FIRE—TRIANGLE
   (Mars also rules a water sign, which is an upside down triangle, in the alchemical design).

A—ALEPH—AIR—CIRCLE

L—LAMED—LIBRA, AIR—CIRCLE

This can be drawn in a design that looks like figure 13–B.

We can also spell the name with Tarot keys and colors using the chart in chapter two (see figure 1–B on page 15). The Tarot keys corresponding to the Letters in this name are the Sun (*Resh*, figure 13–C), the Tower (*Peh*, figure 13–D), the Fool (*Aleph*, figure 13–E), and Justice (*Lamed*, figure 13–F). It can take a variety of forms, depending on the symbols one chose from the Tarot keys, but a sample design might look like this:

Figure 13–C

Figure 13–D   *Figure 13–E*   *Figure 13–F*

RESH—SUN—ORANGE—SUN SYMBOL

PEH—TOWER—RED—TOWER SYMBOL

ALEPH—FOOL—YELLOW—WHEEL SYMBOL FROM FOOL'S DRESS

LAMED—JUSTICE—GREEN—SYMBOL OF THE SCALES

This design may look like figure 13–G.

Figure 13–G

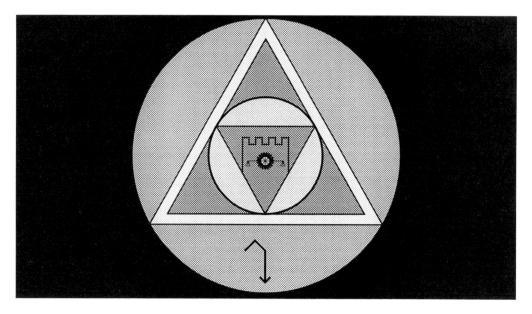

Figure 13–H

We can then combine these two talismans into one piece, and it will look something like figure 13–H. With the knowledge gained from using magical squares and the Rose kamea, we may choose to add sigils appropriate to need or desire.

This method works with any Hebrew word, or words or names translated into Hebrew—if one has a Tarot deck with the Hebrew letters written at the bottom. (For example, Case's Tarot, or see the book, *Archetypes on the Tree of Life*, listed in the bibliography). It can also reveal the many intricacies of the symbolism in the Qabalah and Tarot.

The word in Hebrew which means bow or rainbow is *qesheth* (QShTh). This is an important word that is attributed to the Temperance Key of the Tarot (see figure 13–I), because it signifies the arrow which goes directly up the Middle Pillar of the Tree of Life, and also the rainbow of promise pictured in most Tarot decks behind the image of Michael the Archangel. This angel signifies the Higher Self, which is preparing the personality for the great transformation that the soul undergoes in becoming so totally absorbed in God that it loses all sense of self. This is represented by the metaphor of the arrow which has been released from the bow and finds its way directly into the heart of the mystic. There are many other layers of mystical and alchemical interpretation, but our principal purpose is talisman-making.

How do we go about connecting with the energy this Archetypal Key represents through talismanic artwork?

Figure 13–I

Figure 13–J *Figure 13–K* *Figure 13–L*

We first have to choose the word we want to spell symbolically. We can choose the angelic name (*Michael*), as in the example above, but this time we will use the word *QShTh*, composed of *Qoph*, *Shin*, and *Tau*. The three Tarot keys that correspond to these letters are the Moon (see figure 13–J), the Judgement Key (see figure 13–K), and the World (see figure 13–L). They symbolize the combined power of the waters of the subconscious (Moon) with the fires of purification (Judgement), which are grounded on the Tau cross of the World.

Figure 13–M

Figure 13–N

For this we can use the tattwa symbols of fire, water, and earth. The design with tattwa symbols alone may look like figure 13–M. There are no hard and fast rules, although you may want to follow the order of the spelling which goes from inside out. We can make a flashing color tablet of this figure by limiting our colors to blue and orange, since blue is the principal color of the Temperance Key, associated with Sagittarius and Jupiter.

There are endless ways to work with this one design alone. One may choose to paint it in the colors represented by the Hebrew letters using the chart in chapter two (see figure 2–B on page 15). We can use violet for the moon (Qoph), red for the triangle (Shin) and indigo for the square (Tau). Or one could paint them in the traditional colors of the tattwa elements, silver/white for the moon, red for the triangle, and yellow for the earth. Finally, we can embellish it with figures chosen from the corresponding Tarot keys, as we did in the first example of Raphael.

It already has a moon (Qoph), so we can add the cross on the banner of the angel in the Judgement key and the wreath around the dancer in the World key. It will then look like figure 13–N.

We may want to paint it using all the colors of the spectrum, since all colors are represented in the rainbow, as well as adding an arrow, since these are important symbols in the Temperance key, when we use the letters QShTh to describe it. If one wanted to work with the energies of this key, one could also use the word *Samekh*, which means support. This is the Hebrew letter most frequently attributed to Temperance. The amazing thing about working with the Hebrew letters is that one can spell them: they contain other letters, and so the process opens up many possibilities for understanding the meanings of any single Hebrew letter by taking it apart and spelling it with Tarot keys and/or elements. (See chapter two, figure 2–A, [page 12] for spelling of Hebrew Letters.)

Using the above examples, the student should have no trouble figuring out how to create a talisman spelling this word, using the charts in chapter two that explain which Hebrew letters are related to colors, elements, and Tarot keys. These are very personable tattwa/talismans that lend themselves to many creative designs while still employing traditional Qabalistic symbolism. One of the meanings of the Tarot key we have just been discussing is experimentation and verification. With enough experimentation with these techniques, Qabalah tells us, more secrets are divulged and the full spiritual import of their meanings become personally verified.

Figure 13–O

Chapter 14

USING TATTWAS FOR HEALING AND BALANCING

*The next time you see a flashing point of light on a television advertisement, or
a point of light that scintillates accompanied by a single pinging note of music,
please remember that the advertiser has just implanted what amounts to a direct-
ive in your subconscious mind; he has just polluted your aura with junk energy.*

—David Tansley, *The Rainment of Light*

The principles of using sound and color, both for healing and for maintaining
emotional and physical health are ancient and are the foundation upon which the
modern use of tattwas employed by Dr. Case and others is based. Chapter One
examined the variety of techniques that tattwas—or any systematized method of colored
talismanic mandalas—can be utilized, along with names of writers who have employed
the tattwa-meditation symbols for various purposes.

In this chapter we are just going to focus on the relationship of specific tones and
colors for creating talismans using the tattwas alone. These are primarily based on the
theosophical tradition, which influenced Case considerably in his work with sound and
color. Even though certain tattwa-like designs may symbolize a specific planetary energy,
they do not draw upon other kinds of symbolism such as number and astrological symbols, as we saw in earlier chapters where we created talismans based primarily on the
Sephiroth. These tattwas correspond to the zodiacal and planetary energy of the paths of
the Tree and use the traditional five tattwa elements in different combinations.

Goethe felt that colors were the sufferings of light, and Corine Heline in her *Healing
and Regeneration Through Color* (1987) explains:

> Sacrifice is the keynote of all progression in every round of life from the atom to God.
> The White Light, containing all colors within itself, lowers its vibration rate (sacrifices
> itself) to produce the spectrum (p. 9).

An exhaustive exploration into color healing is not the focus of this book, but some background material is included here so that the student may grasp the underlying principles upon which this tattwa-meditation is based.

Paracelsus felt that the body was composed of a visible substance that was subject to corruption, and a more etheric substance, which was not. Health of the physical body was brought about by reharmonizing it with its etheric vehicle that provided the elements necessary to overcome the malady. Since his time, many auric healers have espoused the mental and physical benefits of projecting colors into a person's aura through thought transference. Numerous investigators of aural phenomenon during the past two centuries, many of whom claimed to be psychic, sought to describe the magnetic atmosphere surrounding the physical body.

In 1911, W. J. Kilner sought to separate himself from the mystical aspects of aura reading. He concluded in his laboratory speculations that surrounding the human body is an envelope with three definite parts that under certain conditions can be seen. He developed a method called the *Kilner screen*, still used today, to view the aura, and wrote about actual rays that shot out at right angles from the body in projections, the colors of which were defined by the health of the body. The aura of a healthy person presents a symmetrical, web-like appearance through the screens, while an unhealthy one is spiny, blotched, or broken (1965).

His work was followed by Oscar Bagnall who in 1937 discovered that no aura emanated from a dead thing. By the twentieth century, the development of colored glass for treatment of diseases was finding numerous adherents in writers who sought to combine scientific inquiry with esoteric philosophy. Today there are many who incorporate color therapy as an adjunct to holistic healing.

Part two of this chapter reviews a more modern understanding of the electro-magnetic properties of color. For an in-depth study in color healing one can look at the works of J. Dodson Hessey, and E. D. Babbit, as well as the more esoteric writers who examine this subject, *e.g.*, Rudolf Steiner, Madame Blavatsky, and Corine Heline. I also recommend Theo Gimbel (1980) and Brugh Joy (1979) for more modern applications.

We now know that the *corona discharge* (a fancy word used by scientists, who don't believe in auras) can be photographed through Kirlian photography. These electrical emanations captured many times on film also show a definite lack or dominance of certain colors, depending on certain conditions (such as stress, health, even what a person is presently thinking). This auric field is often called the bioplasmic body, and is thought to comprise only one layer of the aura. In other words, it is not nearly as fully developed as what can be seen clairvoyantly. For an excellent examination of newer developments using science and clairvoyance, see the work of Dr. Shafica Karagulla (1967), who diagnosed many of her patients with the aid of psychics who could read auras. Another interesting development in energy photography is called the *Schlieren system*, now used by a number of doctors to study heat convection currents of the body. In this heat envelope or halo can be seen not only many shimmering colors, but actual bacteria, which seems to breed in the lower auric field before invading the body.

Corine Heline has said that the correct use of color will be the preventive against epidemics in the coming new age and "will replace the present barbaric custom of vaccination" (1987, p. 35). It has been thought by nearly everyone working in this field that the etheric body needs to be cleansed and healed in order for the physical body to reflect optimum health. We do not know for sure, but we can only presume that this same concept was understood by the ancient healers as well. Although the relationships between the planets, colors, and tones may have been known and used before Pythagorus, it was the Pythagoreans who perfected the art and left it as part of the Greek legacy. They discovered the correspondences by stretching strings of varying lengths and thicknesses to posts, the distance of which were in turn determined by the relative size and distance of the planets. Thus evolved the phrase *music of the spheres*, and Pythagoras was famous for using music, color and poetry to cure diseases. We could today utilize these same principles by employing simultaneous use of the specific tone of the planet with its corresponding color and positive affirmations.

Dr. Case gave the relationship of specific tones and colors with the planets and zodiacal signs in his book, *The Tarot*, but did not explain how to use this information. Like many occult teachings, it was thought that esoteric principles such as these were subject to abuse if they fell into the wrong hands. For this reason blinds have always been a part of many occult teachings; for example, in Blavatsky's scheme, Saturn, which is there connected to green, and Venus, connected to indigo, should be reversed.

Because others published their findings on the correct relationships between colors, tones, and planets independently, Dr. Case later said that the essentials of this esoteric knowledge long kept secret are now public property; I have seen numerous charts over the years that seem to coincide with remarkable similarity. *Archetypes on the Tree of Life* (Compton, 1991) gives the scales of the planetary chakras and the zodiacal signs that correspond to Case's interpretation. He made numerous refinements to Blavatsky's system, in essence correcting her blinds. Later we will employ this scheme for the background of our tattwa constructions.

In his article on Agrippa (1949), Karl Nowotny says:

❖ Preparing the Tattwas

> From the doctrine that elements of the soul are mingled in arithmetic proportion, (and) those of the body in geometrical (proportion). . . he concludes that it is numbers themselves—which term includes such arrangements as magic squares—which act directly upon the soul, while the. . . geometrical figures have peculiar powers over man's body (p. 197).

It does not seem unreasonable that geometric mandala-like forms have proven so beneficial for use in the development of tattwa-meditation techniques in the western tradition over the past 100 years or so. Three of the tattwa colors—red, blue, and yellow—are the primary colors, and therefore their corresponding opposites, as well as other combinations, such as with indigo and violet, become possible when painted on the tattwa cards. The twenty talismanic cards on pages 168–187 are the combination of the twelve

Zodiacal Sign	Letter	Color	Tone
Aries	Heh	Red	C
Taurus	Vav	Red-orange	C sharp
Gemini	Zain	Orange	D
Cancer	Cheth	Yellow-Orange	E flat
Leo	Teth	Yellow	E
Virgo	Yod	Yellow-Green	F
Libra	Lamed	Green	F sharp
Scorpio	Nun	Green-Blue	G
Sagittarius	Samekh	Blue	A flat
Capricorn	Ayin	Blue-Violet	A
Aquarius	Tzaddi	Violet	B flat
Pisces	Qoph	Red-Violet	B

Figure 14–A

zodiacal signs and the eight planets we have covered thus far in our explorations. The student can photocopy these for use in making talismanic mandalas. We are also employing an alternative version of coloring the tattwas based on Blavatsky's interpretation. With these we will have a full range of color that, when used together, create a proper balance for the harmonizing of the etheric body.

This whole technique is simple, yet quite powerful, and can be done in about twenty minutes once all of the talismanic tattwas and other preparations have been made. First, color the tattwa cards in the correct colors. Make sure the colors are vibrant, pure, and uniform. You can use paints or magic markers, but crayons or colored pencils are not advised. When the tattwa figure has been colored, you mount it on construction or poster paper corresponding to the color of the background, or paint the back if done on a large enough frame. Each complete figure should be about 8"x11", similar to the ones used for the talisman-mandalas we described earlier.

When you have the twenty tattwa cards completed, mount them so that you can view them one by one in the order given at the end of this chapter. These designs correspond to the colors, Hebrew letters, and tones in Figures 14–A and 14–B.

Red is traditionally associated with the triangle and fire and therefore it will be found in the designs of the fire signs. It is the first form by which Deity usually manifests, such as the burning bush and tongues of fire, and signals an immediate opening of consciousness and vibrant, active life. Fire was an element thought to be particularly numinous in the ancient world, and vestal virgins were endowed with the task of making sure the sacred flame was never extinguished.

Red can also shift to its opposite, green, and in esoteric literature, the true occult color, or that kept secret from the profane, is often given as the complementary color. The simple design on page 19 (see figure 2–G) is very revealing in terms of uncovering this secret of the mystery of complementary relationships in color. Goethe, in his *Theory of Colour*, spoke of how the opposites incline toward one another:

> (Through meditation) a deep secret will begin to dawn on us. . . and we shall scarcely be able to hold ourselves back from acknowledging that when we see them bringing forth here below, the green is there above the red that we are beholding, on one side the earthly, and on the other side the heavenly creations of the Elohim (1970).

Planet	Letter	Color	Tone
Saturn	Tau	Blue-violet	A
Sun	Resh	Orange	D
Mars	Peh	Red	C
Jupiter	Kaph	Violet	B flat
Venus	Daleth	Green	F sharp
Moon	Gimel	Blue	A flat
Mercury	Beth	Yellow	E
Pluto	none	Silver White	silence

Figure 14–B

Green is the color of both nature and resurrection, and is used behind or within any triangle painted red.

Blue is the color of the circle and symbolizes air. It describes the sea and the sky, and it's energy, being expansive, lifts upward and outward. It is a symbol of freedom from the house of the body, reaching toward infinity. Its complementary color is orange, and it is utilized in the air signs.

Yellow is generally attributed to a square and represents earth. It symbolizes clarity, definition, and the ability to make something concrete. It will be found in the designs of the earth signs. It also revitalizes the physical body in a particular way when meditated on properly. This color is connected to the production of a substance in the body that adepts secrete for longevity and about which the alchemists have long spoken. This is a very useful color for stimulating the development of this secretion. Blavatsky gives yellow-orange for the square symbol, and therefore its complementary color is either violet or indigo. These three are the primaries and their complements.

The moon symbolizes water and to it is attributed either white or shades of violet or blue. It signifies the emotional nature as well as the spark of revelation from the unconscious. Its symbol is incorporated in the water signs.

The egg shape represents akasha and is most often painted indigo or black. It is the color of Saturn and its shape includes mysteries on the Tree of Life relating to Daath and Yesod, as well as its original mother, Binah. (The Yesod seal, it will be recalled, mimics Binah's magical seal.) It symbolizes the most hidden aspects of occultism, and death and the blackness of the Unknown Night. It holds the key of recapitulation of a new consciousness dawning in our age. We find it in the tattwa of Capricorn (ruled by Saturn), Libra (where Saturn is exalted), and especially in Aquarius, whose keynote is universality. Figures A and B incorporate these colors along with the particular vibration of the zodiacal signs and planetary colors and tones. With the exception of Daath, these relate to the Letter-paths on the Tree, not the planetary Sephiroth. Pluto, however, has been assigned to Shin (Judgement) by some, if the student wants to experiment with this.

I suggest working with the tones in one of two ways. Either use a pitch-pipe to intone the correct note and then silently hum it to yourself for a full minute while simultaneously meditating on the corresponding tattwa-talisman, or you could prepare ahead of time a twenty-minute tape (since each tattwa meditation lasts one minute) wherein the corresponding notes are intoned for a minute each. You could use a pitch pipe for doing this, which is best if you make sure it is not played unevenly (which makes it go off key),

Zodiacal Signs and Corresponding Body Parts:

Aries: Ailments affecting the cerebral hemisphere of the brain, organs of the head, eyes and ears.

Taurus: Neck, throat, larynx, tonsils, carotid arteries, and jugular veins.

Gemini: Shoulders, arms, lungs, thymus, and upper ribs.

Cancer: Stomach, diaphragm, lactase, and thoracic duct.

Leo: Heart, spinal chord, and aorta.

Virgo: Large and small intestines and pancreas.

Libra: Kidneys, skin and the suprarenals.

Scorpio: Bladder, urethra, the genital organs, rectum, and descending colon.

Sagittarius: Hips, thighs, femur, illium, illiac arteries and veins, and sacral region (lower part of spine).

Capricorn: Knees, bones (in general), and certain skin eruptions.

Aquarius: Limbs from knees to ankles, and varicose veins.

Pisces: Maladies principally of the feet and toes.

Figure 14–C

or you may play it on a harmonium or some other instrument, as long as you are sure it is presently in tune. It is best to check it against a pitch pipe if doing this.

I find the second method works best; then I can relax and not think about finding the correct tone at the end of every minute and can hum, om, or chant something simple with the tone as I meditate on the tattwa card. At the end of each tone, I simply replace the tattwa with the next card. When you have spent a few sessions using the cards in this way you may want to vary the technique by allowing some time—say, fifteen seconds—at the end of each minute to shut your eyes and reflect on the after image. This may seem like a simple technique, but it is one of the most powerful ways to use magical talismans. You should adjust the timing of your humming or chanting accordingly. It is fine to spend the period with your eyes shut in silence. After a while you will get into the rhythm of this. Don't become passive and go off into some nowhere land. Count to yourself for fifteen seconds if necessary, and then return to the next card, or go on to the next card as soon as the after-image fades. You could also leave a fifteen-second period of silence on the tape in between tattwa keys.

The first twelve tattwas associated with the zodiacal signs are related more to the body; the last eight vibrate to the interior planetary chakras. (The chakras are not glands or organs. They are centers of consciousness.) I conclude the whole operation with certain affirmations that the student would do well to devise for him or herself. You may also use certain tattwas separately, but you should do this with caution. It is better to work in a balanced way; too much focus on one chakra in particular may also affect other areas you may not be interested in treating.

For those interested in the zodiacal signs and their corresponding body parts, figure 14–C briefly lists associations that Corine Heline offers in her book *Healing and*

Inherent Tendencies Aroused by Zodiacal Tattwas:

Aries: Aggressive, energetic

Taurus: Decisive, determined

Gemini: Diffusive, intellectual

Cancer: Tenacious, nurturing

Leo: Organizing, creative

Virgo: Analytical, detailed

Libra: Uniting, artistic

Scorpio: Solidifying, intense

Sagittarius: Inspirational, freedom-loving

Capricorn: Retentive, self-disciplined

Aquarius: Concentrative, theoretical

Pisces: Relaxing, sensitive

Figure 14–D

Regeneration through Color (p. 35). It must be noted that she uses some different color correspondences. All of the correspondences used in this book, including this chapter on tattwas, are Qabalah based and relate to what is known as the King color scale (with the exception of Pluto/Daath, which is not here given as a path correspondence, as are the others.) Although Mathers (1971) seemed to think that the tattwas related more to the Queen scale, he also noted that this use tends to make one more passive. We feel that the uses developed here help maintain concentration and are more effective than the twenty-five designs originally developed in the Golden Dawn.

The chart in figure 14–D lists some corresponding mental and emotional states aroused by stimulating these zodiacal tattwas. The following section lists the overall effects produced by stimulation of the planetary chakras, based on color. I have found them to be much more powerful and effective than those that base their correspondences on an eastern tradition—for example, the rainbow chakra meditation. The rainbow, in the western tradition, is in the body, not the chakras, or interior planets, as can be plainly deduced by studying the Tree. (It is in her discussion of the tattwas that Blavatsky says the prismatic or rainbow scale is "a false reflection, a true Maya" [1980, p. 398]).

The student should study the charts in figures A and B closely, concentrating on discovering their meaning, particularly the chart in figure 14–B. It is not a random arrangement of colors. Keep in mind the principles discussed earlier about complementary colors, and the hermetic principle, "As above, so below." What happens when they are done in this order? They also stimulate these corresponding colors.

The silver-white at the end is not really a chakra; it is the absent Daath. It corresponds to the shell or aura of the etheric body, and is visualized as surrounding all of the chakras, which are flashing in the shining colors attributed to them. As Alice Bailey said:

> Think of the etheric body as a shimmering body of light, a reflector of the conditions of all the other subtle bodies, and the network that connects to the physical body. It is here that we find the key.

❖ The Occult Uses of Color

In this section we will examine some of the reasoning behind this kind of occult use of sound and color, as well as how the planetary energies relate to the interior chakras. Examine the following associations:

Saturn/Indigo Ray: Corresponds to the first or root chakra; associated with the tone A; energy reservoir of the body, often called Kundalini; stimulates deliberation and concentration; also rules skeletal system; deficiency causes eccentric personality, inability of system to rid itself of wastes; it is the ray of introspection and the color that bridges the finite and the infinite.

Sun/Orange Ray: Corresponds to the heart chakra; tone D; a high energy state that is also somewhat relaxed; related to breathing and helpful in relief of pain; good for mental energy and recuperation from fatigue; excessive use can cause fevers; acts as a tonic; stimulates discrimination, guidance in making decisions; powerful for visualizing when healing others.

Mars/Red Ray: Corresponds to prostatic ganglion, also rules adrenals; tone C; active in motor centers of the brain, muscles, and reproductive system; used for depression, anemia, poor circulation, sluggishness, timidity; too much can cause agitation; stimulates energy, strength, activity, challenge.

Jupiter/Violet Ray: Corresponds to solar plexus; A sharp; a calming and soothing agent; directs sympathetic nervous system; acts as a cardiac depressant; connected to arteries, veins, sacral area of spine; acts as tonic to liver and mammary glands; stimulates lofty visions, transcendence, spiritual ideals; dissolves discord; also transformative, bestows patience in suffering.

Venus/Green Ray: Connected to throat chakra, thyroid, and parathyroids; tone F sharp; healer and harmonizer; builds vitality; good for headache and nervous tension; offers refreshment, pleasure, and balance; connected to emotions, love of beauty, and artistry; stimulates creative imagination; too much can cause emotional excess and sensation seeking.

Moon/Blue Ray: Connected to pituitary (brow) chakra; tone A flat; cooling and calming; good for inflammations, fevers, agitation; harmonizes certain physical conditions, especially related to rhythms in the body; organizing principle for all cells; center for telepathy; deficiency causes lack of coordination on cellular level as well as the psychic level; good for treating diseases of the skin and abnormal growths; stimulates retentive memory; too much causes over-sensitivity.

Mercury/Yellow Ray: Connected to pineal gland and cerebrum; tone E; cleanses and purifies entire nervous system; mental stimulant; assists in producing an important aid for digestion called chyle; also connected with longevity; deficiency can cause depression; excess can lead to indecision; stimulates alertness and positive thinking.

Pluto/Silver-White Ray: Connected to etheric-astral body; acts as transmitter to the great unknown; harmonizes all other chakras and brings them to point of transformation beyond the body and outside the world of concept and form. The silence of the great abyss. The highest point of awareness of consciousness as an individualized or separated consciousness.

Please note that they are given in the order in which they are to be stimulated.

If the student finds it frustrating that these relationships differ from another system he or she may be used to, then testing the tradition is in order. You can only find out what works best for you by trial and error. However, this system has been consistently tried and used experimentally for a good part of this century. The reason that some of the tones differ from those given in other esoteric schools—particular prior to the 20th century—is that international pitch has displaced the earlier use of concert pitch.

What used to be called concert pitch was not a sufficient enough standard for musical pitch because it varied too much from place to place. Sometimes old organs in Europe differed from one another by several semitones. According to the pitch used then (prior to the standardization of international pitch), the note marked middle C on our scale gave forth the sound we now call C sharp. In other words, the pitch has risen over time.

Therefore when Blavatsky says that green corresponds to F, it really means it corresponds to what we presently know as F sharp. Likewise red used to correspond to B; now we call it C. So those who reprint charts that follow some of those given in the older theosophical tradition are off simply because of this change in the notes, not because the tones themselves are different. They simply need to be adjusted to the standard we now use. The reason it is important to use a pitch pipe is that tones have a way of going off key in most instruments quite easily. This is why instruments have to be tuned.

Musical tones are very instrumental in creating the vibratory patterns of our reality. If sand is sprinkled on a glass plate attached to a vertical support and a violin bow is drawn across the edge of the plate, each different tone will produce a corresponding geometric pattern. The tattwas serve as excellent meditation mandalas because they comprise the basic elemental structures from which all other geometric forms are composed. These geometric forms are themselves limitless and are the determinants of all organic structure in the mineral, vegetable, and animal kingdoms. We can see the beautiful geometric shapes of a crystal with the naked eye and the intricate patterns of molecules and atoms with high-powered x-ray microscopes.

The permutations of these five basic tattwas can be related to combined influences of the elements and planets they represent, but are more arbitrary than the correspondences derived from working with the talismans in the first part of this book. What is most important is the relationship between the tones and the colors—the shapes simply are the containers for the combinations of these particular vibrations. They serve to hold the elemental vibration of the planet or zodiacal sign and they act as a focus of concentration so the color can be more vividly visualized in the after-image.

The planetary chakras can also arouse other emotional and mental states, and here are some of the findings of Mathers' (1971) work with the tattwas:

For help with memory: Saturn (Tau), called "Great One of the Night of Time."

For development of the imagination: Jupiter (Kaph) or Venus (Daleth).

To work on discernment of truth: Mercury (Beth).

For wandering mind, lack of focus: Mercury or moon (Gimel) (If unable to focus because of temptation, use Daleth).

To strengthen personal resolution: Mars (Peh), but use with caution.

In addition, Case gives some other uses:

For prosperity: Violet, Jupiter chakra, tone A sharp.

For establishing equitable settlements or to bring an end to disputes: Green, tattwa corresponding to Libra, tone F sharp.

For harmony in personal relationships: Orange, tattwa corresponding to Gemini, tone D.

For establishing deeper relationship with your H.G.A.: Blue, tattwa corresponding to Sagittarius, tone A flat.

For transcending rigid patterns of behavior: Red, Mars chakra, tone C.

Someone who has developed an excellent meditation system using the tattwas as representations of the Hebrew Letters and Tarot Archetypes is Emahmn. Many of his tattwas-symbols correspond to those given in this book, but for a complete examination of his tattwas and their relationships, see his wonderful *Book of Correspondences,* listed in the bibliography. He also has a nice set of Tattwas cards available for coloring. Here are some of the uses given in his *Book of Correspondences* for the seven planetary chakra tattwas:

Saturn: Used to develop understanding and comprehension, thoughtfulness, tolerance and temperance, and the ability to define, limit, and create.

Sun: Develops vitality and optimism, productivity and fertility, a warm and affectionate nature, and dignity and distinction.

Mars: Use for initiative and leadership, strength and courage, determination, willpower, foresight and keen reasoning.

Jupiter: Prosperity, generosity, expansiveness, self-confidence, happiness and fortune, higher comprehension, the ability to reach Akashic records.

Venus: Creativity and imagination, ability to visualize, healthy emotions and desires, artistic talent, appreciation of beauty.

Moon: Develops memory, elasticity and adaptability, and a calm and sedate nature.

Mercury: Intelligence, concentration, discernment, ability to communicate, self-respect, assertiveness, and mental quickness.

His tones, by the way, correspond to those given by Dr. Case.

I don't know if the early Golden Dawn magicians used tones in connection with the tattwas designs, but they certainly facilitate their usefulness, perhaps in an exponential way. Colors and sounds are themselves actual forces, not stagnant dead things in our world. They are very potent tools for the serious occult student. All ancient magical traditions have used sounds or mantras as part of their meditation practice, and the work of Dr. Hans Jenny, who developed a science known as cymatics, has visually demonstrated that oscillating frequencies in the audible range create patterns that mimic cellular division and spinal function.

We now know that energy is propagated through space in the form of electro-magnetic waves. The whole spectrum of electro-magnetic energy contains seventy or more octaves, beginning at one end with radio waves, which are very long, and on the other end with x-rays, gamma rays, and cosmic rays, which are very short. The sun's spectrum covers the relatively long waves of infrared light through visible light, to the shorter ultraviolet light waves. Many of these electromagnetic properties have found their way, through such modern technologies as x-rays, radium rays, and laser surgery, into doctor's offices and hospitals and are useful in diagnosing and treating disease.

Visible light is also of vital importance in the proper development of plant and animal life. Some studies have concluded that visible light penetrates the skulls of sheep, dogs and other mammals, and perhaps many internal organs as well. There is a good body of evidence that points to both the benefits and the hazards of certain kinds of light waves. For instance, prolonged exposure to pink light will cause rodents to die, plants will flourish under blue light but will not grow under green light, and blue light consistently reduces blood pressure in humans.

But modern science (especially in America) has neglected, for the most part, to develop the scientific inquiry of visible light (which composes about one-sixtieth of the electro-magnetic spectrum) in the same way it has invisible light waves. Part of this is that our post-Enlightenment age still regards many of these practices as superstitious; and used without other proper resources, or with too simple an esoteric formula, one may well draw some superstitious conclusions.

I personally do not believe that focus on the astrological associations linking the various parts of the body to specific colors is the most effective way to treat maladies arising in that body part, if the technique of meditating on the rainbow spectrum mentioned earlier in this chapter is separated from the whole. Even though the astrological correspondences are helpful in forming a variety of mental associations, it is not as simple as shining a red light on one's head for a headache or a blue light on the hip for arthritis or sciatica. In experimental studies, yellow has been shown to be more effective in treating arthritis, sciatica, or neuritis, followed by blue or violet light, and red is certainly not good to meditate on to relieve a headache.

The point in using these exercises as a holistic method of harmonizing the etheric and physical bodies is to use the whole spectrum so the combination of sound and color works on the whole body. We do not need to consciously understand what is working on what for the technique to be effective. Dr. Case never advocated shining colored lights on specific body parts; rather, he suggested immersing oneself in the color completely in the imagination through the after-image. In the case of the rainbow meditation or the chakra meditation, the whole body is infused with the desired color through the eyes and the imagination. This is an important distinction from attempting to direct color to a specific area.

Although traditional medicine presently refuses to direct sufficient attention to the curative properties of sound and color, there is a large body of accumulating evidence that much of what was thought by the ancient esoteric philosophers from Pythagoras to Paracelsus is beginning to bear fruit scientifically. It has been demonstrated that if a person is subjected to a given color for as little as five concentrated minutes, both his or her mental as well as muscular activity changes.

Used together, certain tones and colors can alter our behavior. The occult student should re-read the quote at the beginning of this chapter and heed it accordingly. Tansley was referring to subliminal programming, where light phenomenon has been used to influence the subconscious in a very systematic way for quite some time. One of the great benefits of doing the twenty minute meditation outlined here is that it cleanses and strengthens the etheric web, which is continually being assailed by our modern pollutants and technologies.

Numerous practitioners in the field of alternative medicine have incorporated various aspects of color therapy as an adjunct to their practice based on results of both laboratory experiments and their own research. What few have attempted to do, however, is combine the influences of sound vibration with light vibration.

I highly recommend that the student experiment with the method described here. Simple as it sounds, the combination of using these two electromagnetic frequencies together is a potent tool. Feel free to experiment with shades. There are, in esoteric theory, seven varying shades or "color notes" for each of the seven planetary colors. Only your own research will bear fruit meant specifically for you.

What I have found to be remarkably effective is to make the tape I described earlier and then play it through a good set of stereophonic earphones while doing the color meditation. Do this and eventually the associations between the colors and the tones become automatic. Soon you will only have to look at a certain color and you will begin to hear the internal tone that corresponds to it. I have found this to be an extremely effective way of working with the energies of the Tarot keys as well. The vibration of each Key also has its own frequency, and whenever I hear a tone in meditation, I check to see what Tarot key or chakra it corresponds to, because it usually signifies what kind of energy will be moving in my life within a short time. In other words, when the subconscious becomes well acquainted with the associations of various sounds and colors, it speaks back to us using this language. When the student has a good grasp of talismanic associations, many interesting techniques can be employed that will greatly enhance his or her Qabalistic work. The student will see that, done correctly, exercises with the tattwas helps develop the ability to see auras. Consistent work invariably proves this, but it must be remembered that the talismans themselves—no matter what variety—are only doors that when meditated on lead one inside, for this is where all true masters have said that we will find the Light of God.

The figures on pages 168–187 are tattwas that can be photocopied and colored for personal use, according to the color keys and designs given in figures 14–E and 14–F, on pages 166–167.

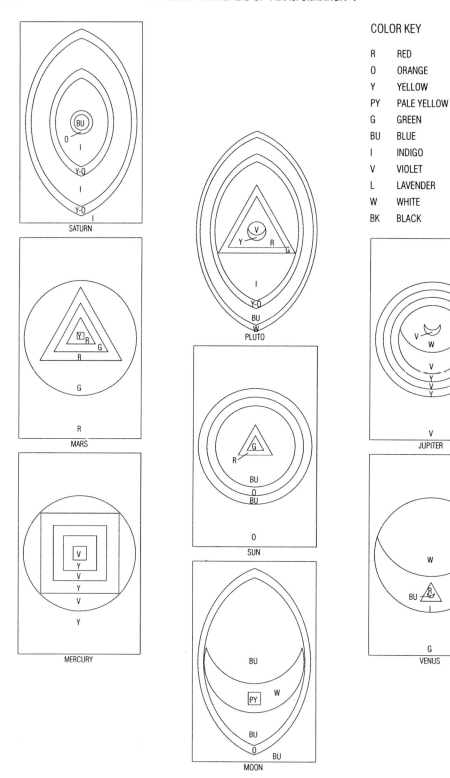

Figure 14–E

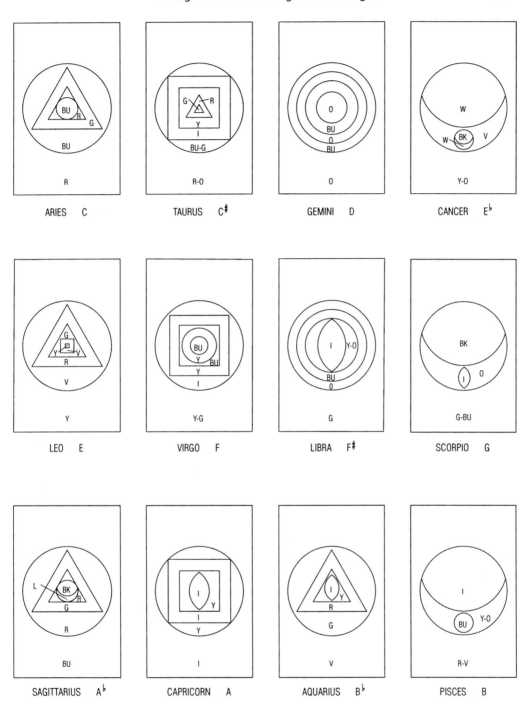

Figure 14–F

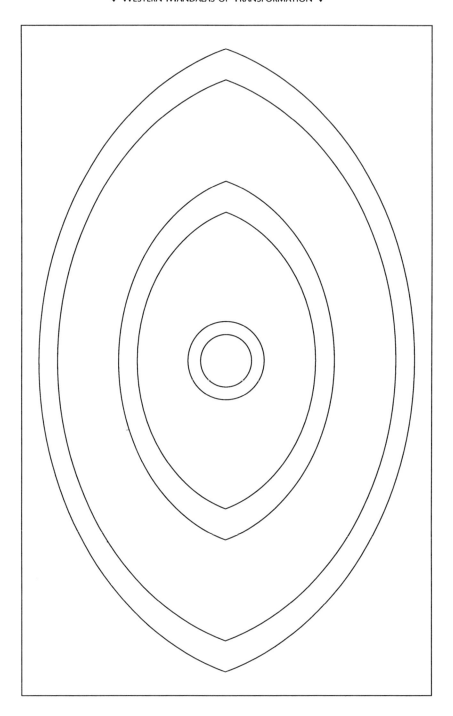

❖ Saturn ❖

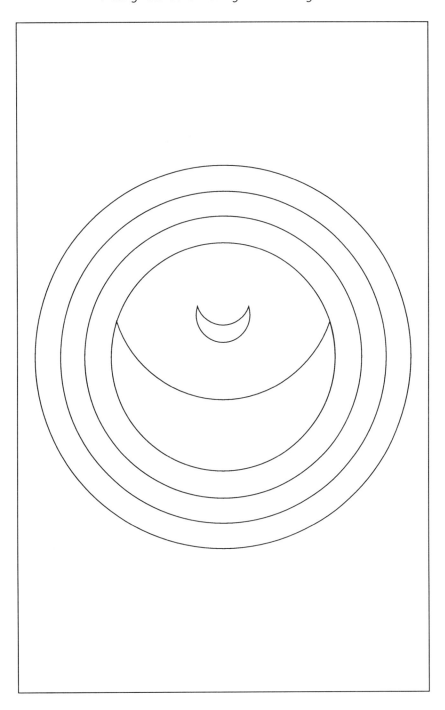

❖ Jupiter ❖

❖ Mars ❖

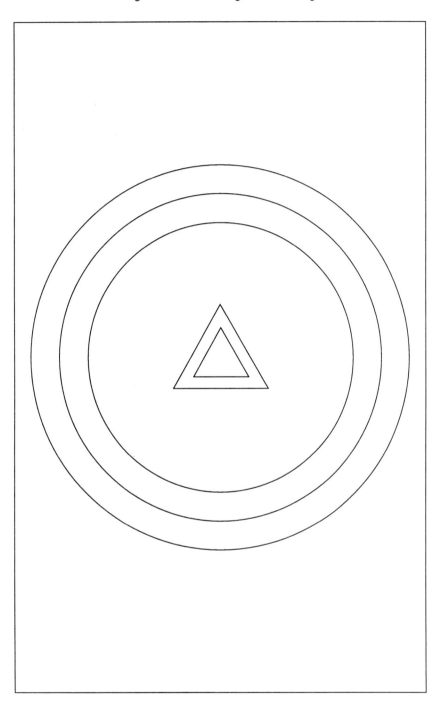

❖ Sun ❖

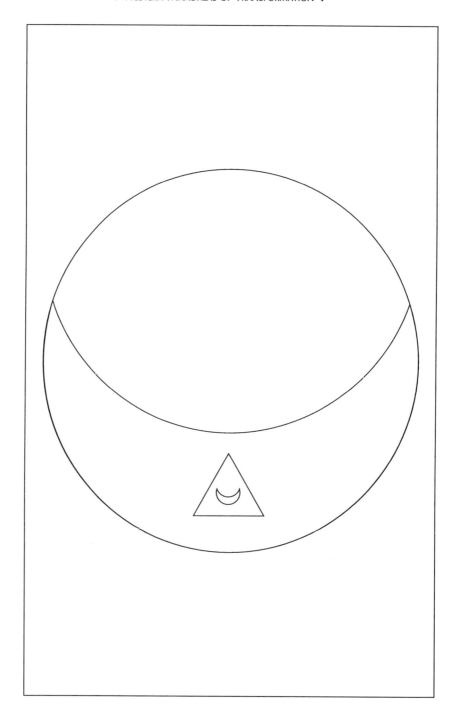

❖ Venus ❖

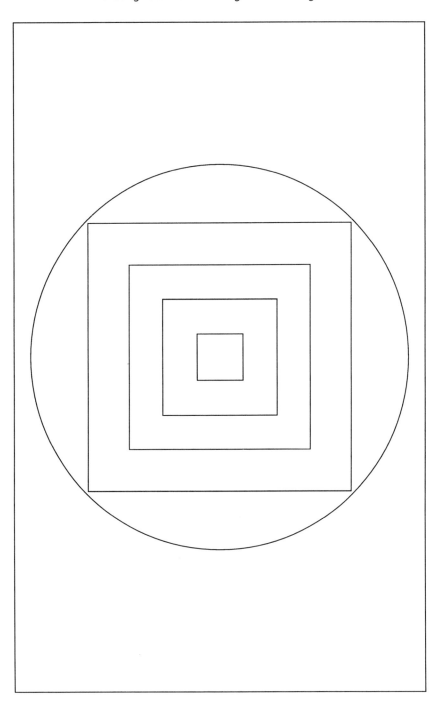

❖ **Mercury** ❖

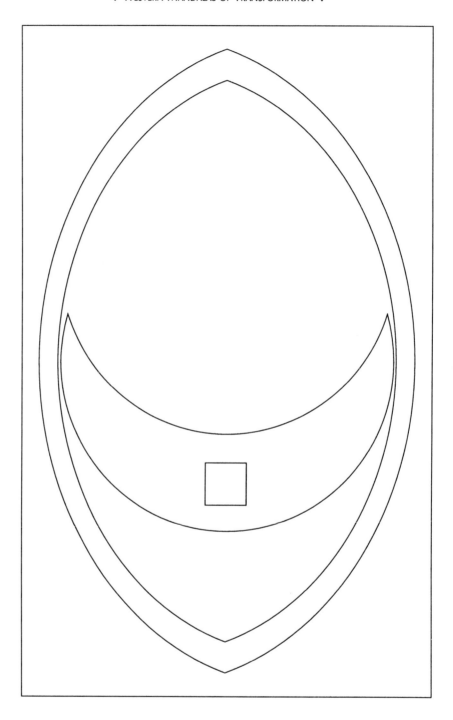

❖ **Moon** ❖

❖ Pluto ❖

❖ Aries—Tone: C ❖

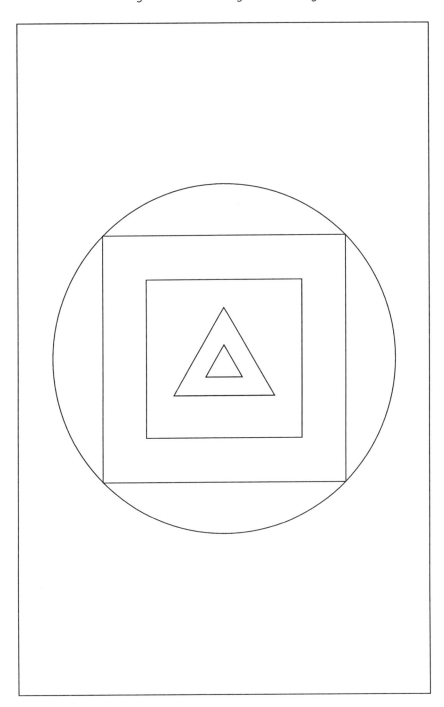

❖ **Taurus—Tone: C-sharp** ❖

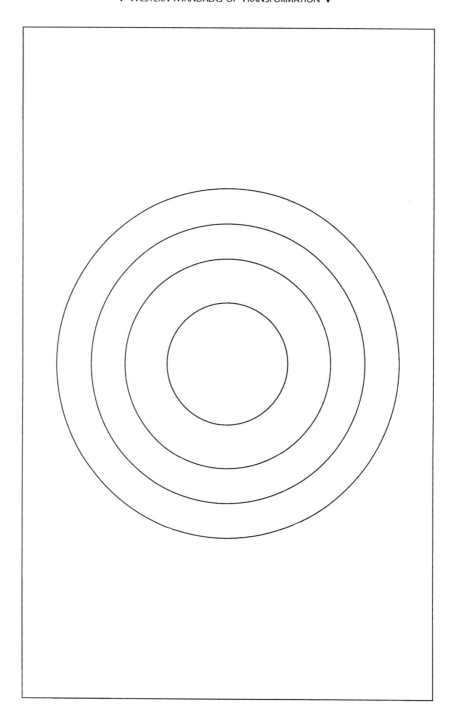

❖ Gemini—Tone: D ❖

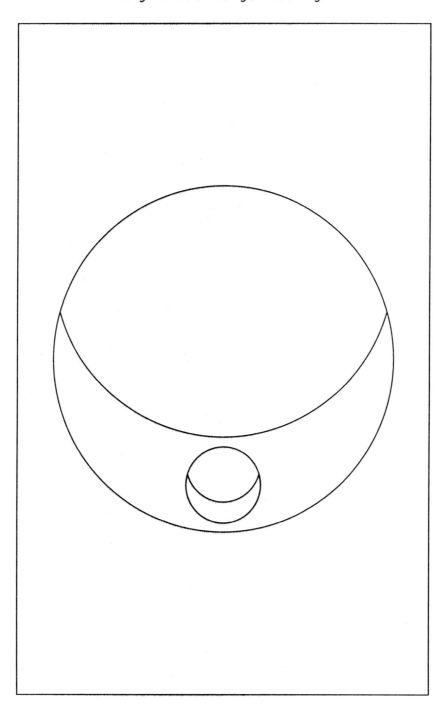

❖ **Cancer—Tone: E-flat** ❖

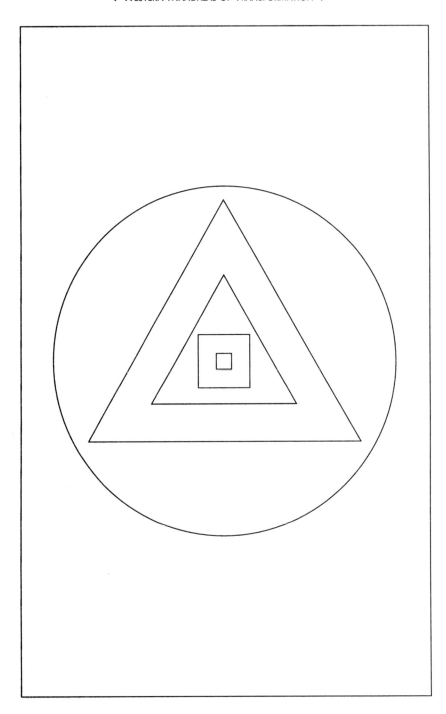

❖ Leo—Tone: E ❖

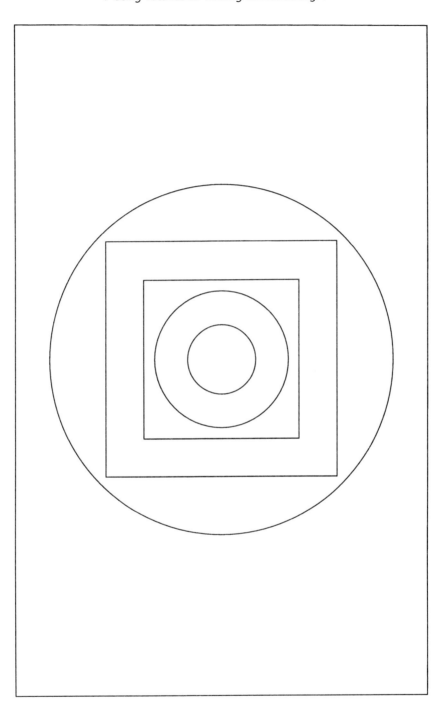

❖ Virgo—Tone: F ❖

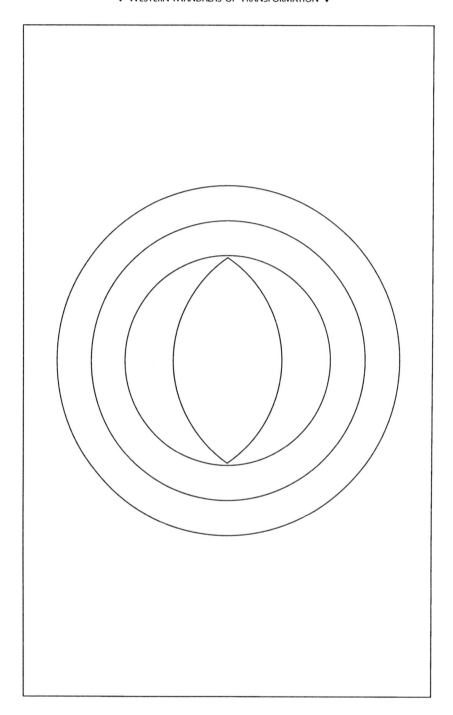

❖ **Libra—Tone: F-sharp** ❖

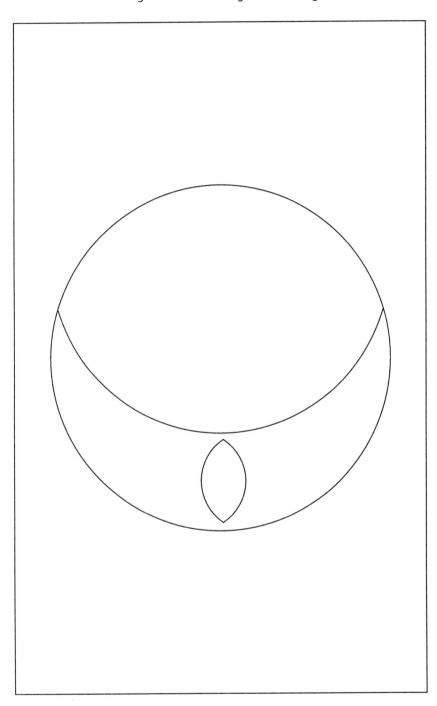

❖ **Scorpio—Tone: G** ❖

❖ Sagittarius—Tone: A-flat ❖

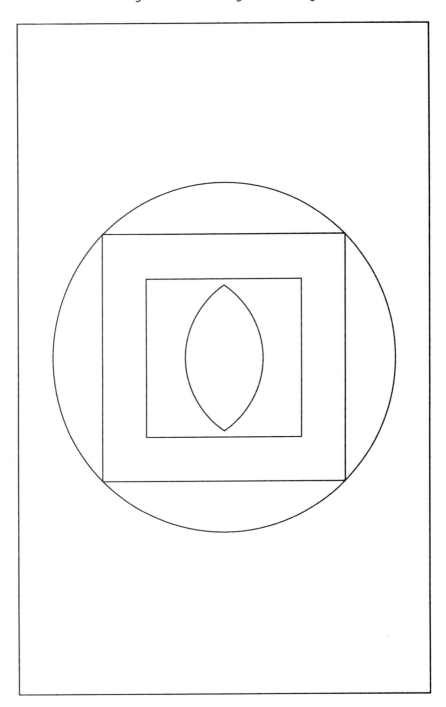

❖ **Capricorn—Tone: A** ❖

❖ **Aquarius—Tone: B-flat** ❖

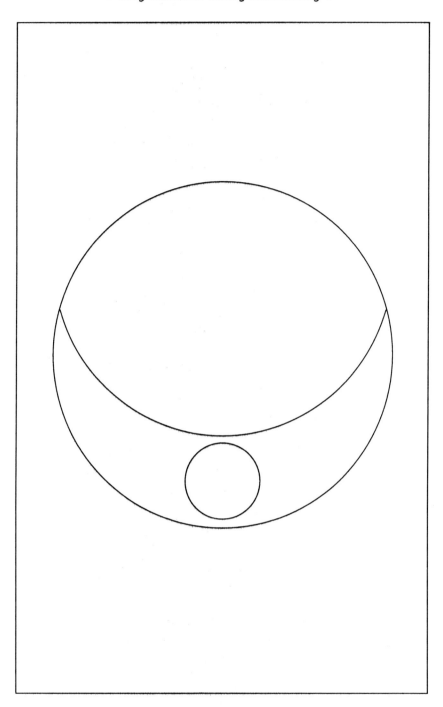

❖ **Pisces—Tone: B** ❖

Chapter 15

CONSECRATION

The following are suggestions for consecrating your finished talisman, as well as some incense recipes for fumigation. You may consecrate your piece any way you like; just follow the proper correspondences pertaining to the talisman (which the student should have a very good grasp of by this point) and use full consciousness and will. You may need to review sections of the first few chapters to make sure you have included all the necessary correspondences in your finished piece, and to explore whether you want to include elements like astrological timing and prayers. It is fine to compose your own prayers; for those who want to include consecration prayers or rituals that have been utilized in the Golden Dawn tradition, I highly recommend the books by Chic and Sandra Cicero, listed in the bibliography.

The primary elements important in consecration are meditation combined with color breathing, and fumigation with correct incense mixtures. I have grown my own herbal and other incense ingredients for many years, and I also pay attention to timing when harvesting. If you cannot use ingredients that you personally harvest, make sure you buy them from someone whose herbs and incenses are as pure as possible. Use essences instead of fragrances for oils, and buy in bulk if you can (*i.e.*, loose herbs, flowers). The more the incense is commercially packaged, the less the essence of the spirit is still present. Some gums and oils are only available in foreign countries; in that case you may need to order them from a good supplier.

To begin: Place the talisman in the center of a triangle. This may be one created by you in the astral world, *i.e.*, created in your imagination, or you may actually draw it or mark it in a part of the room, perhaps using three stones.

Close your eyes and try to cease your thoughts, clearing your mind of anything except your present purpose (to consecrate) and intention (relating to the talisman). Take several deep breaths to cleanse your thought field, and when sufficiently relaxed, begin to imagine the color you are charging the talisman with in your aura.

The color corresponding to the talisman is determined by the particular planetary seal, or else by the color most appropriate to the angel or vibration you are working with, if doing a talisman of a Name (as explained in chapter thirteen). Determine the numerical vibration in harmony with your purpose—for example, six, yellow, and the Sun. Breathe in deeply and steadily for a count of six and visualize yourself gathering the color you need. Hold for a count of six, and while you do, see the color yellow flooding through your whole being. Then, when breathing out, visualize the color yellow filling your aura and the aura of the talisman you are infusing with your power.

After doing this for an appropriate number of breaths, in this case, six or a multiple of six (twelve, if you wish to do it longer), then perform the second part of the exercise, specifically done to charge the talisman. Open your eyes and with outstretched hands, gather in an imaginary ball of yellow light with one sweeping gesture, ending with closed hands together, as in a gesture of prayer. Then rub your hands together rapidly, which will generate a feeling of warmth and energy. Imagine you are generating yellow sparks of electric light with each second you rub your hands together; after about ten seconds, hold your hands over the talisman itself, infusing it with your energy and intention. You may have a tingling sensation in your fingers as you imagine streams of yellow light permeating the aura of the talisman itself. Finish by actually running your fingertips lightly over the whole talisman, firmly repeating your purpose and chanting clearly the God-names and spirit-names on the talisman itself. Finally, pass the talismanic image through the incense compound that has been prepared ahead of time. You may refer to the incenses attributed to specific planets from the chart in figure B on page 26 (see chapter three) and the chart in figure E on page 17 (see chapter two) for construction of angelic or other names using incenses. It is always exciting to mix your own blend (check the chart in figure H on page 33 in chapter three for best times), but here are some time-honored magical planetary mixtures:

❖ Saturn:

1. Myrrh gum or resin, Cypress (wood or oil), Rue oil (one drop), Violet flowers, Pine

2. Storax gum, Elm wood, Musk, Civit, Cassia

3. Mandrake root, Henbane, Musk, Scammony resin, Civit

❖ Jupiter

1. Copal gum, Cedar wood, Hyssop, Orris root

2. Galbanum gum, Saffron, Ash or oak wood, Poplar leaves, Cinquefoil

❖ Mars

1. Benzoin, Dragon's blood resin, Helleborne root, Pepper, or Tobacco

2. Pine wood, Holly, dried Absinthe, Sulfur (pinch), Galangal

❖ Sun

1. Saffron, Aloeswood, Wood of Balsam, Ambergris oil

2. Cinnamon, Frankincense, Yellow Sandalwood, Heliotrope flowers

3. Laurel, Cloves, Frankincense, Acacia flowers, Vanilla

❖ Venus

1. Benzoin, Red Sandalwood, Nutmeg, Damiana, Rose

2. Lign Aloes, Myrtle, Mint or Verbena, Galbanum, Rose

❖ Mercury

1. Mace, Vervain, Clove, Storax

2. Marjoram, Aspen, Lime flowers, Lemon peel

3. Lavender, Mastic, Narcissis, Bayberry

❖ Moon

1. Camphor, Jasmine, Olibanum, Onycha

2. An Artemesia (preferably wormwood), White Sandalwood, Lign Aloes, Ylang-Ylang oil

3. White Poppy, Galbanum, Gardenia, Lotus

❖ Pluto

1. Dragon's Blood, Mandrake, Benzoin, Dittany of Crete, Sulphur

2. Tears of Olibanum, Red Storax, Lign Aloes, Myrrh

A word of caution as well as encouragement: mandalas are to be meditated on. They don't hang on your wall and make magic. The talismans in this book were primarily devised to help you unlock doors to the Source inside of you that is the Reservoir of Light and Truth. Use them for this purpose and they will never become invested with the power to possess you.

Remember, never use the techniques of talisman creation to harm another of God's creatures. You must align yourself with the highest good to be an effective occultist, or disaster will result. If followed correctly, much of the information in this book can connect you with great sources of power. One of the great affirmations of the *Pattern on the Trestleboard* is, "All the power that ever was or will be is here now." You can be a center of expression for it, if your will has been sufficiently purified.

I would like to close with a quote by the first Golden Dawn chief, S. L. Mathers, who once said:

> To establish closer and more personal relations with the Lord Jesus, the Master of masters, is, and ever must be, the ultimate object of the teachings of our Order... The powers we teach our disciples to use are bestowed by Him according to His promise (1971, p. 213).

—*A. L. : Aktrial pro Logos*

✤ APPENDIX ✤

A magic square, or kamea, is a square array of numbers in which all the numbers in every vertical column, horizontal row, and corner-to-corner diagonal add up to the same sum. Figure A shows a third-order magic square, *i.e.*, a square with three cells along each side. A fourth-order magic square has four cells along each side, and so on.

There is only one third-order magic square. The numbers in the 3x3 square can be rotated and mirrored to make it seem as though there are more than one third-order square, but the rotated and mirrored versions are not counted as different, because the numbers maintain the same relationship to each other independent of whether the square is set on its head or its side or viewed from behind. There are 880 magic squares of the fourth-order, not counting rotated and mirrored versions. Perhaps more surprising, French mathematicians in the seventeenth century were able to construct 549,504 different fifth-order squares, and it is theorized that more than 13,000,000 are possible (Fults 1979).

Such large numbers may seem staggering and even unbelievable until we bring them into perspective. In a 4x4 square, for example, how many different arrangements of the numbers one through sixteen are possible, whether they form magic squares or not? Let us begin with an empty 4x4 square. The number one can be placed in any one of the cells, so there are sixteen possible locations for one. The number two can be placed in any one of the remaining cells not occupied by one, so there are fifteen possible locations for two.

4	9	2
3	5	7
8	1	6

Figure A

The number three can be placed in any one of the remaining cells not occupied by one or two, so there are fourteen possible locations for three, and so on for all the numbers up to fifteen. Finally, there will be only one empty cell left for sixteen to occupy. Therefore, the number of different arrangements of the numbers one through sixteen in a 4x4 square is: 16x15x14x13x12x. . .x3x2x1=20,922,789,888,000 approximately. Dividing this number by eight to discount rotations and mirrorings gives us 2,615,348,736,000. Now, with such a large number of possible arrangements, it is not too difficult to believe that 880 of them are magical. The same procedure yields similar results for fifth-order magic squares.

Obviously, the traditional kameas selected by Agrippa are not the only possible kameas of the fourth through ninth orders. On the other hand, when we trace their theosophic extensions, few kameas produce planetary seals which are endowed with beauty and symmetry. The seals and flashing color tablets we have chosen for Mars and the Sun are based on fifth and sixth-order kameas which are different from Agrippa's. The reason for our choice is the beauty, symmetry, and power of their designs.

When considered in terms of their construction, magic squares are divided into three major categories: odd-order, double-even-order, and single-even-order. Along each side of an odd-order magic square there are an odd number of cells, such as three, five, and seven. Along each side of a double-even-order magic square there are an even number of cells, which can be divided evenly by four, such as four, eight, and twelve. Along each side of a single-even-order magic square there are an even number of cells, which can be divided evenly by two but not by four, such as six, ten, and fourteen.

Odd-order magic squares are relatively easy to construct. The traditional kameas of Agrippa are generated by the following rule: Begin by placing one in the cell directly below the center cell of the square (figure B). The rest of the numbers follow in order, i.e., two, three, four, etc., and are placed diagonally one cell down and one cell to the right of the cell occupied by the previous number. For example, two is placed diagonally one cell down and one cell to the right of the cell occupied by one. The next number, three, should be placed diagonally one cell down and one cell to the right of the cell occupied by two, but two is on the bottom edge of the square, so there is no cell for three to be placed in. Since the magic square has edges, the rule for generating it says that if the numbers run off the bottom of the square, put them at the top instead: three is still placed one cell to the right of two, but it is placed in the top cell of the vertical column. The next number, four, should be placed diagonally one cell down and one cell to the right of three, but three is on the right edge of the square, so there is no cell for four to be placed in. When the numbers run off the right side of the square in this manner, put them on the left side instead: four is still placed one cell below three, but it is

11	24	7	20	3
4	12	25	8	16
17	5	13	21	9
10	18	1	14	22
23	6	19	2	15

Figure B

placed in the far-left column. The number five is placed diagonally one cell down and one cell to the right of four. The number one occupies the cell that six should go in. When this situation occurs, place the number two cells below the cell occupied by the previous number. In this case, place the number six two cells below the cell that is occupied by the number five. The rest of the magic square can be generated by following the rule as described, except for one other special situation: the diagonal from the upper left to the lower right corner, numbers eleven through fifteen. The next number in the series, in this case sixteen, is placed two cells down from the top of the far-right column. This rule will generate all of Agrippa's odd-order magic squares: 3x3, 5x5, 7x7, and 9x9.

There are other rules, similar to this one, which will also generate odd ordered magic squares of any size. Some of these other rules, which may have been known to Agrippa, begin by placing one along an outer edge of the square. It is pure speculation on my part, but one reason Agrippa may have chosen the rule described above is that it places one as near to the center as possible. The numbers whirl round and pass through the center, and the final number returns to the center: This is suggestive of an individual's spiritual journey.

The image of numbers whirling round the center is enhanced by conceiving of the magic square as being constructed in a different manner, but by the same rule. We imagine that the magic square is rolled up to form a cylinder (like paper towels are rolled up to form a cylinder): first horizontally, so that the top edge of the square wraps around and just touches the bottom edge; and then vertically, so that the left edge of the square wraps around and just touches the right edge. We begin, as before, by placing one in the cell immediately below the center cell. We place the number two diagonally one cell down and one cell to the right of one. Then, by imagining that the top row of cells is wrapped around so it is below the bottom row of cells, three can be placed diagonally one cell down and one cell to the right of two. Next, by imagining that the left column of cells is wrapped around so it is to the right of the right column of cells, four can be placed diagonally one cell down and one cell to the right of three. We can imagine the numbers continuing in this manner, whirling round and round the center, until their final return.

In chapter seven (see figures B, F, and K), we show an alternative to Agrippa's traditional kamea for our flashing color tablet of Mars. The alternative kamea, taken from Andrews (1917), produces a fiery pattern that conveys the Mars energy more powerfully than Aggripa's. Unlike the traditional kamea, the alternative is generated by following the moves of a knight (the chess piece) as it progresses from cell to cell within the square. Mars is the god of war, and a knight is a warrior. Thus, even the rule generating the alternative square is related to Mars.

In chess, the knight's move resembles the shape of a capital L: In a single move, a knight moves two squares in one direction, and one square at right angles to the first direction. For example, in a single move a knight can jump two squares forward and one square to the right of its original position.

10	18	1	14	22
11	24	7	20	3
17	5	13	21	9
23	6	19	2	15
4	12	25	8	16

Figure C

4	3	2	1
8	7	6	5
12	11	10	9
16	15	14	13

Figure D

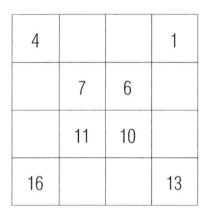

Figure E

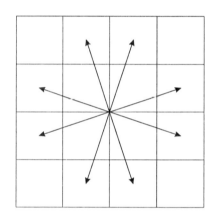

Figure F

To generate the alternative kamea, begin by placing the number one in the center cell of the top row as shown in figure C. The next number, in this case two, is placed two cells up, and one cell to the right of the number preceding it. Since one is in the top row, there are no squares above it in which to place two. In this situation we follow the same general scheme as explained above: If the numbers run off the top of the square, we imagine the bottom edge of the square wrapped around to touch the top edge; if the numbers run off the right side of the square, we imagine the left edge of the square wrapped around to touch the right edge. Following this scheme, the number two is placed in the second row up from the lower edge of the square, and one cell to the right of the number one. The next move of the knight places the number three two cells above and one cell to the right of the number two. The knight continues to advance two cells up and one cell to the right with every move. With a little experimentation and study of figure C, the reader will be able to construct the entire Mars kamea generated by the knight's move.

4	14	15	1
9	7	6	12
5	11	10	8
16	2	3	13

Figure G

Figure H

8	7	6	5	4	3	2	1
16	15	14	13	12	11	10	9
24	23	22	21	20	19	18	17
32	31	30	29	28	27	26	25
40	39	38	37	36	35	34	33
48	47	46	45	44	43	42	41
56	55	54	53	52	51	50	49
64	63	62	61	60	59	58	57

Figure I

8			5	4			1
	15	14			11	10	
	23	22			19	18	
32			29	28			25
40			37	36			33
	47	46			43	42	
	55	54			51	50	
64			61	60			57

Figure J

Double-even order magic squares are perhaps the easiest to construct. As described by Andrews, the first step is to write the numbers in order (one, two, three, etc.) beginning with one in the top, left cell and progressing to the right and down, row by row, until all the cells are filled. However, Agrippa used Hebrew letter-numbers which read from right to left. So, to construct the traditional kameas, we begin in the upper right cell and progress to the left and down. In figure D the fourth order square is shown at this stage of construction. All the numbers in the cells of the corner-to-corner diagonals are now in place, as shown in figure E. In order to complete the square, all the other numbers are simply mirrored across the center, as indicated by the arrows in figure F. The completed traditional kamea of Jupiter is shown in figure G.

Larger double-even order magic squares require a little more effort to construct. Figure H shows a checkerboard pattern composed of shaded and white squares. Each of the squares contains four cells. Within the checkerboard there are three heavily outlined concentric squares: one is 4x4 cells, one is 8x8, and one is 12x12. To construct Mercury's

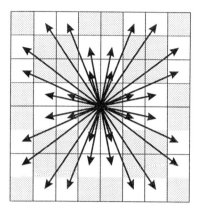

Figure K

8	58	59	5	4	62	63	1
49	15	14	52	53	11	10	56
41	23	22	44	45	19	18	48
32	34	35	29	28	38	39	25
40	26	27	37	36	30	31	33
17	47	46	20	21	43	42	24
9	55	54	12	13	51	50	16
64	2	3	61	60	6	7	57

Figure L

6	5	4	3	2	1
12	11	10	9	8	7
18	17	16	15	14	13
24	23	22	21	20	19
30	29	28	27	26	25
36	35	34	33	32	31

Figure M

6					1
	11			8	
		16	15		
		22	21		
	29			26	
36					31

Figure N

eighth order kamea, write the numbers in order from one to sixty-four, beginning in the upper, right corner of the 8x8 heavily outlined square (see figure I). All the numbers in the shaded squares of the checkerboard are in their correct positions (see figure J). All the numbers in the white squares need to be mirrored across the center as indicated by the arrows in figure K. The result is Mercury's traditional kamea as shown in figure L. For those interested in constructing larger magic squares, the checkerboard pattern and this process can be extended indefinitely to 12x12, 16x16, etc.

Single-even order magic squares are the most difficult to construct. The first step in constructing the traditional 6x6 kamea of the Sun is the same used in constructing the double-even order magic squares, described above. Beginning in the upper, right cell and progressing to the left and down, write the numbers in order from one to thirty-six, as shown in figure M. The numbers along the diagonals (shaded cells) are in their correct locations (see figure N). All the other numbers must be mirrored across the center, as indicated by the arrows in figure O. The result is shown in figure P. At this point, using

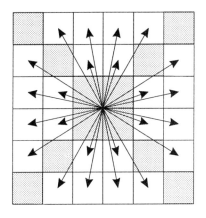

6	32	33	34	35	1
25	11	27	28	8	30
19	20	16	15	23	24
13	14	22	21	17	18
7	29	9	10	26	12
36	2	3	4	5	31

Figure O   *Figure P*

empirical methods, it is possible to determine that all the numbers in the shaded cells (which are laid out symmetrically relative to the corner-to-corner diagonal, one through thirty-six) are in their proper locations. The next step requires inspection and attention to detail. In figure P, a heavy cross divides the square into four quarters. By inspecting the numbers in the unshaded cells, we discover that some are arrayed symmetrically across the heavy, horizontal center line. They are: twenty-five through seven, twenty through fourteen, and thirty-three through three. The remaining numbers in the unshaded cells are arrayed symmetrically across the heavy, vertical center line. They are: thirteen through eighteen, nine through ten, and two through five. When both of the numbers in each of the symmetrical pairs are mirrored over to their counterpart's location, the result is Agrippa's kamea (see figure Q).

The theosophic extension produced by Agrippa's sixth-order kamea is intense, but it is not symmetric, harmonic, or beautiful. In fact, of the three categories of magic squares, those of the single-even order are the least likely to be symmetrical. This is due, at least in part, to their largely empirical construction. Although some can be constructed by fol-

lowing completely mechanical procedures, most cannot. It is curious that the only single-even order kamea on the Tree is at its center, the Sun: symbol of an enlightened consciousness which can be attained only through our developing higher mental abilities. These same abilities are needed, at least to some small degree, in the construction of the Sun's kamea—which cannot be created by rote. Following mechanical procedures cannot raise one's consciousness to the level of the Sun. Thus, the largely non-mechanical construction of a single-even order magic square is not misplaced in assigning a 6x6 kamea to the sixth Sephirah.

6	32	3	34	35	1
7	11	27	28	8	30
19	14	16	15	23	24
18	20	22	21	17	13
25	29	10	9	26	12
36	5	33	4	2	31

Figure Q

Although the kamea we have chosen for the Sun does not produce a symmetrical seal and flashing color tablet, its lack of symmetry is offset by its dynamism. Used in meditation, the flashing color tablet derived from figure F in chapter eight (see page 101) is very powerful, producing a moving, spinning effect; although the underlying square is only semi-magical, *i.e.*, the diagonals do not add up to 111. The fully magical square of the same basic design (see Andrews) is less symmetrical, but in meditation it has its own dynamic effect, appearing active in three dimensions as shown in chapter eight (see figure K on page 102).

Dynamism is an appropriate attribute of the Solar seal. Vibratory forces come from all sides of the Tree toward the center. The Sun must be in tune with all these disparate entities in order to balance them. To be in tune with all of the Planets, as well as the Moon, the Galaxy, and the Primordial Point, the Solar vibration must be complex in its Beauty. Like Bach's polyphonic "Musical Offering," it must sing several separate songs simultaneously, even as in superposition the songs coalesce in a singular masterpiece.

—Lloyd Nygaard

✤ BIBLIOGRAPHY ✤

Agrippa von Nettesheim, Heinrich Cornelius. *La Philosophie Occulte*. Edited and translated by F. Gaboriau, based on the Levasseur translation (1727) from the series "Les Classiques de l'occultisme." Paris: Editions Traditionnelles, 1962.

———. *Three Books of Occult Philosophy*. Edited by Willis Whitehead. NY: Samuel Weiser, 1971.

———. *Of Occult Philosophy: Magical Ceremonies, Book 4*. Edited and translated by Robert Turner. Gillette, NJ: Heptangle Books. 1985.

———. *De Occulta Philosophia*. Ed. by Perrone Compagne. NY: E. J. Brill, 1992.

———. *De Occulta Philosophia: Libre Tres*. Colonias, 1533. (Microfilm: Biblioteca Apostolica Vatican L.IX 39)

Albertus, Frater. *Seven Rays of the QBL*. York Beach, ME: Samuel Weiser, 1985.

Andrews, W. S. *Magic Squares and Cubes*. Chicago: Open Court Publishing, 1917.

Anonymous. *Meditations on the Tarot*. Rockport, MA: Element Books, 1985.

Babbitt, Edward. *The Principles of Light and Color*. NY: University Books, Inc., 1967.

Bagnall, O. *The Origin and Properties of the Human Aura*. York Beach, ME: Samuel Weiser, 1975.

Bailey, Alice. *Letters on Occult Meditation*. NY: Lucis, 1948.

———. *Esoteric Healing*. NY: Lucis, 1979.

Bardon, Franz. *The Practice of Magical Evocation*. Wuppertal, West Germany: Dreter Ruggeberg, 1991.

Barrett, Francis. *The Magus*. Secaucus, NJ: Citadel Press, 1967.

Bennet, Alan. "A Note on Genesis." *Equinox*, Vol. 1, No. 2. NY: Samuel Weiser, 1972.

Benson, William, and Oswald Jacobs. *New Recreations with Magic Squares*. NY: Dover, 1976.

Ben-Yehuda's English-Hebrew, Hebrew-English Dictionary. NY: Pocket Books, 1964.

Blavatsky, H. P. *A Synthesis of Science and Religion.* Wheaton, Ill.: Theosophical Publishing House, 1980.

Case, Paul Foster. *The Book of Tokens.* Los Angeles: Builders of the Adytum, 1934.

———. *The Tarot.* Richmond, VA: Macoy, 1947.

———. *The True and Invisible Rosicrucian Order.* York Beach, ME: Samuel Weiser, 1985.

Cicero, Chic and Sandra Tabatha Cicero. *The New Golden Dawn Ritual Tarot.* St. Paul, MN: Llewellyn, 1991.

———. *Secrets of a Golden Dawn Temple.* St. Paul, MN: Llewellyn, 1992.

Compton, M. C. *Archetypes on the Tree of Life.* St. Paul, MN: Llewellyn, 1991.

Conway, David. *Magic: An Occult Primer.* NY: E. P. Dutton & Co., 1973.

Critchlow, Keith. *Islamic Patterns: An Analytical and Cosmological Approach.* NY: Thames & Hudson, 1976.

Davis, Paul. *The Mind of God.* NY: Simon & Schuster, 1992.

d'Olivet, Fabre. *The Hebrew Tongue Restored.* Translated by Nanyan Redfield. NY: G. P. Putnam's, 1921.

Emahmn. *The Book of Correspondences.* Raleigh, NC: Emahmn, 1991.

Falkner, Edward. *Games, Ancient and Oriental, and How to Play Them.* NY: Dover, 1961 (republished from 1892 edition, unabridged).

Fidler, David. *Jesus Christ Sun of God: Ancient Cosmology and Early Christian Symbolism.* Wheaton, IL: Quest Books, 1993.

Fortune, Dion. *The Mystical Qabalah.* York Beach, ME: Samuel Weiser, 1984.

Frater U. D. *Practical Sigil Magic.* St. Paul, MN: Llewellyn, 1991.

Fults, J. L. *Magic Squares.* La Salle, IL: Open Court, 1979.

Gimbel, Theo. *Healing Through Color.* Essex, England: C. W. Daniel Co., 1980.

Godwin, David. *Godwin's Cabalistic Encyclopedia: A Complete Guide to Cabalistic Magick.* St. Paul, MN: Llewellyn, 1989.

Goethe, Johann W. von. *Theory of Colour.* Boston: M. I. T. Press, 1970.

Gray, William. *The Talking Tree.* York Beach, ME: Samuel Weiser, 1977.

———. *The Ladder of Lights.* Dallas: Sangreal Foundation, 1968.

Hessey, Dodson. *Color in the Treatment of Diseases.* London: Rider & Co., 1966.

Heline, Corine. *Healing and Regeneration Through Color.* Marina del Rey, CA: DeVorss, 1987.

Huntley, H. E. *The Divine Proportion.* New York: Dover Publications, Inc., 1970.

Jonas, Hans. *The Gnostic Religion.* Boston: Beacon Press, 1963.

Joy, Brugh. *Joy's Way.* Los Angeles: J. P. Tarcher, Inc., 1979.

Karagulla, Shafica. *Breakthrough to Creativity.* Santa Monica, CA: De Vorss, 1969.

Kilner, Walter. *The Human Aura.* NY: University Books, 1965.

Knight, Gareth. *A Practical Guide to Qabalistic Symbolism.* Vol. 1. Toddington, Cheltenham: Helios Books, 1965.

Knorr von Rosenroth, Christian. *Kabbala Denudata.* Vol. 1 and 2. Hildesheim and NY: Georg Olms Verlag, 1974. (Reprint of Abrahami Lichtenthaleri edition, Sulzbaci, 1677).

Levi, Eliphas. *Transcendental Magic.* Translated by Arthur E. Waite. York Beach, ME: Samuel Weiser, 1972.

Locks, Gutman. *The Spice of Torah—Gematria.* NY: Judaica Press, 1985.

Marks, R. W. *The New Mathematics Dictionary and Handbook.* New York: Bantam Books, 1964.

Mathers, S. L. MacGregor. *Astral Projection, Ritual Magic and Alchemy.* Edited by Francis King. London: Neville Spearman, 1971.

———. *The Book of the Sacred Magic of Abramelin, the Mage.* NY: Dover Pub. 1975.

———, trans. *The Kabbalah Unveiled.* York Beach, ME: Samuel Weiser, 1983.

———, trans. *The Key of Solomon the King.* York Beach, ME: Samuel Weiser, 1989.

Michell, John. *Dimensions of Paradise.* London: Harper & Row, 1988.

———. *View Over Atlantis.* NY: Ballantine Books, 1969.

Ophiel. *The Art and Practice of Talismanic Magic.* York Beach, ME: Samuel Weiser, 1979.

———. *The Art and Practice of Caballa Magic.* NY: Samuel Weiser, 1977.

Nowotny, K. A. "The Construction of Certain Seals and Characteristics in the Work of Agrippa of Nettesheim." *Journal of Warburg Institute,* XII. London, 1949, pp. 46-57.

Ousley, S. G. *The Science of the Aura.* London: Fowler & Co., 1949.

Pixley, O. *The Armour of Light.* Toddington, Cheltenham: Helios Books, 1971.

Regardie, Israel. "The Art of True Healing." *Foundations of Practical Magic.* Wellingborough, Northamptonshire: Aquarian Press, 1979.

———. *The Complete Golden Dawn System of Magic.* Phoenix, Arizona: Falcon Press. 1984.

———. *Garden of Pomegranates.* St. Paul, MN: Llewellyn, 1985.

———. *The Golden Dawn,* Vol. 3 and 4. River Falls, WI: Hazel Hills Corp., 1970.

———. *How to Make and Use Talismans.*Wellingborough, Northamptonshire: The Aquarian Press. 1981.

———. *The Middle Pillar.* St Paul, MN: Llewellyn, 1970.

Richards, G. *The Chain of Life.* Rustington: L. Speight, Ltd. 1954.

Schubert, Hermann. *Mathematical Essays and Recreations.* Translated by Thomas McCormack. Chicago: Open Court Pub., 1899.

Simon, W. *Mathematical Magic.* New York: Charles Scribner's Sons, 1964.

Steinbrecher, Edward. *Inner Guide Meditation.* Sante Fe, New Mexico: Blue Feather Press, 1978.

Stenring, Knut, trans. *Sefer Yetzirah.* NY: KTAV Publishing House, 1970.

Tansley, David. *Subtle Body: Essence and Shadow.* London: Thames & Hudson, 1977.

Vince, Leo. *Talismans, Amulets, and Charms.* London: Regency Press, 1977.

Waite, A. E. *The Book of Ceremonial Magic.* New Hyde Park, NY: University Books Press, 1961.

———. *The Holy Kabbalah: A Study of the Secret Tradition of Israel.* New Hyde Park, NY: University Books, 1960.

Stay in Touch

On the following pages you will find listed, with their current prices, some of the books now available on related subjects. Your book dealer stocks most of these and will stock new titles in the Llewellyn series as they become available. We urge your patronage.

To Get a Free Catalog

You are invited to write for our bi-monthly news magazine and catalog, *Llewellyn's New Worlds of Mind and Spirit*. A sample copy is free, and it will continue coming to you at no cost as long as you are an active mail customer. Or you may subscribe for just $10 in the United States and Canada ($20 overseas, first class mail). Many bookstores also have *New Worlds* available to their customers. Ask for it.

In *New Worlds* you will find news and features about new books, tapes and services; announcements of meetings and seminars; helpful articles; author interviews and much more. Write to:

Llewellyn's New Worlds of Mind and Spirit
P.O. Box 64383-170, St. Paul, MN 55164-0383, U.S.A.

To Order Books and Tapes

If your book store does not carry the titles described on the following pages, you may order them directly from Llewellyn by sending the full price in U.S. funds, plus postage and handling (see below).

Credit card orders: VISA, MasterCard, American Express are accepted. Call toll-free in the USA and Canada at 1-800-THE-MOON.

Special Group Discount: Because there is a great deal of interest in group discussion and study of the subject matter of this book, we offer a 20% quantity discount to group leaders or agents. Our Special Quantity Price for a minimum order of five copies of *Western Mandalas of Transformation* is $79.80 cash-with-order. Include postage and handling charges noted below.

Postage and Handling: Include $4 postage and handling for orders $15 and under; $5 for orders over $15. There are no postage and handling charges for orders over $100. Postage and handling rates are subject to change. We ship UPS whenever possible within the continental United States; delivery is guaranteed. Please provide your street address as UPS does not deliver to P.O. boxes. Orders shipped to Alaska, Hawaii, Canada, Mexico and Puerto Rico will be sent via first class mail. Allow 4–6 weeks for delivery. **International orders:** Airmail—add retail price of each book and $5 for each non-book item (audiotapes, etc.); Surface mail—add $1 per item.

Minnesota residents please add 7% sales tax.

Mail orders to:
Llewellyn Worldwide, P.O. Box 64383-170, St. Paul, MN 55164-0383, U.S.A.

For customer service, call (612) 291-1970.

Prices subject to change without notice.

THE THREE BOOKS OF OCCULT PHILOSOPHY
COMPLETELY ANNOTATED, WITH MODERN COMMENTARY—
THE FOUNDATION BOOK OF WESTERN OCCULTISM

by Henry Cornelius Agrippa,
edited and annotated by Donald Tyson

Agrippa's *Three Books of Occult Philosophy* is the single most important text in the history of Western occultism. Occultists have drawn upon it for five centuries, although they rarely give it credit. First published in Latin in 1531 and translated into English in 1651, it has never been reprinted in its entirety since. Photocopies are hard to find and very expensive. Now, for the first time in 500 years, *Three Books of Occult Philosophy* will be presented as Agrippa intended. There were many errors in the original translation, but occult author Donald Tyson has made the corrections and has clarified the more obscure material with copious notes.

This is a necessary reference tool not only for all magicians, but also for scholars of the Renaissance, Neoplatonism, the Western Kabbalah, the history of ideas and sciences and the occult tradition. It is as practical today as it was 500 years ago.

0–87542–832–0, 1,024 pgs., 7 x 10, softcover $39.95

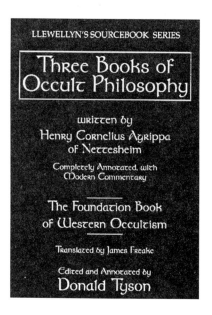

THE KEY OF IT ALL
BOOK ONE: THE EASTERN MYSTERIES
BOOK TWO: THE WESTERN MYSTERIES
AN ENCYCLOPEDIC GUIDE TO THE SACRED LANGUAGES
& MAGICAL SYSTEMS OF THE WORLD

by David Allen Hulse

The Key of It All series clarifies and extends the knowledge established by all previous books on occult magick. *Book One* catalogs and distills, in hundreds of tables of secret symbolism, the true alphabet magick of every ancient Eastern magickal tradition. *Book Two* does the same for every ancient Western magickal tradition. Unlike the current rash of publications which do no more than recapitulate Regardie or Crowley, *The Key of It All* series establishes a new level of competence in all fields of magick both East and West.

Book 1: 0-87542-318-3, 592 pgs., 7 x 10, tables, charts, softcover   **$24.95**
Book 2: 0-87542-379-5, 592 pgs., 7 x 10, tables, charts, softcover   **$24.95**

THE GOLDEN DAWN JOURNAL
Book II: Qabalah—Theory & Magic

Edited by Chic Cicero and Sandra Tabatha Cicero

Book Two: Qabalah—Theory & Magic explores the various aspects of this mystical system, both ancient and modern. These include the history and evolution of the Qabalah, inquiries into how the Qabalah is used for spiritual growth, traditional techniques of Gematria, Merkabah mysticism and Angel magic, comparisons between Qabalistic philosophy and the sciences of Astrology, Alchemy, and Psychology, investigations into the Goddess and feminine energies on the Tree of Life, Sphere-workings, Telesmatic magic, explorations into the Qabalistic aspects of Golden Dawn magic, and new Qabalistic rituals for today's practicing magicians.

- **The ABC's of Qabalah**—Harvey Newstrom
- **The Tree of Life: Jacob's Extending Ladder**—Gareth Knight
- **Sacred Images: A Qabalistic Analysis of the Neophyte Formula**—William Stoltz
- **The Restoration and Alchemy**—Steven Marshall
- **The Qabalistic World-view Behind the Golden Dawn System of Magic**—George Wilson
- **The Tree of the Sephiroth**—Donald Tyson
- **This Holy Invisible Companionship: Angels in the Hermetic Qabalah**—Adam P. Forrest
- **The Sacred Feminine on the Tree**—Madonna Compton
- **She Dances on the Tree**—Oz
- **The Equilibration of Jehovah: A Ritual of Healing**—M. Isidora Forrest
- **Shebilim Bahirim (The Bright Paths)**—Mitch and Gail Henson
- **Structural Implications in the Sepherot**—Sam Webster
- **Qabalistic Ritual**—Dolores Ashcroft-Nowicki
- **The Astrological Kaballah**—Lisa Roggow

1–56718–851–6, 456 pgs., 6 x 9, softcover $16.00

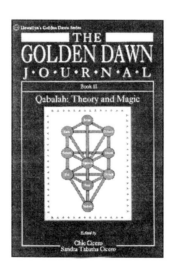

THE GOLDEN DAWN JOURNAL BOOK III
BOOK III: THE ART OF HERMES

Edited by Chic Cicero and Sandra Tabatha Cicero

Book Three: The Art of Hermes focuses on Hermetic magic, upon which all Western occultism for the past five centuries is based. Hermes Trismegistus is the god of wisdom of the Graeco-Egyptian philosophers who lived in Egypt in the early centuries of the Christian era. He is linked with alchemy, medicine, magic and the mysteries. All secret schools and orders in the West that claim an occult tradition (such as Freemasonry) may be loosely linked with Hermes. The editors trace the course of the Hermetic tradition from ancient Egypt, through Greek philosophy and the Greek Mystery religions, Gnosticism, Neoplatonism and the Kabbalah, down to the modern occult revival and the Golden Dawn.

- **Hermes: Chief Patron of Magick**—William Stoltz
- **The Emerald Tablet of Hermes and the Invocation of the Holy Guardian Angel**— Lon Milo DuQuette
- **The Hermetic Isis**—M. Isidora Forrest
- **Logos Revealed: Hermetic and Kabbalistic Influences on the Renaissance Humanists**—Madonna Compton
- **God-Making**—Donald Tyson
- **The Hall of Thmaa: Sources of the Golden Dawn Lodge System**—John Michael Greer
- **The Pillar of Osiris**—Adam P. Forrest
- **Invocation of Hermes Trismegistus and the Vision of the Poimandres: Two Ritual Pathworkings**—Oz
- **Of Hermes Mercurius**—Sam Webster
- **Images of Growth in the Hermetic Arts**—Gareth Knight
- **Magical Notebooks: A Survey of the Grimoires in the Golden Dawn**—Mitch and Gail Henson
- **Women, Qabala, and Masonry**—Fran Holt-Underwood

1-56178-852-4, 360 pgs., 6 x 9, softcover   **$20.00**

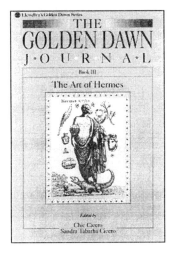

GODWIN'S CABALISTIC ENCYCLOPEDIA
COMPLETE GUIDANCE TO BOTH PRACTICAL AND ESOTERIC APPLICATIONS

by David Godwin

One of the most valuable books on the Cabala is back, with a new and more usable format. This book is a complete guide to cabalistic magick and gematria in which every demon, angel, power and name of God... every Sephiroth, Path, and Plane of the Tree of Life... and each attribute and association is fully described and cross-indexed by the Hebrew, English, and numerical forms.

All entries, which had been scattered throughout the appendices, are now incorporated into one comprehensive dictionary. There are hundreds of new entries and illustrations, making this book even more valuable for Cabalistic pathworking and meditation. It now has many new Hebrew words and names, as well as the terms of Freemasonry, the entities of the Cthulhu mythos, and the Aurum Solis spellings for the names of the demons of the Goetia. It contains authentic Hebrew spellings, and a new introduction that explains the uses of the book for meditation on God names.

The Cabalistic schema is native to the human psyche, and *Godwin's Cabalistic Encyclopedia* will be a valuable reference tool for all Cabalists, magicians, scholars and scientists of all disciplines.

1–56718–324–7, 832 pgs., 6 x 9, softcover $24.95

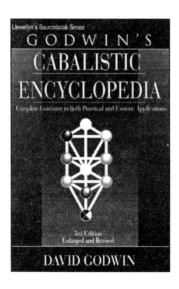